2002

Reelpolitik

Recent Titles in the
Praeger Series in Political Communication
Robert E. Denton, Jr., General Editor

REELPOLITIK

Political Ideologies in '30s and '40s Films

Beverly Merrill Kelley,
with John J. Pitney, Jr., Craig R. Smith,
and Herbert E. Gooch III

Foreword by Steve Allen

Praeger Series in Political Communication

Westport, Connecticut
London

Library of Congress Cataloging-in-Publication Data

Reelpolitik : political ideologies in '30s and '40s films / Beverly
 Merrill Kelley . . . [et al.] ; foreword by Steve Allen.
    p.   cm.—(Praeger series in political communication, ISSN
 1062–5623)
   Includes bibliographical references and index.
   ISBN 0–275–96018–8 (alk. paper).—ISBN 0–275–96019–6 (pbk. :
 alk. paper)
   1. Motion pictures—United States—Political aspects.   I. Kelley,
 Beverly Merrill.   II. Series.
 PN1995.9.P6R44   1998
 791.43'658—DC21   98–16909

British Library Cataloguing in Publication Data is available.

Library of Congress Catalog Card Number: 98–16909
ISBN: 0–275–96018–8
    0–275–96019–6 (pbk.)
ISSN: 1062–5623

First published in 1998

Praeger Publishers, 88 Post Road West, Westport, CT 06881
An imprint of Greenwood Publishing Group, Inc.

Printed in the United States of America

The paper used in this book complies with the
Permanent Paper Standard issued by the National
Information Standards Organization (Z39.48–1984).

10 9 8 7 6 5 4 3 2 1

To my mother, my first and best teacher, who introduced me to the magic of movies

To Jonathan, my soul-mate, who blesses me more than he'll ever realize

To Herb, Craig and Jack, all brilliant writers, whose generosity empowered a rank amateur to realize her dream

To Mr. Steve Allen, with the hope that the rest of the book lives up to his prefatory remarks

Contents

Series Foreword

Those of us from the discipline of communication studies have long believed that communication is prior to all other fields of inquiry. In several other forums I have argued that the essence of politics is "talk" or human interaction.[1] Such interaction may be formal or informal, verbal or nonverbal, public or private, but it is always persuasive, forcing us consciously or subconsciously to interpret, to evaluate, and to act. Communication is the vehicle for human action.

From this perspective, it is not surprising that Aristotle recognized the natural kinship of politics and communication in his writings *Politics* and *Rhetoric*. In the former, he established that humans are "political beings [who] alone of the animals [are] furnished with the faculty of language."[2] In the latter, he began his systematic analysis of discourse by proclaiming that "rhetorical study, in its strict sense, is concerned with the modes of persuasion."[3] Thus, it was recognized over twenty-three hundred years ago that politics and communication go hand in hand because they are essential parts of human nature.

In 1981, Dan Nimmo and Keith Sanders proclaimed that political communication was an emerging field.[4] Although its origin, as noted, dates back centuries, a "self-consciously cross-disciplinary" focus began in the late 1950s. Thousands of books and articles later, colleges and universities offer a variety of graduate and undergraduate coursework in the area in such diverse departments as communication, mass communication, journalism, political science, and sociology.[5] In Nimmo and Sanders's early assessment, the "key areas of inquiry" included rhetorical analysis, propaganda analysis, attitude change studies, voting studies, government and the news media, functional and systems analyses, technological changes, media technologies, campaign techniques, and research techniques.[6] In a survey of the state of the field in 1983, the same authors and Lynda Kaid found additional, more specific areas of concerns such as the presidency, political polls, public opinion, debates, and advertising.[7] Since the first study, they have also noted a shift away from the rather strict behavioral approach.

A decade later, Dan Nimmo and David Swanson argued that "political communication has developed some identity as a more or less distinct domain of scholarly work."[8] The scope and concerns of the area have further expanded to include critical theories and cultural studies. Although there is no precise definition, method, or disciplinary home of the area of inquiry, its primary domain comprises the role, processes, and effects of communication within the context of politics broadly defined.

In 1985, the editors of *Political Communication Yearbook: 1984* noted that "more things are happening in the study, teaching, and practice of political communication than can be captured within the space limitations of the relatively few publications available."[9] In addition, they argued that the backgrounds of "those involved in the field [are] so varied and pluralist in outlook and approach, . . . it [is] a mistake to adhere slavishly to any set format in shaping the content."[10] More recently, Swanson and Nimmo have called for "ways of overcoming the unhappy consequences of fragmentation within a framework that respects, encourages, and benefits from diverse scholarly commitments, agendas, and approaches."[11]

In agreement with these assessments of the area and with gentle encouragement, in 1988 Praeger established the series entitled "Praeger Series in Political Communication." The series is open to all qualitative and quantitative methodologies as well as contemporary and historical studies. The key to characterizing the studies in the series is the focus on communication variables or activities within a political context or dimension. As of this writing, over seventy volumes have been published and numerous impressive works are forthcoming. Scholars from the disciplines of communication, history, journalism, political science, and sociology have participated in the series.

I am, without shame or modesty, a fan of the series. The joy of serving as its editor is in participating in the dialogue of the field of political communication and in reading the contributors' works. I invite you to join me.

Robert E. Denton, Jr.

NOTES

1. See Robert E. Denton, Jr., *The Symbolic Dimensions of the American Presidency* (Prospect Heights, IL: Waveland Press, 1982); Robert E. Denton, Jr., and Gary

Woodward, *Political Communication in America* (New York: Praeger, 1985; 2d ed., 1990); Robert E. Denton, Jr., and Dan Hahn, *Presidential Communication* (New York: Praeger, 1986); and Robert E. Denton, Jr., *The Primetime Presidency of Ronald Reagan* (New York: Praeger, 1988).

2. Aristotle, *The Politics of Aristotle,* trans. Ernest Barker (New York: Oxford University Press, 1970), p. 5.

3. Aristotle, *Rhetoric,* trans. W. Rhys Roberts (New York: The Modern Library, 1954), p. 22.

4. Dan Nimmo and Keith Sanders, "Introduction: The Emergence of Political Communication as a Field," in *Handbook of Political Communication,* eds. Dan Nimmo and Keith Sanders (Beverly Hills, CA: Sage, 1981), pp. 11–36.

5. Ibid., p. 15.

6. Ibid., pp. 17–27.

7. Keith Sanders, Lynda Kaid, and Dan Nimmo, eds. *Political Communication Yearbook: 1984* (Carbondale, IL: Southern Illinois University: 1985), pp. 283–308.

8. Dan Nimmo and David Swanson, "The Field of Political Communication: Beyond the Voter Persuasion Paradigm," in *New Directions in Political Communication,* eds. David Swanson and Dan Nimmo (Beverly Hills, CA: Sage, 1990), p. 8.

9. Sanders, Kaid, and Nimmo, *Political Communication Yearbook: 1984,* p. xiv.

10. Ibid.

11. Nimmo and Swanson, "The Field of Political Communication," p. 11.

Foreword

As we near the year 2000 it seems to be the general perception, among all but the Sensitivity Impaired, that our nation is in a state of social dislocation that is perhaps unprecedented. Whether there are any totally new problems is questionable; the old, classic problems seem especially exacerbated. The general unease is detectable even as regards the long-recognized political divisions. Most Americans grasp the obvious distinction between Left and Right and have at least a hazy understanding of how to use the words "liberal" and "conservative" in a coherent conversation, but a smaller number know that ours is a time of strange bedfellows and that the two large political camps are raucously subdivided. For example, Ralph Nader on the Left and Pat Buchanan on the Right agree that the North American Free Trade Agreement was a bad idea that, while it might do some good for poor foreign nations, will provide few benefits for our own.

Another illustration: The FBI, the CIA and the nation's law-enforcement agencies generally, both federal and local, have long been perceived as essentially conservative institutions. But in the present climate they are being most heatedly criticized—often even physically attacked—by that element of the far Right that characterizes its own political philosophy as populist.

Parenthetically, it's interesting how all the key words of political identification have a rather noble sound. The terms "liberal" and "liberalism," rooted as they are in the concept of freedom, certainly have an attractive ring. And, given that every society has certain traditions and practices well worth conserving, the same is true of the word "conservative." Just so, populism, which purports to represent the people, could hardly have a better etymological pedigree. Unfortunately, when these and other labels are applied to the practical cases, the seeming nobility and clarity may become confused and tarnished. Perfectly fair questions do arise. For instance, how can Populists claim to truly represent the American people when their numbers are so small that, at least as of 1998, they are able to elect no one at all to major office? And those who are not members of one or another of the common political divisions can easily summon up critiques of their opponents. It is not many years in the past, after all, that William F. Buckley told us that the threat of liberalism was far more serious than that of communism, and this was at a time when by no means only conservatives were so apprehensive of Marxism that some almost frothed at the mouth when they considered it.

The world is grateful that communism eventually collapsed, which happened not because of anything whatever done by the American Right but simply of its own crushing weight. Nevertheless its dissolution was a dammed long time coming and its eventual defeat was small comfort to the millions who suffered and died under its heel. To this day it is quite probably that most Americans never did understand that the logical enemy of communism is not conservatism but capitalism, given that both are economic concepts.

And of the small number of Americans who did grasp the point of the contrast, fewer still were aware that it was capitalism, in the form of its weaknesses and excesses, that had given rise to communism in the first place.

Well, enough—for the moment anyway—of confusion. We must be grateful for any instruction that diminishes it, and this stimulating study can be of help in that regard, even though its focus is so narrow as to concentrate on evidences of political bias in motion pictures.

Inevitably the films of director Frank Capra come to mind in this connection. Although I am far from a student of that talented gentleman's work, I have generally perceived it as essentially a combination of conservative and middle-of-the-road elements. And this, of course, is why certain Capra films have been so long beloved. His most popular picture, *It's a Wonderful Life*, starring Jimmy Stewart and Donna Reed, is obviously sympathetic to long-cherished social ideals. The same may be said of *Mr. Smith Goes to Washington*.

On the other hand, Capra was obviously no great respecter of the super-rich and socially mighty. This is particularly clear in one of my favorite films, *Meet John Doe*, which starred Gary Cooper, in which the actor, despite his personally heroic image, played a poor fellow, down on his luck and so socially obscure as to be almost invisible. But his essential innocence and decency stand in sharp contrast to the corrupt, cynical characters who manipulate him for their own selfish purposes.

There is more than enough meat in all this to provide many nourishing meals for casual students or serious social analysts. Those conservatives who are religious—which means practically all of them—cannot possibly be admirers of Ayn Rand, the goddess of libertarianism (another of those noble words that require closer scrutiny), given that Ms. Rand herself had nothing but contempt for religion generally and Christianity specifically. All such currents washed through the creative Hollywood community; the studies in this collection remind us of that important fact.

Both an economic collapse and a global war endured during the Golden Age of the silver screen heightened political awareness and sharpened the extremes by which Americans sought to locate themselves on the political landscape. The choice between ultimately resorting to strong, even elitist leadership versus governance by "the people," populism, however vaguely envisioned and nostalgically inspired, harks back to the debates between Hamilton's Federalists, who embraced a strong central government, led by visionaries with keen expertise in the affairs of state, and Jefferson's Republican-Democrats, who opted for a more decentralized and weaker government guided by the common man, presumably grounded in simple common sense. Frank Capra emphasized the latter in *Mr. Smith Goes to Washington* (1930) while Orson Welles insinuated the former in *The Magnificent Ambersons* (1942).

Because it was a time of emergency and unemployment, the Depression seemed to call for a strong man and a Hamiltonian strategy for running the country. Trust in leadership from on high to solve our problems during the decade following the stock market crash was pointedly established in *Gabriel over the White House* (1931). La Cava's tribute to benevolent fascism was counterpointed by Welles's incisive portrait, *Citizen Kane* (1942), which bore a penetrating witness to the noxious nature of fascist totalitarianism.

Movies reflect political choices, not with looking-glass clarity, but often as shadowed, displaced and distorted. Moviegoers expect entertainment, after all, not education, so the student of political thought has to do a bit of deciphering, "deconstruction," as they say on campuses these days. If a few million people actually pay good money to see a film, this bit of pleasure is *ipso facto* a commodity whose popularity says something about the society as a whole—for better or worse—whatever else it might convey about individual taste and understanding.

Another pair of options, isolationism and interventionism, provide the means by which Americans have attempted to understand our engagement with the world. Our self-sense of unique moral destiny is rooted in an initial founding by Puritans as a Christian utopia, followed by a rounding as a radical experiment in democracy. There seems to be a particular and peculiar emphasis on America as a moral experiment. Should we keep to ourselves, avoiding the "entangling alliances" that

Washington and Jefferson feared, or should we share, perhaps sometimes even impose, our virtue on others, for their own good? Is our current urge to keep to ourselves, in an age of international conflict, the path of virtue?

There is always the nagging moral question as to whether it is truly right to simply turn our backs on the murderous cruelty that leads to suffering by millions in so many parts of the world. In the context of this troubling philosophical question we must never forget that, had isolationist sentiments prevailed in the 1940s, the horrors perpetrated by Hitler and his philosophical allies would have been perpetuated, perhaps even to the present period. Such questions are of particular relevance to those who consider themselves Christians since it is obvious that Christianity's preachment of universal love and social concern cannot possibly be harmonized with the views of those who say that we must simply ignore all forms of human suffering that take place outside our borders.

In the wake of disillusionment with the results of World War I, and our self-absorption in dealing with the Great Depression, the 1920s and 1930s proved a period of isolationism. Pearl Harbor, however, changed our minds, quickly and with a vengeance. Two films provide parentheses for understanding American attitudes toward foreign policy in the 1930s. The first, *All Quiet on the Western Front* (1930), in recounting the tale from the enemy's point of view, underlined the case for isolation in one of the most dramatic depictions of the dehumanizing futility of war ever recorded. The second, *Casablanca* (1942), often considered the most beloved of movie romances, though its script's authors were Jewish, actually debated the wisdom of America's impending interventionism under the guise of a tragic love triangle.

Americans are notorious for their commitment to interpreting new ideas in terms of what de Tocqueville popularized as individualism. The term stretches to encompass both a highly singular as well as a collective response to dealing with political and economic problems. King Vidor illustrates this definition of individualism with both *Our Daily Bread* (1934) and *The Fountainhead* (1947). With the shock of the Depression, the tradition emphasizing *laissez faire* capitalism appeared insufficient and the New Deal seemed to pose a compromise short of the collectivist extremes of socialism and communism. Big government was redefined as the employer of last resort, agent of common purpose and financial angel, priming the pump of economic expansion. In *Our Daily Bread*, Vidor demonstrates the manner in which the American imagination, steeped in the language of individualism, attempted to understand and explain the need for a more collective response to the painfully evident economic collapse of society.

Fifteen years after making *Our Daily Bread*, Vidor undertook the filming of Ayn Rand's libertarian tract, *The Fountainhead*, so utterly and ideologically contrary to collectivism. How could the same individual direct two films with such diametrically opposed political viewpoints? Because Americans perceived individualism as receptive to communal endeavors as long as collective is defined in terms of teamwork, not revolution.

The American attempt to reason about politics requires a language that is not only elastic and porous, but capable of pragmatic shape-shifting. Throw away your texts strictly proposing ideological *isms*, we sometimes are tempted to say. American political ideologies appear to have flourished in darkened theaters during the '30s and '40s. As history cycles Santayana-like toward the millennium, we might profitably look back to see forward. Education, after all, can be entertaining. Seen any old movies lately?

Steve Allen

Gregory La Cava directing Walter Huston in *Gabriel over the White House*. Courtesy of the Academy of Motion Picture Arts and Sciences.

Chapter One

Introduction: Purpose, Methodology and Background

Beverly Merrill Kelley

PURPOSE

Reelpolitik: Political Ideologies in '30s and '40s Films was stimulated by the 1996 year-long centennial celebration of American film at California Lutheran University. Initially, student reaction to a compulsory viewing of a series of 1930s and 1940s flicks as a requirement for courses in political science, English, communication arts and history was (in the most polite language one can muster) "highly resistant": "But these movies are really *old*." "They are in black and white." However, after the first film netted a handful of converts, word-of-mouth gained increasingly larger audiences, some individuals actually volunteering to spend their time at Richter Hall and admittedly enjoying themselves.

Why? Well, the faculty who delivered the pre-film lectures were hand-picked among those scholars who self-identified as amateur silver screen aficionados, and they were paid a nominal honorarium for their efforts. Second, professors were permitted to choose among their favorite classic films and cover whatever material they believed significant to the moviegoers. Third, the audiences were brought in as collaborators in the analysis via post-movie discussions. Last, while one should never underestimate the placebo effect engendered with quantitative study results (students do occasionally tell teachers what they want to hear), there appeared to be significant evidence this media generation was learning with an eagerness and effortlessness unanticipated by the instructors. They seemed to be enchanted with a dramatized portrayal of ideology and the entertaining ethos of the medium.

Parlaying enchantment into more effective educational pedagogy prompted proposing this book as a teaching tool for classes in American government, political science and film criticism. The proffered text seems to have three things going for it: The ideologies are organized into opposing pairs (a built-in impetus for discussion); 1930s and 1940s American films reflect a relevant portion of our history and culture in an engrossing manner; and, except for a few closet *American Movie Classics* addicts, these movies should prove a novel cinematic experience for the students.

METHODOLOGY AND BACKGROUND

Why limit the period covered by this book to the 1930s and 1940s? This book was envisioned as merely the first in a series on American film. Dividing this country's cinematic output into twenty-year (generational) increments allows for the opportunity to probe deeply within discrete time periods for the shifting focus between individual and community, which is the focus of the final chapter. Movies produced prior to 1930, for the most part (even D. W. Griffith's *Birth of a Nation* often fails to lock in the attention of film majors) lack fully developed plot lines, sophisticated production values and ready availability on video. Two subsequent volumes, the second covering the 1950s and 1960s and the third the 1970s and 1980s, are planned for future publication.

Political films still go unrecognized as a genre, at least as delineated by most critics, since they take the same subject matter, namely political ideas, yet utilize a wide range of vehicles to deliver the message. The format and use of conventions in a screwball comedy like *The Front Page* differ wildly from those in a thriller like *The China Syndrome*, a melodrama like *Pinky* or a biography like *Norma Rae*. Furthermore, some critics would argue that musicals and westerns qualify as political because of a shared emphasis on individualistic achievement, faith in leadership and system of competition with more conventional political movies. The waters of political film, in the broadest sense, are too muddy to separate into distinguishable streams.

To avoid being sucked into the endless quagmire that results when one links "political" as a descriptive adjective to cinema, it was decided to limit the focus of this book to "political ideology," defined as "integrated assertions, theories and aims that constitute a governmental policy." While arguably 90 percent of the movies produced during the 1930s and 1940s were "political," including social issues parading as such, the eight films in this volume fell within fairly stringent parameters.

Since suitability as a teaching tool was paramount, availability on video was a must. This eliminated such intriguing examples of communist and anticommunist propaganda as Michael Curtiz's *Mission to Moscow* and William Wellman's *Iron Curtain*. Yet in light of a claim by

American Movie Classics that 90 percent of all silent movies and 50 percent of sound films produced before 1950 have disappeared, often decaying into dust, video copies preserve as well as document our cinematic heritage.[1]

Of course the film had to illustrate, on at least several occasions, the gist of the political ideology. Many of the political movies made during the 1930s and 1940s dealt with populism, fascism, communism and interventionism, so it seemed logical to compare and contrast ideologies with their opposites, namely, elitism, antifascism, anticommunism and isolationism.

Despite that fact that "the media elite" are credited with wielding a great deal of power these days, the most difficult doctrine to illustrate was the antithesis of populism because few American filmmakers glorified elitism. The most popular films during the Depression gave us a "rear-window" view of the world of the rich while remaining somewhat critical of the economically privileged. After an exhaustive search, the editor selected *The Magnificent Ambersons*, in which the real star of the movie was the mansion, used by Booth Tarkington and Orson Welles to represent rule by the upper class.

While the subject of many political films has rendered them box office poison, until *Independence Day*, one would be hard pressed to name a handful of political movies that also qualified as blockbusters. A few made acceptable profits by serving as "prestige projects" by significant directors. Choosing critically successful projects guaranteed that they would have sufficient production values to appeal to the sophisticated 1990s motion picture-viewers taking courses in colleges and universities. Frank Capra was deliberately left off the auteur list by the French, yet his movies couldn't be a more resonating reflection of American culture. While Gregory La Cava could hardly be considered a director in the same league as Orson Welles, his film *Gabriel over the White House* makes a wonderful contrast with *Citizen Kane* when filtered through the political doctrine of fascism. Selecting a film other than *Mr. Smith Goes to Washington* to pair with *Kane* broke new ground in criticism and analysis.

Historical accuracy was considered as well. For example, *Casablanca*, opening as it does via a newsreel, was rushed into release just after the Allies invaded North Africa, rendering the film a political statement as well as an accurate chronicle of World War II during 1942. Second, *Citizen Kane* recounted the biography of William Randolph Hearst with docudrama-like artistic license. Last, you can't beat Clarissa Saunders from *Mr. Smith Goes to Washington* as a guest lecturer on the "art of the filibuster" as well as "congressional procedure."

The length of the film was an important consideration. The eight movies range from seventy-four to 125 minutes, thus making it possible to view each of them within one or two typical classroom periods.

Individualism versus community, originally intended as an additional ideological category, was discovered in all subsequent ideological pairs under consideration in this book. The tension between the individual and community is the single most significant factor in identifying these films as essentially American. This country was founded by dissatisfied individualists, who, while reluctant to separate from the mother country, decided that the tyrannies of George III left no other option. The framers of the Declaration of Independence and the Constitution codified the kind of community considered ideal.

The pendulum between individualism and community swung wildly back and forth in the course of 200 years. American history follows the power shifts from the utopians of the left to idealists of the right as each group attempted to make its respective ideology the law of the land. For the most part, successful leadership coalesces somewhere in the middle. Historian Robert Dallek, author of the forth-coming *Hail to the Chief— The Making and Unmaking of American Presidents*, speaks of a kind of schizophrenia we suffer as essentially a middle-class, middle-of-the-road populace, despising strong centralized authority (which runs counter to our individualism) yet desiring consensual community.

Submitting the pairs of ideologies—populism/elitism, fascism/anti-fascism, communism/anticommunism, interventionism/isolationism— to further scrutiny through the lens of individualism/community gives even more depth to discussions engendered by the classic movies. Americans of every political stripe, priding themselves on both bootstraps and boosts, independence and connection, personal responsibility and safety nets, have found common ground and no "ism" has ever shaken the sturdy foundation provided by the Founding Fathers.

Is the purpose of movies merely to entertain? In the days when movie moguls like Sam Goldwyn called the shots, he admonished his writers to call Western Union if they wanted to deliver a message. Each of the films selected for this book suffered the wrath of critics, was boycotted by interest groups opposed to the ideology exemplified or was threatened by political figures. "It's only a movie," countered the industry, yet that excuse convinced no one.

Whether you loved or hated *American President* depended in part on whether or not you were offended by the send-up of the conservative Right. On the other hand, Frank Capra couldn't make anything but a box office hit during the 1930s; the time was right for his populist philosophy. Bottom line: if political films do make an impact on the audience that impact is impossible to evaluate. There are the exceptions like *JFK*, which mobilized viewers into pressuring President Clinton to open up secret files, but academia could certainly use a device to measure political effects.

Even if a movie deals only peripherally with politics, it socializes us to political ideas, values and behavior. With parents increasingly abdicating responsibility as their child's primary teacher, the media have taken on that task, and film (arguably even more than television) has become the most effective agency. In 1964, Marshall McLuhan, in *Understanding Media*, pontificated, "The medium is the message." While his theories may have fallen out of favor today, his claim evidences film's persuasive superiority. The movie has plenty of time (the average film runs 120 minutes) to package novel-length political messages into larger-than-life metaphor, a sure-fire way to bypass reason and travel directly to one's emotions. Television, temporally restricted to narrating shorter stories, tends to favor a persuasive process less dependent on myth, fantasy and rhetorical vision simply because television appeals to the lowest common denominator. Financed primarily by advertising, television requires huge homogeneous audiences. Multiplexes, which charge $6.50 or more per ticket, allow the moviegoer to self-select into smaller, narrower interest groups.

Further, the use of stars allows the movie to "borrow" the charisma of the actor/actress, tacking it to the persuasive message. Film legends score far higher on the credibility meter than do mere television folk. Margaret Farrand Thorpe, writing in 1939, dubbed Hollywood and its constellation of stars the "standard of reference" for the 85 million Americans who filed into theaters each week.[2] Celebrated not only on screen but in print and on radio, these popular-culture figures inspired more adoration than anyone who came before them. Most of the stars in these eight political films are largely unfamiliar to the students who are going to be viewing these movies. That is not to say that the considerable talents of Jimmy Stewart, Joseph Cotten, Orson Welles, Walter Huston, Gary Cooper, Patricia Neal and Humphrey Bogart would not impress students or that their performances would fail to hold up even after more than fifty years.[3]

NOTES

1. *American Movie Classics* Cable Network appeal for film preservation.

2. Margaret Farrand Thorpe, *America at the Movies* (New Haven, CT: Yale University Press, 1939), 113.

3. Each author was asked to incorporate his or her own answers to the following questions in the course of each chapter:

1. Why is this a classic film?

2. What did this ideology look like in terms of American politics, government and history?

3. Is this film historically accurate?

4. What influence did the director have on this film?

5. What was the audience reaction at the time of its premiere?

6. How does this film compare with its ideological opposite?

Jimmy Stewart and Jean Arthur in *Mr. Smith Goes to Washington*. Courtesy of the Academy of Motion Picture Arts and Sciences.

Chapter Two

Populism in *Mr. Smith Goes to Washington*

Beverly Merrill Kelley

Two company towns, Washington, D.C., and Hollywood, California, sprouted up around prestige, power and performers. Both Babylonian offspring are mutually suspicious, as is typical of sibling rivals. Each takes turns accusing the other of nefarious acts ultimately leading to the end of civilization. To my mind, the constant bickering between the nation's capital and Tinseltown belies one of America's great romances and I predict, just as in a 1930s screwball comedy, we will find the two in a clinch by the final reel. In fact, in striving for coexistence, the cities have worked out a 1990s codependency, with Hollywood passively taking the heat for destroying family values and hallowed traditions, while aggressively portraying politicians as iniquitous idiots and lecherous loons. Even though it took pot shots at the nation's best and the brightest, Hollywood voluntarily assumed a "don't ask, don't tell" policy with respect to calling any risqué residents of Congress and the Oval Office by name. Even though it was common knowledge that Louis B. Mayer registered as a Republican and Jack Warner declared himself an ardent fan of Franklin D. Roosevelt, on screen, overt partisanship was *verboten*.

Patriotic fervor might seem anachronistic during the 1990s, especially considering the boisterous cheers that greeted the vaporization of the White House in *Independence Day*. These days, we consider ourselves the aliens in a present-day Cold War with a less-than-candid government. Despite current neo-populism, in which alienation has replaced patriotism, the wee lad sounding out Lincoln's words, as depicted in Capra's little civics lesson, still holds us in awe.

Capra has been roundly criticized for the populist poetry the dauntless Mr. Smith uses to admonish the assembled senators, yet Capra's unequivocal patriotism served the nation in good stead as we slogged through the Depression and prepared for World War II. In 1938, the Axis Powers were on the move. As the world descended into combat, Americans reached into their democratic arsenal for the ideals exemplified by Capra heroes. In the documentary *Frank Capra's American Dream*, John Cassavetes quipped, "Maybe there really wasn't an America, maybe it was only Frank Capra."

FRANK CAPRA

Mr. Smith Goes to Washington is the definitive Hollywood excursion up the Potomac. Frank Capra, realizing his need for total directorial freedom, knew this movie would be his last for Columbia. A message movie, but not profoundly so, the film was written not by Capra's usual partner Robert Riskin but by Sidney Buchman, who had handled some rewrites on *Lost Horizon*. Not only did Buchman's politics lean heavily to the Left, he acknowledged his membership in the Communist Party just in time for the premiere of *Mr. Smith*. Buchman was eventually blacklisted for refusing to name names and fled this country to live the rest of his life in London. No evidence of pink proclivities emerged in *Mr. Smith*, which unabashedly mirrors Frank Capra's conservative ideology.

If you were to look up the term "capraesque" in your dictionary, you would discover two meanings: "idealistic" and "sentimental." Neither definition is a compliment to Capra, seen as idealistic because he romanticized the middle class and derided as sentimental by reviewers who whined that Capra merely animated Norman Rockwell's illustrations. They thought he airbrushed America instead of serving up the unemotional realism then in vogue.

Capra's relentless optimism made him no darling of the commentators, who saved their praise for more cynical cinematic visions. Criticism of his work ranged from charges of tired triteness to downright demagoguery. Capra was accused of trying to impose his vision of "what America ought to be" on the unsuspecting public, not an unusual response of relativists to a moral absolutist. Capra affirmed his detractors' charges by self-deprecatingly referring to his work as "Capracorn."

Depression films such as *Mr. Smith* reflected Capra's roots as a gag writer ("Our Gang" comedies), never straying far from his preoccupation with youthful innocence. Capra spent a considerable amount of time working with Will Rogers, who never met a man or a political zinger he didn't like.

In his best-selling "autohagiography," *The Name above the Title*, Capra summed up his philosophy of filmmaking in the motto, "One man, one film," seemingly synonymous with the definition of "auteur director" first proposed by Francois Truffaut in the mid-fifties. However, the

French New Wavists deliberately left Capra's name off a list that included fellow directors John Ford, John Huston, Alfred Hitchcock and Orson Welles, citing his lack of signatory effects.

While occasionally indulging in cinematic wipes, montage and juxtaposition, Capra was adamant about banning anything in his films that distracted from the telling of the story. Yet one can argue that what was signatory about his work was not his style but his subject matter. Since documenting the American experience doesn't translate easily into French, many American beliefs may appear culturally irrelevant to Parisians in the business of evaluating directors.

A second reason Capra was omitted from the French roster is that, with the exception of *It's a Wonderful Life*, most films produced by Capra after 1948 remain distinctly inferior to his earlier efforts. Perhaps Capra had nothing further to say. At any rate, post-World War II prosperity failed to stir him, and his passion would continue unstimulated until President Lyndon Johnson's "Great Society" gave him pause.

George Lucas might be able to comment on the inverse relationship between overwhelming commercial success and critical acclaim. Between 1932 and 1939, all of Capra's cinematic productions were nominated for "Best Picture" Oscars and enjoyed extraordinary success at the box office. Although Frank Capra graced the 1938 cover of *Time* and was profiled by the *Saturday Evening Post*, he was still regarded as merely an entertaining romantic by the reviewers.

It seems paradoxical that an immigrant born in Bisacquino, Sicily, in 1897 would be tapped by General George Marshall to produce the propagandistic "Why We Fight" series. Frank Capra seemed to catch hold of the American Dream with greater fervor than any native. His family moved to Los Angeles when young Frank turned three (or six, depending on which biography you read). One of seven children, he enrolled in California Institute of Technology's chemical engineering program after his high school graduation. After working his way through school at great personal sacrifice, Capra discovered the Depression pre-empted employment opportunities for engineers, so he served a stint in the army.

Until he broke into films, Capra lived an itinerant life, selling books and working in agriculture up and down California. Although little did Capra-as-populist realize it at the time, a hazily remembered blur of hamlets that served as his temporary digs would coalesce into Jefferson Smith's hometown of Jackson City, Montana.

POPULISM

A recurring political theme, populism,[1] stresses the role of government in defending small voices against the wealthy or powerful. If not rooted in Jeffersonian,[2] Jacksonian and Lincolnesque interpretations of democracy, it certainly bears their imprint. As a political force emerging from the formal protest movement in the 1890s, populism seems to be ideologically ambiguous. Economic populism leans to the Left, viewing wealth and power as unequally distributed. At the same time, cultural populism is positioned decidedly to the Right, with its core support coming from religious fundamentalists. Populism commends neither the liberal solution of handing welfare to the farmer forced off his land nor the conservative solution, which says "I got mine—what's your point?" The idea behind populism is to place self-help in everyone's grasp, so that prosperity percolates up from the bottom as opposed to trickling down from the top.

Unfettered American capitalism exploded after the Civil War. Mark Twain's Gilded Age was marked by rampant materialism, bottom-line morality, government corruption and a total void in environmental responsibility. The rich got richer with the promise of a better life for all—a promise that remained largely unfulfilled.

Predominantly agrarian and decidedly democratic, the have-nots at the poor end of the economic continuum joined the People's Party of America. This alternative to the two major parties promoted grass-roots democracy and the notion that stuffed shirts were to blame for impoverishing the plow-and-overalls crowd. Populists demanded answers to public questions involving the place of minorities, the wave of foreign immigration, women's rights, government's role in shaping social development, monetary policy and tariff protection.[3]

Populism peaked in 1892 with the People's Party unsuccessfully running James B. Weaver for president but electing four senators. In 1896, populists took a leading role in the Democratic Party, later merging with the progressives in promoting the graduated income tax, public ownership of utilities, voter initiative and referendum, the eight-hour workday, immigration restriction and government control of currency as platform planks.

In the last quarter of the nineteenth century, farmers were hard hit by economic distress and social insecurity. These individualistic entrepreneurs, when confronted with the failure of falling crop prices to keep up with rising mortgage payments, joined the Grange during the 1870s and the Farmer's Alliances during the 1880s, banding together to discover new markets or to raise prices by curbing output. In 1890, the economic downturn prompted their political organization against railroads, banks and other monopolies.

In 1896, a Democrat, William Jennings Bryan, emerged as the voice of the populists with his famous speech *Cross of Gold*. Bryan would mark the end of his career by prosecuting a young teacher in the John Scopes "monkey trial," depicted in the 1960 film, *Inherit the Wind*, because Bryan believed "teachers in public schools must teach what taxpayers desire taught."[4] The People's Party backed Bryan rather than trying to over-come the impossible odds against a third-party candidate, which perse-vere a century later. Bryan was defeated by the GOP choice, William McKinley, but his supporters sought comfort in the fact that they still managed to garner electoral votes in twenty-two states even though they were dramatically outspent by the Republicans. A $500,000 contribution by J. P. Morgan and Standard Oil, in fact, exceeded the total netted by all Democratic fundraising. This fact predictably intensified the incessant populist harangue against money (as the root of all evil) as well as cor-ruption on the part of their worthy opponents.[5] Bryan's message advo-cating a return to a more rural, religious America was crippled by its provincialism and fundamentalism, both playing dismally in the cos-mopolitan cities on both coasts. Even though many urbanites agreed with Bryan's economic platform, they felt so threatened by his seemingly radical social issue planks that they supported McKinley. Note to those who fail to learn from history (thus dooming themselves to *Groundhog Day*-like repetition): The closer one comes to undiluted populism, the more likely one is to be regarded as an outlier on the political contin-uum. Despite three unsuccessful attempts at the Oval Office, Bryan did provide Democrats with the rationale for expanding the federal role in the twentieth century. Drawing heavily from insurgent populists, he rec-ognized the need for an activist government to protect the little guy in a power struggle with the economic elite.

While Lawrence Goodwyn views populism as a far-reaching radical movement in *Democratic Promise: The Populist Movement in America*[6] not all members of the historical academy consider populism an ideology. In fact, populism has been depicted as a reactionary response, consumed with grievances so petty and shallow that, with the return of prosperity after 1896, its justification quietly evaporated. Populism has also been regarded as merely a cyclical political mood expressing a free-floating resentment of power, distrust of major institutions and impotent sense of alienation. Populist ideologues seem to burn for fairness, a Sodom and Gomorrah-like cleansing of the country's morals, and, instead of big government, a return to the innate wisdom of the people in dealing with their own affairs. When the original populists failed to survive, historians relegated populism as a subset of conservatism.

Irwin Unger complains that populists simply failed to understand the complexities of their era and their obsession with finances caused them to define monetary control as the source of nearly every difficulty. Re-member the Democrats' rationalization for Bryan's loss? Unger argues that solutions proffered by populists were filtered through an ignorant and limited social vision, which he blamed on their geographic isolation.

Populists did pave the way, although not altogether intentionally, for a more economically accommodating version of reform within both major parties. Republican Theodore Roosevelt championed "the little man" while Democrat Woodrow Wilson promised Americans freedom from corporate tyranny. The defunct People's Party also provided a seedbed for political action through the next fifty years. Populists offered an alternative vision for America: a counterculture, both democratic and localist in thrust. Central to its popularity was the seeming failure of government to make good on the American dream of shared prosperity. The Social Security Act and minimum-wage laws sprang out of an unsated hunger to realize that dream in the twentieth century. The period following the 1929 crash inspired an energetic renewal of rhetorical assault on the monied and privileged, which Roosevelt handily harnessed in plowing through his New Deal.

Populists seemed content to clash over values and ideas that eventually merged with fascism/Nazism on the Right and socialism/communism on the Left, rather than wage a serious fight for political power. The political powers-that-be in the last decade of the nineteenth century simply could not allow populists to become a viable third party alternative. The fact that Ross Perot attracted 19 percent of voters in 1992 still strikes fear in the hearts of Democrats and Republicans alike.[7] Current political consultants maintain the swing voter usually identifies himself or herself as a populist.

The downside of the populist legacy was a revival of anti-Semitism and a plethora of Wall Street conspiracy theories. Demagogues such as Father Charles Coughlin took to the airwaves, catering to the paranoia of 30 million listeners and blaming the Great Depression on bankers who supposedly created an artificial scarcity of money.

The populist impulse persists because it continually draws attention to the gap between American ideals and ruling institutions thought to betray the citizens' trust. One only has to turn to perennial presidential candidate Pat Buchanan, who stridently articulated the increasing anxiety of American workers over corporations exporting jobs overseas, or Ross Perot, the "on again, off again" ultimate Washington outsider, to evidence the persistence of populism.[8]

CAPRA'S BRAND OF POPULISM

Populism as a political ideology was illustrated by several themes running through *Mr. Smith Goes to Washington*. A reverence for the Founding Fathers as well as the documents they authored appears pivotal to Capra's brand of populism. Jefferson Smith reads from both the Constitution and the Declaration of Independence during his Senate filibuster scene. To establish Smith's wide-eyed idealism, Capra allows Smith to realize the number one item on his list of heart's desires, to sightsee in our nation's capital. Capra took his film crew on the kind of D.C. tour bus frequented by millions of annual visitors to document the moving monument montage accompanied by an eye-misting medley arranged by Dimitri Tiomkin opening the film. At his first inaugural speech, Ronald Reagan paid homage to *Mr. Smith* by breaking with tradition and staging his speech at the front of the Capitol. Nearby monuments remained within the vista of the television cameras, thus allowing Reagan to incorporate references in his address.

The Declaration of Independence focuses on inalienable rights and the Constitution frames our democratic ideals; these are not just patriotic symbols, but primary documents delineating populist rights and responsibilities. The sanctity of life was personified by Jefferson Smith's giving up the one hope to clear his name since that meant his Boys Stuff apologists would suffer at the hands of Taylor's thugs. The freedom Jefferson Smith hoped to make meaningful to his Boy Campers was symbolized by Lady Liberty perched on the top of the Capitol dome. Capra took his understanding of the pursuit of happiness from Aristotle's concept of life lived in conformity with virtue; one's right to pursue happiness is confined by the rights of others. Since Boss Taylor's single-minded obsession caused others misery, exercising his right to pursue happiness flew in the face of the Founding Fathers' intent.

The Constitution's significance was realized by metaphors of totalitarian threats to democracy such as police hoses being turned on marchers and hired hoodlums beating up helpless Boy Rangers merely exercising their First Amendment rights. Additionally, German and Italian diplomats were shown lurking in the gallery of the Senate, subtly serving as Capra's harbingers of World War II.

Capra interpreted effective leadership in terms of decency, requiring his heroes to conform to the highest standards of propriety and morality. The driving force behind neo-populism today is crystallized in the American sense of fairness. UCLA's John Petrocik calls it "one of the nation's most important values. Or you could call it something more, the foundation from which our most treasured myths (note connection with Fantasy Theme Analysis) about ourselves arise.[9] Capra's hero is a man of principle, the maxim, "It isn't a principle until it costs you personally," became a litmus test. It was not coincidental that Abraham Lincoln, a man who paid the ultimate price for his ethical code, served as Jefferson Smith's silent mentor.

Although Capra's primary intent was to provide entertainment, he was genuinely concerned with the moral impact of his films: "It sounds sappy but the underlying idea of my movies is actually the Sermon on the Mount—a plus value of some kind along with the entertainment. I think if you read the Sermon on the Mount to anyone a little removed from an ape they would warm up to it."[10] Capra's sentiment is best illustrated by the scene in which a little boy (representative of the child-like faith advised by the Bible) reads the Gettysburg Address aloud to his immigrant grandfather from the marble walls of the majestic Lincoln Memorial.

Jefferson Smith learned the value of decency from his father. Clayton Smith, an ardent champion of the underdog, boasted that lost causes were the only kind worth fighting for. Jefferson was also taught to keep his word, so when he vowed, "I'll do nothing to disgrace this office," he was prepared to keep that pledge at any cost. A recent president learned the hard way that unrealized campaign promises bear consequences. George Bush's "read my lips, no new taxes" was transformed into a bill stamped "payment now due" by the American public, who denied him a second term.

Last, populists distrust power and oppose the economic elite, Washington D.C., and academia as a matter of course. Populists depict themselves as anti-materialist, anti-big government, anti-intellectual, anti-media and anti-technology.

Anti-materialist

The Capra populist, unlike the 1890s folk who begged for a bureaucratic buffer against the economic elite, applauds the acquisition of money in the presence of a level playing field, as long as the vantage point of wealth isn't used to look down on others. America is supposed to be a nation without a class system. From the Capra perspective, even lower than "the snob" is the wealthy soul who abdicates control over his life by constantly worrying about what other people think. The original sin in the populist version of the Scriptures is hypocrisy. The Capra ideal is an individual who is honest and humble. While love of money may remain the root of all evil (Capra doesn't let go of that notion any more than the 1890s populists did), his heroes are content to responsibly give away any excess left after securing a comfortable life. Dependence is seen by Capra as just another means of controlling others. Populists prefer empowerment to control. You only have to look to Mr. Deeds's "two acres and a cow" or George Bailey's Building and Loan alternative to Potter's Field for illustrations of Capra's interpretation of the admonition, "Instead of giving a man a fish, teach him how to fish."

Anti-big Government

Capra departs from the 1890s populists in that he rejected Franklin Roosevelt and his bloated bureaucracy. He employed Jefferson Smith to symbolize a voice crying out in the wilderness. The Willow Creek Dam Appropriations Bill would have lined the pockets of Boss Jim Taylor and

Senator Paine as well as literally flooding Smith's fresh air camp for boys. A Capra populist would argue that a country peopled by the "good neighbors" to whom Smith appealed during his stirring filibuster scene would have no need for federal handouts. Private-sector schemes such as sweat equity (Habitat for Humanity) or Bush's "thousand points of light" would prove more effective once dependence-inducing big government (welfare reform) gets out of the way.

Anti-intellectual

Capra believed that academia is full of liberal, so-called experts, who mistakenly trust in government to solve society's problems. He believed that intellectuals complicate, while wisdom inherent in the people[11] simplifies. In addition, Capra observed that the ivory tower dweller who deliberately isolates himself from the common man keeps coming up with meaningless "isms" or unworkable big ideas such as communism or fascism, which, instead of enriching humanity, exact a costly toll in terms of human life.

Anti-media

Keeping in mind that television didn't exist in 1939, the press and radio remained acceptable to populists as long as the marketplace of ideas wasn't co-opted by any single viewpoint. However, Capra doubted the marketplace could stay free for long, which he illustrated by rendering Smith's Boy Rangers helpless in their battle to disseminate the truth. Capra divides the press as creators of public opinion into mendacious miscreants like Taylor and responsible journalists who explain and expose. In fact, the convention party preamble from the 1890s populists might well serve as actual dialogue for *Mr. Smith Goes to Washington*.

> We meet in the midst of a nation brought to the verge of moral, political and material ruin.... The newspapers are largely subsidized or muzzled.... The fruits of the toil of millions are boldly stolen to build up colossal fortunes for a few unprecedented in the history of mankind, and the possessors of these, in turn, despise the republic and endanger liberty.[12]

In the classic filibuster scene, the press assumes the role of the "reactive character," guiding while dissecting the dramatic flow. The press performs as a Greek chorus by silently inquiring "Is he winning?" "Is he losing?"

Radio was represented by CBS "anchor," Hans Von Kaltenborn,

whose highly rated news reports were enhanced by personal commentary and declaimed by an affected British accent. Playing himself, Kaltenborn lauds, with tongue in cheek, "democracy in action."

If you have any question about how Capra felt about the Fourth Estate, look for a profile of a rat-faced reporter callously announcing a senator's death or Smith's ill-fated press conference in which acerbic agenda-setters play him for the stooge.

Anti-technology

The dangers inherit in the rush to advance science were rarely considered by the ruling institutions. Touted as a means of improving American life, "progress" became the operative word. Capra underscores his disdain for technological development by cleverly juxtaposing images of the massive network of presses against the Boy Rangers' primitive hand operation or contrasting Taylor's bellowing one-way telephone conversations with Smith's homing pigeons silently winging back to his hometown.

FANTASY THEME ANALYSIS

American film has proved to be a dramatist's *tabula rasa* for the etching of dream and fantasy imagery. Ernest G. Bormann identified "rhetorical vision" as a highly persuasive device dominating this country's effective political campaigns from Jefferson's "tree of liberty" to Franklin Roosevelt's "New Deal" to Clinton's "bridge to the twenty-first century." In line with his "fantasy theme analysis" theory,[13] Bormann observes that compelling communicators merge critical pieces of information into a "dramatic scenario" that recollects a past event or presents a fantasy of the future. Capra merely extended the political stump to your local Bijou. In *Mr. Smith Goes to Washington*, Jefferson Smith, perceived by the party machine as ignorant and naive, is selected to succeed a senator who dies unexpectedly. Smith's secretary, Clarissa Saunders (Jean Arthur) wises up Smith and he decides to confront Boss Jim Taylor (Edward Arnold) but discovers, to his chagrin, that he is seriously outgunned. Corrupt Senator Joseph Harrison Paine (Claude Rains), who, because of a lifelong bond with Smith's father, would like to jump to Jeff's defense when the neophyte legislator is framed by Taylor, ends up selling out Smith in order to save his own skin.

At first, Roosevelt's 1935 shift to the Left merely tormented Capra.[14] Then the blowout 1936 election served as a wake-up call. Historian Maury Klein believes "Capra's instinct for convincing audiences that his world was the way life should be lived was uncanny. To it he added topical relevance that fashioned mythical portraits of an America in which people longed to believe."[15]

The "land of opportunity" theme is tied to the middle-class work ethic and is best exhibited by the ruggedly independent farmer yeomen fomenting the populism movement of the 1890s as well as the frugal and hard-working immigrants in Capra's own family tree. New York Governor Mario Cuomo played the same motif when he referred to the bleeding feet of his workaholic father in his 1984 Democratic keynote address. California Governor Pete Wilson, in his aborted try for the 1996 GOP presidential nomination, elevated his naturalized grandmother (Kate Barton) to counterpoint the teeming masses of illegal immigrants he held accountable for overburdening the taxpayers of California. This fantasy theme, in contrast to a New Deal-like redistribution of wealth, permits the equitable access of "opportunity to" (as opposed to "guarantee of") the American Dream. Jefferson's reverie consisted of a summer camp where boys could escape the cities, independent of government largess. The retreat was to be financed by nickels and dimes donated by the kids themselves. Coupled with Horatio Alger mythology, this fantasy theme preaches an anti-victimization doctrine in which one is encouraged to rise a single bootstrap at a time. However, a wise politician (such as Newt Gingrich, in hindsight) might choose to temper populism's single-minded emphasis on self-help with a touch of compassion.

Optimistically labeled "good will toward men," the second fantasy theme conjures up images of the Yuletide season. Aristotle credits universal good will as one of the components of *ethos* or (the current term) "credibility." Capra reinterpreted Aristotle by noting that there's nothing wrong with America that can't be cured by behaving as one who has his neighbor's best interests at heart. Capra would have the Golden Rule made manifest thus; Jefferson Smith pleads for "plain, ordinary, everyday kindness, a little looking out for the other fella," in his famous filibuster attempt. Furthermore, "doing unto others," as Capra would have it, does not necessarily mean developing a rigid code of conduct or adhering to a mainstream religious belief system.

The third fantasy theme takes delight in the simple life. While relocating to Walden Pond would be unnecessary, conspicuous consumerism and collecting expensive evidence of one's success are anathema to the Capra hero or heroine. The most valued gift one person can bestow upon another in Small Town, USA, is the present one has made with one's own hands. Jefferson Smith's mother sends Clarissa a jar of her homemade strawberry preserves to affirm Clarissa's relationship with her son. Standing in opposition to the popularly perceived image of former President George and Barbara Bush as elitists was the touching tableaux published in *Time*. Here was the first couple in their White House four-poster, with a passel of grandchildren snuggled under the covers.

Andrew Bergman attributes the popularity of *Mr. Smith Goes to Washington* to the way the film reconciled the irreconcilable: "[It] created an America of perfect unity: all classes as one, the rural-urban divide breached; love, decency and neighborliness ascendant. It was an American self-portrait that proved a bonanza."[16]

The fourth and final fantasy theme, "log cabin to White House," is derived, of course, from the mythology of Abraham Lincoln, our sixteenth and arguably most popular president. The Boy Rangers boasted that Jefferson Smith knew all of Honest Abe's words by heart. This theme gives credence to the populist belief that political leaders who come from humble beginnings are best suited to represent the people. Candidates who boast, "I was born in a log cabin I built with my own hands" aside, populist presidential candidates from William Jennings Bryan to Jimmy Carter understood that the individual best able to understand the crises and concerns of the citizenry rarely emerges from the elite.

THE CAPRA HERO AND HEROINE

The new millennium seems to be ushering in a decline of the nation-state, with even Democrat Bill Clinton espousing the demise of big government. As we move to a more global society and the federal government increasingly turns more control over to state and local governments, futurists are predicting a civic renaissance. Urbanites are rushing to relocate in small towns and neo-populism is on the rise. Ronald Reagan's 1980s rhetorical vision of the "shining city on a hill" and "morning in America" resonated with voters. The fortieth president's populist hero mythology is distilled in these two lines from his first Inaugural speech: "Those who say that we're in a time when there are no heroes—they just don't know where to look. . . . You meet heroes across a counter—and they're on both sides of that counter."[17]

Capra, some forty years earlier, also chose the members of his audience as his heroes and heroines. During the Depression, while other directors gave us glimpses into the world of the economic elite, Capra, like King Vidor in *Our Daily Bread*, lifted up working stiffs. Instead of playing off the war between the sexes, the cinematic couples demonstrated mutual respect, often exchanging teacher and student roles. Clarissa tutors Jefferson through the legislative labyrinth while he exemplifies good triumphing over evil to the shell-shocked survivor of a thousand psychic wars. In fact, Capra's string of box-office hits can be best explained by the fact that he placed the folks in the seats up on the screen.

The origins of the Capra hero arose out of a screen character he was assigned to develop for Mack Sennett's production company: "The character I evolved for [actor] Harry Langdon was a very selfless man, who hadn't got any allies, his only ally was God, his only protection was his own goodness, and what he did was to love everybody."[18]

Jefferson Smith qualifies as a fully formed Capra hero, tackling seemingly impossible odds while bestowing his love wholeheartedly on the heroine (once he figures out who the heroine is). A self-sacrificing servant, Mr. Smith succeeds through his innate goodness. Even though Boss Taylor is able to push around the media throughout Montana, it is Smith's adherence to his principles despite the cost that eventually wins over the vice president (Harry Carey) and the rest of the Senate. During the twenty-three-hour and thirty-minute speech that culminates in a dead faint, you observe Jimmy Stewart (who often wryly observed that Capra makes you pay for his happy endings) either slumped over or leaning on the desk, emblematic of debilitating discouragement. Yet, momentarily distracted by Clarissa's less-than-subtle prompting from the gallery or when he calls to mind the righteousness of his cause, he abruptly pulls himself up to full six-foot stature. Capra's seamless edits between the speech and the Senate chamber audience, particularly his focus on the vice president, who allows his amusement to become evident in his expression, telegraphs Smith's ultimate victory.

During the course of the film, Smith's faith in himself develops from "local boy fights Sweetwater forest fire" to a one-man crusade against evil Boss Taylor, in much the same way as staving off a sheep-stealing bear girds little David to run his goliathan gantlet. The biblical metaphor is indeed appropriate here because Capra intended his protagonist to be a Christ-like figure and filled his movie with references to the Good Book: Dis Moore's (Thomas Mitchell) mocking allusion to a "jesting Pilate," Senator Paine's Judas-like suicide attempt, Smith's recitations from the New Testament in the filibuster scene as well as his philosophy of life which he boiled down to three words, "Love thy neighbor."

It was no accident that Capra recycled the same actors and actresses in his films. Unknowingly pioneering a Stanislavsky-like directoral method, Capra eschewed "acting" as such, encouraging instead cast members, from extra to ingenue, to simply play themselves. Capra alternated between Gary Cooper and Jimmy Stewart, who both bore a physical resemblance to Capra's idea of a hero, to fill the "savior" role in five of his movies:

> Cooper is the more mature person, at least he gives you that impression. He also gives you the impression of being a more solid, earthy person. He's simple, but he's strong and honest, and there's integrity written all over him. When you're dealing in the world of ideas and you want your character to be on a higher intellectual plane than just a simple man, you turn to persons like Jimmy Stew-

art because he has a look of the intellectual about him. And he can be an idealist. So when you have a combination of an intellectual who is also an idealist, you have a pretty fine combination.[19]

Capra's heroes are boyish in their lack of pretension and polish. First smitten by Senator Paine's daughter, Jefferson Smith can't seem to hold on to his hat in her presence. Capra calculatingly assigns Daniel Webster's desk to the freshman senator. The irony of a flustered Smith, delivering his maiden speech from the seat of one of America's greatest orators, was not lost on the film-going audience. Smith's inarticulate and clumsy delivery invited comparison with his role model, the suavely sophisticated "Silver Knight." Ironically, Senator Paine is also a quintessential Capra villain.

Smith's irrepressible enthusiasm and optimism, typical of the Capra hero, prompted his plan to draft a "how-hard-could-it-be" Senate bill by pulling an all-nighter with Ms. Saunders. Still feeling guilty for colluding with inside-the-Beltway journalists to embarrass Smith, Clarissa is forced to assist her clueless congressman. However, realizing that even heroes must exist in the real world, Capra took great pains to exact a faithful representation of the machinations required to shepherd a legislative package through the process. Many critics noted that this movie does a more effective job of instructing the uninitiated in government than any high school or university course. Capra makes the procedure for appointing a senator, the filibuster as parliamentary device, and the role of vice president come alive. Capra also used the character of Clarissa to articulate his faith in the system. The legislative branch of government works just fine, thank you very much; any failure is due to the occasional bad apple momentarily fooling the voters.

The Capra hero rarely departs from his small town roots, idiosyncrasies are tolerated, and folks are able to distinguish between respecting authority figures and holding them in awe. Jefferson Smith doesn't stop to weigh the unintentionally comic effect his duck calls might have on the Washington press corps; he was asked to demonstrate one of his God-given talents and he complied. Frank Capra resisted conformity his entire life. In fact, becoming an indistinguishable part of the whole was one of his greatest fears: "I don't like to see these youth conform so to each other. I'd rather see some individuals. That was the common man idea, I didn't think he was common, I thought he was a hell of a guy. I thought he was the hope of the world."[20] In the remainder of his films, Capra continued to probe for the uniqueness of every human being.

Capra's heroine, on the other hand, originated in the cynical, wisecracking character played by Clark Gable in earlier Capra films. Generous to a fault, street-smart women were popular with the men in the 1930s and 1940s. It was not unusual to hear a male fan confess he could picture himself marrying someone like Jean Arthur. Capra himself thought she was a "warm, able, lovable kind of woman who has a very feminine drive. I think of her as a woman who always is looking for that man who she could give her whole life to, but who can't seem to find him. A tough gal with a heart of gold."[21]

Even though they are tough enough to survive a daily prowl through big city jungles, Capra heroines immediately melt when touched by the inherent innocence and goodness of the Capra hero. Clarissa Saunders, closely modeled after Capra's wife, Lu, may have initially betrayed him to his enemies but she rallies round in the end, coaching Smith through his moment of truth, as wedding bells echo in her ears.

Capra preferred the conclusion to *Mr. Smith Goes to Washington* in which Taylor and his machine are handily destroyed. He went along with the ending, picked by preview audiences, that redeems Senator Paine (denied, like John Doe and George Bailey, the solution of suicide) but remains noncommittal about the fate of Boss Taylor.

While his films embraced the champion who refuses to sell out in the face of enormous pressure, Capra himself was more like Paine than Smith. Joseph McBride's well-documented biography concludes that Hollywood had successfully seduced Capra in much the same way that a tenured politician becomes incrementally compromised by Washington. He contends that Capra, who successfully posed as a self-righteous populist, secretly admired Benito Mussolini and nursed anti-Semitic attitudes.

AUDIENCE RESPONSE

The most important premiere of *Mr. Smith Goes to Washington* (October 16, 1939) was held in Philadelphia's historic Constitution Hall. Capra's guest list included members of the House and Senate as well as generals, admirals and, of course, the cream of Washington society. When the lights came up at the end of the film, there was only a faint smattering of applause. At the Press Club reception afterward, newsmen lashed out at Capra for disclosing the existence of graft in the nation's capital to a worldwide audience but what particularly ticked off these journalists was the movie's portrayal of a reporter, Dis Moore (Thomas Mitchell), as an alcoholic.

The Senate as a whole hated the movie. Majority Leader Alben W. Barkley of Kentucky, claiming to speak for the entire body, insisted that the film characterized senators as crooks. A third of the politicians in attendance walked out of the film, shocked by the depiction of lobbying in Congress. Critics, mainly politicians and the media elite, called it a disservice to democracy. U.S. Ambassador to Britain Joseph P. Kennedy's urgent and confidential cablegram insisted the film ridiculed the republic, struck a blow at the morale of America's allies, could be construed as pro-Axis propaganda and should be withdrawn from distribution in Europe. A few months later, when all reviews were in, the overall reaction was generally favorable. Frank Capra collected the press clippings and shipped them off to Kennedy,[22] feeling vindicated by the support from even the anti-Nazi contingent in Europe.

Mr. Smith Goes to Washington cleaned up at the 1939 Academy Awards, securing an Oscar for Lewis R. Foster as "Best Original Story" as well as nominations for "Best Picture" and "Best Director" for Capra, "Best Actor" for Jimmy Stewart, "Best Supporting Actor" for both Harry Carey and Claude Rains and "Best Screenplay" for Sidney Buchman. Most movie patrons were hardly surprised, much less shocked, at the prospect of corruption in government yet remained as hopeful as Capra that democratic principles were more powerful than those who would abuse positions of trust.

This film is rediscovered with each new generation of film-goers. Pop culturists call up old reviews of *Mr. Smith Goes to Washington* as a basis of comparison whenever a political film opens. They usually come up with a yet another timely insight into the uneasy relationship between the national seat of power and the entertainment capital of the world. I'll further predict anyone who shucks an ear of this Capracorn will make the same observation: "They just don't make movies like *Mr. Smith Goes to Washington* anymore!"

NOTES

1. Populism has always been with us to one degree or another. The basic idea is that the people have an essential wisdom that guides them in their rebellions against the elite. I ran across three controversies in my research: first, whether populism is an actual ideology; second, whether the definition of populism requires revealing its dark side, including anti-Semitism, distrust of immigrants, and conspiracy theories about Wall Street; and third, whether the defeat of populism disqualifies it as a true political/cultural alternative. I've tried to include notions representative of each point of view without attempting to resolve the disputes.

2. Thomas Jefferson, while actually an elitist (based in agriculture), shared a distrust of the Bank of the United States and big business with the 1890s Populists. However, Jefferson relied heavily on the immigrant vote and supported generous policies toward them.

3. Iain McLean, *The Concise Oxford Dictionary of Politics* (Oxford, England: Oxford University Press, 1996), 392.

4. George McKenna, *American Populism* (New York: G. P. Putnam & Sons, 1974), 130.

5. Gene Clanton, *Populism: The Human Preference in America 1890–1900* (Boston: Twayne, 1991), 160.

6. Irwin Unger, "Points of View: Were the Populists Backward Looking?" in *Firsthand America: A History of the United States*, edited by Virginia Bernhard, David Burner, Elizabeth Fox-Genovese and John McClymer, 3rd edn., vol. 2 (St. James, New York: Brandywine Press, 1993); and Lawrence Goodwyn, *Democratic Promise: The Populist Movement in America* (New York: Oxford University Press, 1976).

7. William Grieder, *Who Will Tell the People: The Betrayal of American Democracy* (New York: Simon and Schuster, 1992).

8. According to a 1995 Time/CNN poll, 74 percent of those polled believe the present tax system benefits the rich and is unfair to the ordinary working man or woman, as quoted in John Petrocik, *Los Angeles Times* (February 17, 1996), A20.

9. Ibid.

10. Geoffrey T. Hellman, "Thinker in Hollywood," *The New Yorker* 16 (February 24, 1940), 23–28.

11. Terry Christiansen, author of *Reel Politics*, makes an interesting observation: "The film has been labeled 'populist' because it seems to show faith in the 'the people' but its message is more complicated, perhaps darker, than that. It shows faith in one man—Smith, as Everyman—but it's hard to see how the film shows faith in a public that is so easily manipulated. Even the faith in one good man does not stand up to scrutiny. . . . Smith and the people are saved by Paine's crisis of conscience and bad aim."

12. John D. Hicks, *The Populist Revolt* (Lincoln, NE: University of Nebraska Press, 1961), 436.

13. For a complete compilation of Bormann's original work and that of some of this students, see John Cragan and Don Shields, *Applied Communication Research* (Prospect Heights, IL: Waveland Press, 1981). See also Dan Nimmo and James Combs, *Mediated Political Realities* (New York: Longman, 1983).

14. In her biography, *No Ordinary Time*, Doris Kearns Goodwin argues that Roosevelt did not come to the presidency with a liberal agenda. Chief among his platform planks were a balanced budget and a plan to rescue capitalism from the Great Depression. Roosevelt excoriated "economic royalists" (self-interested big businessmen) for their obstruction to the economic recovery, allying with a resurgent labor movement, a network of professionals, intellectuals (within and outside academe) and a colossal contingent of clergy.

15. Maury Klein, "Laughing Through the Tears: Hollywood Answers to the Depression," in *Hollywood's America: United States History Through Its Films*, edited by Steven Mintz and Randy Roberts (St. James, New York: Brandywine Press, 1993), 87–92.

16. Andrew Bergman, *We're in the Money* (New York: New York University Press, 1971), 132.

17. Ronald Reagan, "First Inaugural," *New York Times* (January 20, 1981), 1.

18. Jeffrey Richards, "Frank Capra and the Cinema of Populism," in *Movies and Methods: An Anthology*, edited by Bill Nichols (Berkeley: University of California Press, 1976), 68.

19. Richard Glatzer, "A Conversation with Frank Capra," in *Frank Capra*, edited by Richard Glatzer and John Raeburn (East Lansing: University of Michigan Press, 1974), 35.

20. The American Film Institute, "Frank Capra: One Man—One Film," in *Frank Capra*, edited by Richard Glatzer and John Raeburn (East Lansing: University of Michigan Press, 1974), 19.

21. Glatzer, "A Conversation," 35.

22. Paul F. Boller, Jr. and Ronald L. Davis, "The Playbill: Message Movies," in *Hollywood Anecdotes*, edited by Paul F. Boller, Jr. and Ronald L. Davis (New York: Ballantine, 1987), 310–12.

Chapter Three

Elitism in *The Magnificent Ambersons*

Beverly Merrill Kelley

When Mr. George Minafer and Miss Lucy Morgan exchange pleasantries during their initial rendezvous, George mentions his Uncle Jack, the Honorable Jack Amberson, that is. Unfortunately for the callow swain, George's unbridled arrogance impressed the object of his affection more than did his pretentious name-dropping. The offhand remark, "The family always liked to have someone in Congress—it's sort of a good thing in one way," was one of many quietly telling moments depicting life on the aristocratic plane in the film *The Magnificent Ambersons*, based on the 1918 Pulitzer Prize-winning novel by Booth Tarkington.

BOOTH TARKINGTON AND ORSON WELLES

Newton Booth Tarkington (1869–1946), who bore a striking resemblance to Bob Dole, was elected as a Republican to the Indiana Legislature in 1902. His subsequent disenchantment with politics provided fodder for two novels highly critical of congressional corruption, *The Gentleman from Indiana* and *In the Arena*. The precursor to George Minafer, the spoiled heir to the Amberson fortune, can be found in Tarkington's Hoosier boy in *His Own People*, who receives his comeuppance while traveling abroad. The conflict between materialism and the romanticism of those enmeshed in the past in *The Magnificent Ambersons*, while painting a wry portrait of the Indianapolis stuffed-shirt set, furnishes a compassionate cinematic depiction of elitism as well. Tarkington meant the locals' regard for the magnificence of the Amberson manse to be somewhat ironic since its grandeur was an expression of vulgarity. Yet the tragedy of the Ambersons was not their insulation from tech-

Joseph Cotten dancing with Dolores Costello, and Tim Holt with Anne Baxter on the stairs in *The Magnificent Ambersons*. Courtesy of the Academy of Motion Picture Arts and Sciences.

nological progress but their insistence on clinging to the materialism of an earlier age.

In making this film, Orson Welles (director, producer and screenwriter), would hardly overlook one of his abiding passions—politics. Ronald Brownstein, writing in *The Power and the Glitter*, reports: "But Welles was an uncompromising, impatient, militant liberal who believed in the Popular Front strategy of alliance with communists, lamented Roosevelt's 'political caution,' mourned his decision to drop Henry Wallace from the ticket, and hoped FDR would break with the Southern Democrats to form a truly 'liberal party.' "[1] After *Citizen Kane* and *The Magnificent Ambersons*, Welles was writing a political column, conducting lecture tours on the East Coast, and considered running for the Senate in 1946.[2] He proved a staunch supporter of Roosevelt and the New Deal, probably because he was a beneficiary. The federal government made possible the production that brought him national prominence: *Macbeth*, for the Negro Theater Project in Harlem. John Houseman and Orson Welles were also commissioned by the WPA's Federal Theater to start their own production company, the Mercury Theater, which would eventually prompt George Schaeffer to invite Welles out to Hollywood.

The plutocratic Tarkington attended all the right schools—Phillips Exeter Academy, Purdue and Princeton—but he failed to obtain his diploma, victim of the Greek proficiency requirement. However, Princeton eventually bestowed an honorary master's degree and doctorate on their distinguished dropout.

Had not the effects of a lifelong habit of chain-smoking, advanced age and cataract-induced blindness intervened, it would have preferable for Tarkington to have written the screenplay for *The Magnificent Ambersons* instead of Orson Welles. Not only was he an established playwright, the genial Tarkington served up sarcasm in a much more subtle sauce and seemed more at home depicting Midwestern life and morals (*Ambersons*, with *Growth* and *Penrod*, constituted his life-in-a-midland-town trilogy) than *wunderkind* Welles. Biographer Joseph McBride corroborates: "Welles's distance from the characters is slightly greater than Tarkington's, a fact which no doubt accounted for much of the tittering of audiences unable to see the satire" in Welles's version of *Ambersons*.[3]

George Orson Welles, the pampered offspring of a successful gentleman inventor and a concert pianist, might have thought of himself as a populist but he was as much an elitist as George Amberson Minafer. The wealthiest family in Indianapolis is not much different from the wealthiest family in Kenosha. The prodigy quickly established himself playing the piano, acting, drawing, painting, performing magic and writing verse. His mother died when Orson was eight, leaving father and young son to spend the next few years traveling around the world. When they returned to the United States, Orson was promptly enrolled at the exclusive Todd School in Woodstock, Illinois.

Welles was passionate about Booth Tarkington's novel and may have seen Vitaphone's silent film version, *Pampered Youth*, directed by David Smith in 1925. Tarkington's portrait of a turn-of-the-century municipality in Indiana was also attractive to Welles because it mimicked his experience in a hometown loath to change from sleighs to motor buggies.

For Welles to cast himself as kindred *enfant terrible*, George Minafer, in the film, the same part he played in the Mercury Theater of the Air adaptation,[4] seemed a no-brainer. A mature-appearing twenty-seven, Welles may have looked older than his character, yet his privileged childhood, megalomania, natural arrogance and inherent sense of entitlement should have rendered him much more believable in the role than former cowboy movie actor Tim Holt. Welles discovered Holt who was appearing in a small role in *Stagecoach* directed by Welles's favorite, John Ford. Holt was noted for his black, curly hair, an insolent pretty face, a ramrod back, the hint of plumpness and an aggressive masculinity scarcely concealing a vulnerable "feminine side." He conveyed the character's vain cruelty with a haughty strut.

Pampered Youth used two actors, Ben Alexander and Cullen Landis, to play younger and older Georges,[5] which might also have solved the age differential problem in Welles's version of *The Magnificent Ambersons*.

The biggest obstacle was Welles's ill-considered obligation to act in Norman Foster's *Journey Into Fear*, necessitated by an agreement he made to finagle himself out of difficulties encountered while unsuccessfully attempting to pull off *The Way to Santiago*, a political espionage thriller, as the follow-up to *Citizen Kane*. Welles's biographer Robert L. Carringer reports in the chapter on *The Magnificent Ambersons*:

> What happened after *Citizen Kane* is one of the great tragedies of film history.... But in less than a year after the release of *Citizen Kane* Welles found himself in catastrophic difficulties on two major productions that were eventually taken out of his hands altogether. As a consequence he would never be trusted again with a major Hollywood production on his own terms, and from the summer of 1942 to the rest of his life he was the official pariah of the Hollywood system and its most celebrated casualty.[6]

Welles overspent on both RKO projects. *The Magnificent Ambersons*, budgeted at $853,950, cost $1,013,760.46 to make, and *Journey Into Fear* chalked up massive over-runs,[7] ultimately costing George Schaeffer, Welles's only advocate at RKO, his position as head of the studio and Welles, his job, as well.

Less than entranced over the length and the "arty" aspects of *The Magnificent Ambersons*, the sneak preview audiences in Pomona and Pasadena turned in opinion cards reading:

"No, the worst picture I ever saw."

"People like to laff [*sic*], not be bored to death."

"Picture will not be received by the general audience because they as a whole are too darn ignorant [*sic*]."

"I did not like it. I could not understand it. Too many plots."

"Too many wierd [*sic*] camera shots."

"It should be shelved as it is a crime to take people's hard-earned money for such artistic trash as Mr. Welles would have us think. Mr. Welles had better go back to radio, I hope."[8]

The studio panicked. Even Orson's Mercury Theater friends thought the Chekhovian ending was too edgy. His dear friend, Joseph Cotten, wrote this heartfelt note dated March 28, 1942:

You have written doubtless the most faithful adaptation any book has ever had, and when I finished reading it I had the same feeling I had when I read the book. When you read it, I had that same reaction only stronger. The picture on the screen seems to mean something else. It is filled with some deep though vague psychological significance that I think you never meant it to have.[9]

Robert Wise, in a series of complicated switches and reconfigurations, was dispatched to cut the film from nearly two hours to eighty-eight minutes. Orson was in Rio, ineffectively attempting to communicate via telephone and telegraph while tied up with the South American version (requested by the State Department) of *It's All True*. Wise and Mercury Business Manager Jack Moss remained faithful to Tarkington's book to make editing decisions. Screenings for the press were held toward the end of June 1942. Reviewers praised the film's artistic value but the trade press considered it a tough sell. The cut footage was unceremoniously burned and Charles Koerner opened the film cautiously outside New York in August 1942, long past the original Easter date, to "spotty results." Eventually RKO abandoned the film, losing $600,000 on the deal.[10]

A movie poster for *The Magnificent Ambersons* envisions an eight-armed Welles working simultaneously on everything from designing the costumes to conducting the orchestra. The copy reads: "Hollywood's most amazing citizen now brings you his successor to *Citizen Kane*."[11]

What a perfect metaphor for Orson Welles as his own worst enemy. Welles typically blamed others for various delays and overages; he particularly singled out illnesses by cast members and the relatively inexperienced cinematographer, who operated at a painstakingly slow pace. It was, however, Welles who brought about the disastrous outcome by judgments that, in retrospect, appear rash. Because scripting was his weakest suit, his most significant error was crafting the screenplay himself.

Cinematic authorship, the topic of a childish sandbox argument with respect to *Citizen Kane* (debating whether the director is the true auteur), was one of the few noncontroversial aspects during the production of *The Magnificent Ambersons*. Welles wrote the opening montage and blocked out the rest of the novel in a nine-day stint on King Vidor's (*Our Daily Bread* and *The Fountainhead*) yacht, greatly benefiting from having already banged out the radio version on his typewriter. Amalia Kent was whisked off to seclusion on Catalina Island to turn Welles's efforts into conventional screenplay format.

Welles esteemed Tarkington's writing ability, attributing the quality of the overall film to Tarkington's extraordinary ability as a novelist. He lamented the fall from fashion of Tarkington's prairie values and remarked during an interview with Peter Bogdanovich that Tarkington deserved to be taken much more seriously: "What doesn't come from the book is a careful imitation of his style. What was all my own was a third act which took the story into a darker, harder dimension."[12] And, it might be added, most of this act was left on the cutting-room floor. Since Welles had traded away his right to the final cut, the studio exercised its preference for the Tarkington ending.

Orson Welles claimed that his father, Richard Head (Dick) Welles, had been a friend of Booth Tarkington and the author's model for Eugene Morgan (the character played by genial Joseph Cotten as a gentleman of the old school rather than the maverick head of Morgan Motors), "an early automobile fellow with a deep suspicion of what the automobile would do—fascinated by it, and very much afraid of what it was going to do to the world."[13] At this point, it might be appropriate to warn the reader that during an interview with Jean Clay in 1962, Welles crowed: "If you try to probe, I'll lie to you. Seventy-five percent of what I say in interviews is false. I'm like a hen protecting her eggs. I cannot talk. I must protect my work. Introspection is bad for me."[14]

The record shows that Welles's father tinkered with lamps for bicycles (Aunt Fanny Amberson squanders the last of her wealth investing in automobile headlights) but there's no evidence Orson's father had a hand in inventing the automobile. However, both Eugene Morgan and Dick Welles made a fortune in spite of themselves as the sort of inventors who were in it for fun rather than funds. It is hardly surprising that neither Tarkington nor Welles were able to come down hard on people who walked, talked and lived as they did.

In a 1967 interview with Kenneth Tynan, Orson Welles tried to explain himself in this way: "For thirty years people have been asking me how I reconcile X with Y! The truthful answer is that I don't. Everything about me is a contradiction, and so is everything about everybody else. We are made out of oppositions; we live between two poles. There's a philistine and an aesthete in all of us, and a murderer and a saint. You don't reconcile the poles. You just recognize them."[15]

ELITISM AS POLITICAL IDEOLOGY

Elitism,[16] strictly speaking, is a belief in the principle that government ought to be confined to individuals (usually power-based in economic, political, military or academic institutions) who can transcend ordinary circumstances by being positioned to make consequential decisions.[17] Elitism is more often a platonic ideal than a comprehensive and consistent ideological framework. To view elitism as an American political ideology requires a grounding in both democracy and capitalism. Ironically, Athens, traditionally honored as the birthplace of democracy, fails to qualify as "democratic" in the modern sense of the word, which is derived from the Greek *democratia*, meaning "rule by the people." Since women, slaves and resident aliens, 90 percent of the city's population,[18] were excluded from participation in Athenian government, touting itself as the cradle of self-government appears to stretch the truth. That didn't stop Pericles (430 BC), the first ideologue of democracy, from arguing its promotion through the virtues of tolerance and public-spiritedness. Yet despite the persuasive rhetoric of Athens' foremost orator, philosophers Plato and Aristotle could not be counted as fans of democracy. The American founding brought new life to the idea of popular rule.

However, the United States, even in the eighteenth century, would have had almost as much trouble justifying itself as a democracy as did Athens. Jean-Jacques Rousseau, who influenced American revolutionaries, wrote in his 1762 *Social Contract*, "In the strict sense of the term, a true democracy has never existed, and never will exist."[19] Rousseau's observation seems to be the single most significant argument justifying the class politics of elitism. Then as now, a precise definition of who makes up "the people" in "rule by the people," appears to be up for grabs. In fact, any government anywhere on the globe may apply for the designation "democratic," as long as a majority of males are enfranchised.

Democracy has also become synonymous with majority rule, which assumes equal rights by all citizens (one person, one vote) or equal competence, circumscribed by the belief, all things being equal, that the more people who are involved in arriving at a decision, the more likely that decision will be correct.[20] To address the tension between democracy and liberty, said decision should also include safeguards that keep the majority from violating the rights of the minority.

While it might seem inappropriate to link "elitism" and the United States in the same sentence, in practice, political or economic elitism often supplants the democratic ideal in this country. The conflict between elitism and populism is not only important but also inherent in democracy worldwide. According to Jeffrey Bell, author of *Populism and Elitism: Politics in the Age of Equality*, "it explains more of what is happening in the world than the usual distinctions between left and right or socialism and capitalism; it extends in one form or another into virtually every area of human life."[21]

In popular folklore as well as official rhetoric, the seat of legitimate power is believed to be "the great American public," but note the word "idiot," which comes from the Greek *idiotes*, meaning "private citizen," would imply that even in the birthplace of democracy, private citizens are known as idiots. With the ability of the citizenry to rule appearing to negate itself with each succeeding election, this point becomes particularly persuasive in favor of rule by intellectual elites from philosopher-kings to Ivy League brahmins of nineteenth-century America.

Elitism finds roots in the work of Plato, who was born into an aristocratic Athenian family, and the writings of Aristotle, whose father was the wealthy physician to the king of Macedon. Both philosophers remained critical of democracy; the former took exception to yanking away control from experts in governance and reassigning it to populist rabble-rousers while the latter objected to democracy on the grounds that government by the people was, in actuality, rule by the economically disadvantaged, whom Aristotle fully expected to dispossess the rich.

Capitalism traditionally is defined in an economic context, usually in comparison with Marxist notions of production modes. In capitalism, ownership is private and markets determine production and distribution. However, other attributes of the term "capitalism," at least those of a connotative nature, may be from Max Weber's discussion of the "spirit of capitalism," in which he postulates a synthesis of the Calvinistic work ethic with a "can-do" entrepreneurial attitude. "Profit motive," a term also closely associated with capitalism, focuses on the organization of production for markets in a commercial context.

Free competition, for most Americans, remains more a political than an economic concept. The Scottish Enlightenment philosopher and founder of classical economics, Adam Smith, seemingly defends plutocracy in *The Theory of Moral Sentiments* (1759):

> The rich . . . divide with the poor the produce of all their improvements. They are led by an *invisible hand* to make nearly the same distinction of the necessaries of life, which would have been made,

had the earth been divided into equal portions among all its in-
habitants, and thus without intending it, without knowing it, advance the interest of the society, and afford means to the
multiplication of the species.[22]

Yet while Adam Smith pushed a laissez-faire[23] economic policy, he did
not believe as a matter of public policy that the unregulated market was
the best provider of the national defense, public works and education.
He was highly suspicious of both government and nongovernment elites,
especially when they got in bed together. Writing in opposition to mer-
cantilism, which equated wealth with trade surplus, he substituted human labor and ingenuity instead. His conviction that the economic
competence of the common people spawns broad-based growth was not
picked up by one of his successors. For the most part, the sweeping
principles of Adam Smith as articulated in the *Wealth of Nations* (1776)
carried the credibility of holy writ until the 1930s, when no "invisible
hand" seemed evident.

Americans also yearn for blue-blooded leaders, social elitists role-
modeling refinement as opposed to dealing out deft fiscal policy. Over
150 years ago, Alexis de Tocqueville paid a call on nineteenth-century
America in an effort to perceive the progress of the Jeffersonian experiment for himself. He became intrigued with the tension between egalitarian ideals and an entrenched class structure. In *Democracy in America*
he wrote, "The surface of American society is covered with a layer of
democratic paint, but from time to time one can see the old aristocratic
colors breaking through."[24]

Most of the high-profile American revolutionaries, although rebelling
against a political elitist doctrine (divine right of kings), remained essentially elitist themselves, moving easily from position to position atop the
major institutions. That is not to say that elites are incapable of sincere
populist beliefs. The optimism of the upper class was a key factor in the
American Revolution. Yet the hostility between populism and elitism
hinges not on class conflict *per se* but rather on whether the people are
competent to handle their own affairs.

Thomas Jefferson, who usually sounded the popular view that rank,
birth and "tinsel-aristocracy" would shrink into insignificance because
of the abundant opportunities of the New World, refined the traditional
argument favoring aristocracy in an 1813 exchange with John Adams: "I
agree with you that there is a natural aristocracy among men. . . . The
grounds of this are virtue and talents. That form of government is best
that prevents the ascendancy of artificial aristocrats and provides for the
ascendancy of the natural aristocrats, the elite of virtue and talent."[25]
When Jefferson speaks of "natural aristocrats," he supplies a key to understanding a film such as *The Magnificent Ambersons*. In a natural aris-

tocracy, some individuals will rise above others, but their sons and daughters lack the guarantees inherent in a hereditary aristocracy. Deficient in talent or virtue, aristocratic progeny are not immune from falling prey to an economic reorganization that thrusts a newly emerging elite ahead of them.

Prior to the 1930s, political elitism was temporarily sidetracked only twice: The Metropolitan 400[26] couldn't flourish in the face of Jacksonian democracy, demonstrating the ability of popular government to transform from business servant to rival; and during the 1890s, populists organized against railroads, banks and other monopolistic elites.[27] Monopolies became subject to prosecution under the Sherman Anti-Trust Act of 1890. Later merging with progressives, anti-elitists promoted the graduated income tax, public ownership of utilities, voter initiative and referendum, an eight-hour work day, immigration restriction and government control of currency.

The supremacy of corporate economic power began with the congressional elections of 1866 and was legitimized twenty years later when the Supreme Court based its decision to protect and preserve the corporation on the 14th Amendment. American aristocracy was at its zenith in wealth and prestige during what became known as the "Golden Era" of America's ruling elite, around the time referred to in the first line of the film, "The magnificence of the Ambersons began in 1873." The film went on to chronicle the events culminating in the financial ruin of many of the nation's upper echelon.

In *American Capitalism*, John Kenneth Galbraith writes: "Measured by its continuing imprint on actions and attitudes, the Depression clearly stands with the Civil War as one of the two most important events in American history since the Revolution."[28] The crash should have sounded the death knell for elitism. The prevailing principles of American capitalism, based on Say's Law of Markets (contending that production provided the purchasing power to buy whatever was produced), had lulled economists, and through them, politicians and businessmen, and through them, the public (except for those chronically complaining farmers), into a false sense of security.

The crash of 1929 marked a crisis for capitalism, clouding the American economic system's competency, credibility and capacity to endure. Radicals, socialists, political activists and intellectuals, eventually rallying to Roosevelt, were disillusioned by the refusal of elites (attempting to cohere to the remnant of their power) to break through their denial. In fact, the word "depression" was coined by Hoover to minimize the ill-wrought wreckage. No one was fooled, however, and it was the fact that those causing the collapse were shipwrecked, finding themselves alongside the innocent investors and the jobless, which ultimately saved them from retributive class warfare.

As governor of New York in 1932, Roosevelt decried the myth of unfettered private enterprise serving brahministic self-interest. Yet FDR was
an elitist, born and bred. With hordes of Roosevelts on one side and
droves of Delanos on the other, FDR's childhood was a textbook exercise
in conspicuous consumption. Whatever Franklin wanted, Franklin got:
"A pony? As soon as his legs were long enough to straddle its back. A
boat? He had the use of his father's yacht, the *Half Moon*, a Campobello
sea captain to teach him how to handle it and a twenty-one footer of his
own. A gun? His father handed him one at eleven."[29] Sara Delano Roosevelt's single expectation was that her son should become "a respected
citizen of his community just as they were, living quietly and happily
along the Hudson,"[30] not much different from the expectation George
Minafer held for himself. But inspired by "Cousin Theodore" while still
at Groton, FDR pledged his life to public service, a commitment further
cemented during his studies at Harvard.

Many Americans viewed the Great Depression not just as the collapse
of capitalism but as the veritable demise of democracy. In 1929 when
Hoover took office, unemployment averaged 3.2 percent; four years later,
joblessness had shot up to 25.2 percent, with Hoover's high tariff policies
worsening matters. Fault-finding with the stuffed-shirt crowd became
the order of the day: charges of paternalism at the least; totalitarianism
at the worst, with corruption as consequent (condensed by British states-
man, William Pitt,[31] somewhat predating the celebrated Lord Acton admonition) thrown in for good measure. The major reason fascism
flourished elsewhere on the globe was that the unemployed masses with
nothing to lose were willing to trade freedom for security. FDR, a democratic Democrat, stopped considerably short of restructuring society; he
just wanted to get people back to work.

It was Roosevelt's willingness to speak the truth about the condition
of the country that gave the electorate its first inkling of hope. That
optimism formed the basis of his political platform and his popularity.
If the old ideas about capitalism had led to its breakdown, new ideas, it
was argued, would build it back up. British economist John Maynard
Keynes overhauled Smith and Say by turning the spotlight from markets
to capital for investment, sluggish supplies of which were being hoarded
during the deep 50 percent dive in GNP during Hoover's watch.[32] Public
works created by alphabet agencies and deficit spending brought out
hidden stores of idle lucre, increasing in Keynesian fashion, "aggregate
demand for goods and services" and thus creating more wealth for in-
trepid investors.

Media elitist William Randolph Hearst, however, referred to FDR's
plan for recovery as "the Raw Deal."[33] By the 1936 presidential campaign, more than 80 percent of the press opposed Roosevelt, yet he won
by the highest percentage ever. During the campaign and for years after,

many newspapers, including major syndicates, went beyond all legitimate bounds in an effort to disparage the president and the New Deal.[34] Yet FDR's New Deal did not reverse elitist control of politics and economics. No competing center of power arose to challenge the omnipotent corporations. In fact, FDR imported captains of industry, the so-called "dollar-a-year men," to offer guidance to government expanding to elephantine proportions; lamentably, they never left.

The earlier and middle Roosevelt administrations can best be understood as a search for some route within capitalism to reduce unemployment. FDR created the ultimate center ring balancing act: "He subsidized the defaults of the capitalist economy which had simply broken down; and by his rhetoric, he balanced its political disgrace, putting 'economic royalists' in the political doghouse."[35]

ELITISM IN *THE MAGNIFICENT AMBERSONS*

Although *The Magnificent Ambersons* appears to be critical of the controlling class of the wealthy, Welles makes us feel compassion for the figures in the story. The words from the original trailer describing *The Magnificent Ambersons* must have irked those who prided themselves on being descended from those with "all rights of royalty without the responsibilities."

Yet the responsibilities expected of the elite were rigorous and rigidly self-enforced. What George Minafer called "living an honorable life" was defined in what appears to be a highly restrictive moral code. For example, Isabel had to give up Eugene Morgan not merely because he crashed into the bass violin while engaged in a ritualistic serenade but because he had violated a code of behavior that forbade public drunkenness. Lucy Morgan refused to marry George Amberson Minafer because she realized that without work of some sort, he would be violating the code that prohibited idleness, even for the rich.

The Protestant ethic of productive capitalism and the wasteful consumption of capital through the accumulation of useless things stand in diametrical opposition, even for the plutocracy. When George, educated at the finest schools, tells Lucy that he doesn't intend to go into a profession because those types don't know about "real things," Lucy's curiosity is piqued.[36] She follows up with the defining question: "What do you want to be?" George's answer, "A yachtsman," positions him forever in the category of undesirable mate, defective because he would not be able, as Sarah Roosevelt expected of her Franklin, to become "a respected citizen of his community just as they were, living quietly and happily" not on the Hudson but on Amberson Boulevard.

There were a number of unspoken rules to be filed under the "business is business" universal. Some dealt with the nuances of competition; others with situational ethics. During a dinner conversation, Uncle Jack inquires about a horseless carriage shop that has opened outside town, with the Major adding his prediction that either the new entrepreneurs would drive Morgan out of business or the two of them just might join forces against the rest of the town's business owners. Monopolies, though rare for the most part, were regularly prosecuted by the Sherman Anti-Trust legislation passed in 1890. The reference was to the accepted (by elites) practice of collusion. The Sherman law would soon be utilized to prosecute two or more businesses getting together in order to control prices, although proving collusion in court remained difficult.

When all was said and done, however, no one has yet figured out a way to "take it with you." The narration describing Major Amberson preparing to meet his maker could have been written by Frank Capra, it was so consistent with the populist morality. We encounter Major Amberson realizing that all his joys and sorrows, all his wealth and accomplishments count for naught in comparison with facing the Grim Reaper: "For the Major knew now he had to plan how to enter an unknown country, where he was not even sure of being recognized as being an Amberson." It is in the spiritual realm that elitism went wrong, producing the wealthy class who horde their money, who cry "communist" when asked to provide a safety net for the poor, who object to government restrictions of any kind despite the lesson of the Depression, and who get their comeuppance just as Georgie Minafer did when he made that final promenade up National Avenue.

It wasn't that George had not been taught the rules. The twin tenets of capitalism and democracy constituted a symbolic system on which elite social relations were based. Both money and the law became part of a social order based on the abstract elitist ideological principles discussed previously. Thus, money transcends the literal exchange of objects and rules transcend relationships, placing both in a spiritual system of morality.[37]

Isabel Minafer took martyrdom and maternal sacrifice to untoward levels. George knew at some level that he would be expected to contribute to charity and to take on some sort of cause as a member of the plutocracy. However, this was head knowledge as opposed to wisdom of the heart. He was more interested in his entitlements, what he could expect just because he was an Amberson: "Anybody that really is anybody ought to be able to go about as they like in their own town, I should think."

George thought wrong. His violation of rules against risking the lives or property of others when he felt like barreling through town in his pony cart or the impropriety of his house-to-house attempt to clear his mother's name via intimidation was duly noted. Punishment for these offenses would be meted at some point: "There were people, grown people they were, who expressed themselves longingly—they did hope to see the day, they said, when that boy would get his comeuppance."

Both Welles and Tarkington suggested a psychological foundation for George's feelings of megalomania. An only child, a sickly one at that, he had almost died when he was about four months old. That was all Isabel needed to become a textbook "overprotective mother." A so-called "prophetess" of the film, who watched Isabel, along with the rest of the townspeople, choose to marry a man she did not love, predicted she would lavish all her affection on George. George repaid her maternal self-sacrifice by preventing her from marrying Eugene when she had a second chance after Wilbur Minafer's untimely demise. You don't have to be Freud to see the Oedipal conflict spelled out complete with a Greek chorus following the initial montage.

George's father was a nonentity even in premature death, symbolized by the sudden appearance of a black wreath on the door of the Amberson mansion. Welles trained the camera on the townspeople filing past the funeral bier, one remarking how quiet a man he seemed to have been and another commenting, "The town will hardly know he's gone." The parallels to the Depression's prompting a universal need for a father figure are not far-fetched even for the amateur film critic. The audience is invited to explore George's psychological struggle as symbolic of the consequent tension between eschewing the safety and security of omnipotent government with the suffocating act of crawling back into the womb of federal dependency.

Wilbur Minafer remained a relic from a previous age in which agriculture drove the economy, while Eugene Morgan represented new technology and the challenges the inauguration of the industrial age would deliver to the town. Isabel symbolizes the elite who, whether willingly or otherwise, contributed to their own destruction. A mother's vocation is to give up her child, to work herself out of a job. Eugene implores Isabel to let go, realizing at some level that she was incarcerating George in emotional infancy, depriving him of manhood and preventing his departure on a personal journey toward greatness. However, she could release him only in death.

After spurning George for the final time, Lucy makes up a charming little parable about a depraved Indian chief of the They Can't Help It tribe, whose name roughly translates as Chief Rides Down Everything. She tells her father that the chief was the most evil Indian who had ever lived. Rides Down Everything "was unspeakable. He was so proud he wore iron shoes and walked over people's faces with them." The tribe determines that Rides Down Everything's youth and inexperience were no excuse for his conduct and resolves that the community was better off without him. The chief was placed aboard a canoe carried by the current toward the great sea: "And he never got back. They didn't want him back, of course. They hated [Rides Down Everything] but they weren't able to discover any other warrior they wanted to make chief in his place. They couldn't help feeling that way." The extension of the metaphor from rejected suitor to corporate America seems fairly obvious.

In film criticism, the French phrase *mise-en-scéne* refers to the physical setting of the action. In *The Magnificent Ambersons*, the glimpses we get of the privileged world are critical to understanding the film's political ideology.

Orson Welles reads the following as the camera pans across the exterior of the mansion, the real star of the movie:

> Against so homespun a background, the magnificence of the Ambersons was as conspicuous as a brass band at a funeral. There it is, the Amberson mansion. The pride of the town. Well, well. Sixty thousand dollars for the woodwork alone. Hot and cold running water, upstairs and down. And stationary washstands in every last bedroom in the place.

It was the interior, however, that gave the most information about the rarefied air breathed by the Ambersons. The house served as a metaphor for most of what Welles and Tarkington had to say about the upper class. They asked the viewer to interpret the images in the same way that one reads poetry. The camera came in long and low, emphasizing the relationship of the characters to their environment. While the exteriors were shot documentary-style, the interiors were caught in a highly stylized juxtaposition of long and short angles, providing sweeping glimpses of gaudy baroque furnishings, black walnut staircases and, at the opulent Amberson ball, the "last of the great, long-remembered dances that everybody talked about," a dazzlingly ornate Christmas tree. The camera took in the richly flowered wallpaper, shimmering chandeliers, and glowing brasswork along with "the gleaming young heads, white shoulders, jewels and chiffon." Welles reports, "You see, the basic intention was to portray a golden world—almost one of memory—and then show what it turns into. Having set up this dream town of the good old days, the whole point was to show the automobile wrecking it—not only the family but the town." Welles tenderly brushstrokes an American past as visually nostalgic as a cameo brooch.

Relying on the language of the mind, exemplified by fantasy themes such as the land of opportunity discussed in *Mr. Smith Goes to Washington*, or taking delight in a slower and simpler life required audience participation, something the preview audiences in Pomona and Pasadena resisted, and which biographers of Welles explained away by noting that viewers caught up in the war wanted to be entertained instead of being educated.

While there were major overruns in every category of production costs, by far the largest percentage was attributable to the three major sets, consisting of the three floors of the Amberson mansion. A trio of key scenes depended on these larger-than-life settings: the Amberson ball, the dinner party for Eugene Morgan and the confrontation between George and Fanny on the stairs.

The four-sided sets provided "virtual space," so that every camera angle allowed you to see a space beyond the room in which the action was taking place. Usually an editor allows the viewer to provide closure by use of dissolves or fade-to-black. For example, if you see an actor enter a door, that door doesn't necessarily have to lead anywhere; most times it does not, since it is cheaper to construct false fronts. According to Robert Carringer, "The largest single expense in the budget by far was for set construction, $137,265.44. This is hugely expensive—as a percentage of total picture cost it is nearly twice the proportion for *Citizen Kane*, almost three times as much as *Gone with the Wind*, more even than RKO's all-time champion set-centered film, the cathedral in *The Hunchback of Notre Dame*."[38]

Further, Welles wanted the central staircase to dominate the Amberson mansion:

> The heart of a pompous house was its pompous staircase. It's all that imitation-palace business. These people haven't got any royal processions to make, but they wouldn't admit it. I had great-aunts who lived in houses exactly like that one. It even had a ballroom on the top floor just like the Amberson mansion.

Since the ingenue role of Lucy Morgan was one of Anne Baxter's first parts, she was frequently visited on the set by her grandfather, Frank Lloyd Wright. He used to make withering remarks about the baroque atmosphere of the Amberson mansion, remaining incredulous at the taste of people living during that period.

With respect to the cast, Welles made some engaging decisions; many were incestuous, some were inspired, others proved more trouble than they were worth. Welles admitted he had Agnes Moorehead, one of the Mercury players from *Citizen Kane*, in mind for the part of Aunt Fanny as he was writing the screenplay for *The Magnificent Ambersons*. While Moorehead's Aunt Fanny was not quite the character beset by violent mood swings and blessed by the ability to look twenty at one moment and sixty the next (described in Tarkington's novel), Moorehead was able to depict the frustration and misery of her character by high-pitched whining, pointless rage attacks and fits of hysterical weeping. The anecdote in which Welles rehearsed Moorehead so many times for the boiler scene (which merited an Oscar nomination and a Best Actress award from the New York Film Critics) that she ultimately did become hysterical may be apocryphal.

Orson Welles loved Richard Bennett, bestowing on him the compliment: "Greatest lyric power of any actor I ever saw on the English-speaking stage."[39] Bennett was better known for fathering a trio of cinematic luminaries: Barbara, Constance and Joan. Welles found Bennett, then lost from cinematic memory, residing in a boarding house in Catalina. His salad days behind him, Bennett couldn't remember a line, so Welles worked out an arrangement in which he spoke the words, and Bennett repeated them, with the sound editor removing Welles's voice.

In selecting the actress to play Isabel, Welles initially thought of Mary Pickford but asked Dolores Costello to star instead. Welles discovered the former wife of Jack Barrymore living in retirement, and she, like Bennett, often had trouble staying focused on the action. Costello, although still a great beauty, was a trifle old for the part but she conveys her character's delicacy, fragility and genteel quality.

Nearly forty-five minutes were excised from *The Magnificent Ambersons*; what was lost remains debatable. While the missing film was burned, extant copies of the screenplay offer a better idea of what remained unseen by the 1942 audience. Most of the three big scenes remained intact, with modest cuts that never took away from the impact. Some edits were promoted by the unintended tittering of preview audiences when Welles had missed the mark satirically. Redundant or extraneous scenes were chopped so that, for example, you could still get the idea that the automobile transformed a bucolic village into a filthy metropolis without taking up Wellesian film time. Without the scenes related to the Major's futile attempts at thrift, the conflict between the townspeople and the Ambersons, the populist-elitist clash, lacked potency. Numerous references to the polluting effects of the automobile were summarily excised. Welles's prescient warning that technology would destroy the environment as well as the quality of life was lost to the 1942 audiences. Probably the most detrimental cut was the "excision of the great silent sequence when the camera, strapped to the operator's chest, explores the stairs and the empty sheeted rooms in a repeat of the great take with which it earlier explored the same setting filled with dancing and carousing figures."[40]

CONCLUSION

Welles accomplished a great deal in a commercial medium without ever having achieved commercial success. "They will love me after I'm dead," predicted Welles and he was correct.[41]

He harbored, however, more than a few regrets. Both Peter Bogdanovich, Welles's favorite biographer, and Oja Kadar, Welles's companion before his death in 1985, testified that Orson Welles couldn't watch *The Magnificent Ambersons* without his eyes filling up with tears.[42] Thus it would seem the final narration in *The Magnificent Ambersons* was a depiction not only of George Minafer but Welles himself. Like Minafer, in the years following the release of this film, Welles would find himself on a stroll down his own *via doloroso*:

> George Amberson Minafer walked homeward slowly though what seemed to be the strange streets of a strange city. . . . This was the last walk home he was ever to take up National Avenue. . . . Tomorrow they were to move out. Tomorrow everything would be gone. . . . Something had happened, that thing which years ago had been the eagerest hope of many, many good citizens at last; George Amberson Minafer had got his comeuppance. He got it three times filled and running over.

George Amberson Minafer's mutable hometown, first traversed in a pony-cart driven with reckless abandon, mirrors America's development from localized preindustrial communities into a competitive society of industrial capitalism, once described by German sociologist Ferdinand Tonnies as *Gemeinschaft* and *Gesellschaft* in his book *Community and Society*. *Gemeinschaft* (community) is the total experience of intimate, private and exclusive life. *Gesellschaft* (society) is a public life residing in the world itself: "In *Gemeinschaft* with one's family, one lives from birth on, bound to it in weal and woe. One goes into *Gesellschaft* as one goes into a strange country." Coincidentally, both Tonnies and Welles employ the word "strange" to portray an existence in which the sense of community has been lost.[43]

The Amberson mansion provided the vehicle for contrasting 1870s elitism, when a horse-drawn streetcar driver took the time to wait for silk and satin-gowned women to finish dressing, with the urban sprawl of factories belching toxic smoke as well as factory workers who assumed an anonymity much like the cogs in their machines. George Minafer's belief that he ought to be making the consequential decisions for the townspeople, once squarely grounded in the economic superiority of the Ambersons, was based on a false sense of entitlement. American aristocrats such as Minafer made way for the Eugene Morgans, who through personal ingenuity and financial success acquired the "credentials," once possessed by the Ambersons, to assume their rightful places as the city's "most influential citizens."

'Twas ever thus.

NOTES

1. Ronald Brownstein, *The Power and the Glitter, The Hollywood-Washington Connection* (New York: Pantheon Books, 1990), 96.

2. Ibid., 105.

3. Joseph McBride, *Orson Welles* (New York: Da Capo Press, 1996), 62.

4. On October 29, 1939, with Walter Huston as Eugene and Nan Sunderland, Mrs. Walter Huston, as Isabel.

5. McBride, *Orson Welles*, 55.

6. Robert L. Carringer, *The Making of Citizen Kane* (Berkeley: University of California Press, 1985), 122.

7. Ibid., 125–27.

8. Orson Welles and Peter Bogdanovich, *This Is Orson Welles*, edited by Jonathan Rosenbaum (New York: Harper Collins, 1992), 117.

9. Ibid., 121–22.

10. Carringer, *The Making of Citizen Kane*, 127.

11. Ibid., 135.

12. Welles and Bogdanovich, *This Is Orson Welles*, 96.

13. Ibid., 98.

14. Kenneth Tynan, *The World of Orson Welles*, cited in Simon Callow, *Orson Welles, the Road to Xanadu* (New York: Viking, 1993), xi.

15. Ibid.

16. Like populism, elitism has always been with us to one degree or another. Its premise is that people lack the essential wisdom to guide themselves, therefore necessitating governance by a minority elite. I ran across two corollaries to populist controversies in my research: whether elitism is an actual ideology, and whether the definition of elitism requires revealing its dark side, including the propensity of power to corrupt. Again I've tried to include notions representative of each point of view without attempting to resolve them.

17. C. Wright Mills would number churches, families and schools as "adapters" rather than "shapers" in his delineation of the major institutions of society.

18. Jeffrey Bell, *Populism and Elitism: Politics in the Age of Equality* (Washington, DC: Regnery Gateway, 1992), 45.

19. Jean-Jacques Rousseau, *The Social Contract and Discourse* (1762), Book III, Chapter 4 (London: Dent, 1973), 217.

20. The theory of justice underlying twelve-member juries.

21. Bell, *Populism*, 3.

22. Adam Smith, *The Theory of Moral Sentiments* (Indianapolis: Liberty Fund, 1982), 184–85; emphasis added.

23. French for minimal governmental interference in market transactions.

24. Alexis de Tocqueville, *Democracy in America*, edited by J. P. Mayer, translated by George Lawrence (Garden City, NY: Doubleday Anchor, 1969), 49.

25. Jefferson to Adams, October 28, 1813, in Thomas Jefferson, *Writings*, edited by Merrill D. Peterson (New York: Library of America, 1984), 1305–6.

26. C. Wright Mills, *The Power Elite* (New York: Oxford University Press, 1956), 47–70.

27. Michael Kazin, *The Populist Persuasion* (New York: Harper Collins, 1995), 27–46.

28. John Kenneth Galbraith, *American Capitalism: The Concept of Countervailing Power* (Boston: Houghton Mifflin, 1956), 65.

29. Joseph P. Lash, *Eleanor and Franklin* (New York: New American Library, 1971), 169–70.

30. Ibid., 171.

31. William Pitt, "Case of Wilkes" speech, January 9, 1770: "Unlimited power is apt to corrupt the minds of those who possess it; and this I know, my lords, that where laws end, tyranny begins." John Emerich Edward Dalberg-Acton, "Letter to Bishop Mandell Creighton" (April 24, 1881): "Power tends to corrupt and absolute power corrupts absolutely."

32. James P. Pinkerton, *What Comes Next: The End of Big Government and the New Paradigm Ahead* (New York: Hyperion, 1995), 77.

33. Laura Mulvey, *Citizen Kane* (London: BFI Publishing, 1994), 34.

34. William Stott, *Documentary Expression in America* (London: Oxford University Press, 1973), 79.

35. Mills, *Power Elite*, 274.

36. All dialogue from film transcribed by author.

37. Mulvey, *Citizen Kane*, 53.

38. Carringer, *The Making of Citizen Kane*, 130.

39. Welles and Bogdanovich, *This Is Orson Welles*, 127–28.

40. Charles Higham, "Orson Welles as Poet and Historian," in *Hollywood's America: United States History Through Its Films*, edited by Steven Mintz and Randy Roberts (St. James, New York: Brandywine Press, 1993), 126.

41. Welles and Bogdanovich, *This Is Orson Welles*, xxxiii.

42. Carringer, *The Making of Citizen Kane*, 134; and Wells and Bogdanovich, *This Is Orson Welles*, 131–32 (also cited in McBride, *Orson Welles*, 87–88).

43. Ferdinand Tonnies, *Community and Society* (1887) (East Lansing: Michigan State Press, 1957), 33–34.

Chapter Four

Fascism in *Gabriel over the White House*

John J. Pitney, Jr.

On March 1, 1933, *Gabriel over the White House* opened in Glendale, California. In this film, Walter Huston plays President Judson Hammond, a sleazy politico who cheerfully ignores the country's problems until a car crash sends him into a coma. While he lies unconscious, the angel Gabriel inspires him to change his ways. After rising from his sickbed, he puts jobless people back to work, crushes organized crime and gets the world's leaders to sign a global peace treaty. There is just one small catch: To accomplish his goals, he has to dismiss Congress and disregard the Bill of Rights. In short, he becomes a fascist dictator (though one with very nice intentions).

From today's perspective, it is tempting to regard *Gabriel* as a satire or a subtle warning about the corruption of power. The video version's jacket says of President Hammond: "Unfortunately, his zeal for reform is as misguided as his previous indifference was destructive." *Gabriel*'s makers did not intend such a message, and moviegoers did not infer it. Calling it the most important bad film of the year, the reviewer for *The Nation* wrote: "Its all-too-evident purpose is to convert innocent American movie audiences to a policy of fascist dictatorship in this country."[1] The critic overstated his case: *Gabriel*'s first purpose was to make money for MGM. Yet it is revealing that Hollywood would make such a picture, and that cash-strapped audiences would pay to see it.

In the America of 1933, responsible people were talking about dictatorship.[2] A few welcomed it, while others regretfully thought of it as inevitable. Even among the great majority who rejected a full-fledged fascist regime, many favored a temporary suspension of constitutional

Walter Huston delivering a State of the Union address in *Gabriel over the White House.* Courtesy of the Academy of Motion Picture Arts and Sciences.

restraints, so that a strong leader could rescue America from the Depression.

Gabriel over the White House opens a window onto another time, and perhaps it holds a distant mirror to our own.

AMERICA IN 1933

In the early 1930s, America was enduring its hardest days since the Civil War. The Great Depression differed from previous economic slumps, because it was getting worse with each passing year. Recession was one thing, hopelessness quite another.

The unemployment rate in 1933 stood at 24.9 percent, up from a mere 3.2 percent at the time of the 1929 stock market crash. Over those four years, real disposable income per capita had plunged by 28 percent.[3] Worried that the banking system would collapse, people increasingly withdrew their money, triggering the bank failures that they feared.

Looking ahead to a bleak future, millions of American couples chose to postpone or forgo parenthood. The rate of births among every thousand women ages fifteen to forty-four dropped from 89.3 in 1929 to 76.3 in 1933.[4]

During that year, social tension combined with gangland rivalry over the liquor market to produce 9.7 killings for every 100,000 Americans. That figure, more than twice the level of 1910, represented the century's highest murder rate up to that time, a dubious record that would last until 1974.[5] On February 15, 1933, President-elect Franklin Roosevelt nearly joined the murder statistics when anarchist Joseph Zangara fired five shots at him in Miami. Zangara missed, but fatally wounded Chicago Mayor Anton Cermak.

Unrest was building. After angry farmers staged highway blockades in several Midwestern cities, the head of the National Farmers Union told the Senate: "The biggest and finest crop of revolutions you ever saw is sprouting all over the country right now."[6] Communist agitator Mother Bloor came back from a Midwestern tour to say with admiration: "I never saw anything like the militancy of those farmers."[7]

In 1932, thousands of World War I veterans, many of them homeless and unemployed, marched on Washington to demand immediate payment of a bonus that the federal government had promised. This "Bonus Army" settled in makeshift shanties and tents near the Capitol and along the Anacostia River. Claiming that communists and criminals had infiltrated their ranks, President Hoover refused to honor their demands. On July 28, he ordered General Douglas MacArthur (with two obscure officers named George Patton and Dwight Eisenhower) to disperse the Bonus Army and destroy its camps.

Democracy seemed to be failing the challenge of hard times. Although

President Hoover had taken serious steps against the Depression, most people thought that he and other Washington politicians were dithering. Socialist leader Norman Thomas sadly predicted that "the present reckless deflation will go on; the next Congress will try to balance the budget and find that it can't; it will pass legislation for the benefit of the farmers which will knock things even worse out of balance than they are now. . . . Then the cry will go up for stabilization, for a dictator."[8]

That cry was already starting. The June 1932 issue of *Vanity Fair* exclaimed: "Appoint a dictator!" A writer for the mainstream magazine *Liberty* declared: "What we need now is martial law. There is no time for civil law. The President should have dictatorial power."[9] On Capitol Hill, Senator David A. Reed, a Pennsylvania Republican, said:

> I do not often envy other countries their governments but I say that if this country ever needed a Mussolini it needs one now. I am not proposing that we make Mr. Hoover our Mussolini, I am not proposing that we should abdicate the authority that is in us, but if we are to get economies made they have to be made by someone who has the power to make the order and stand by it. Leave it to Congress and we will fiddle around here all summer trying to satisfy every lobbyist, and we will get nowhere.[10]

The invocation of Benito Mussolini was not an accident, in the 1920s and early 1930s, he fascinated many Americans. A onetime socialist newspaper editor, Mussolini broke with the Left to support Italy's participation in World War I. After the war's end, he helped found a new party, won a seat in the Italian parliament, and plotted the seizure of power. Taking advantage of social unrest, he mustered 40,000 blackshirted men to march on Rome in October 1922, and as he expected, the weak-willed government yielded to him rather than fight back. Over the next few years, he tightened his grip on the government and cultivated a public image (not entirely accurate) of an efficient disciplinarian who could make the trains run on time.

Fascist doctrine subordinated individual interests to the unified will of the people, as embodied in the state. Like communism, fascism dispensed with free elections in favor of dictatorial rule; but unlike communism, it preserved private ownership of the means of production, so that the government could exploit capitalism rather than abolish it. Fascism emphasized a passionate form of nationalism: Mussolini envisioned a rebirth of the Roman Empire, and other fascists spoke mystically of serving destiny. Fascists celebrated war and conquest while belittling liberal democracy and bourgeois values.

Fascism had an impressive "amen corner" in the West. Calling Parliament "an unparalleled engine for preventing a country from being governed," George Bernard Shaw praised a number of gentlemen who wanted to get something done, and who were determined that it shall be done. Specifically, he said, "Let us have a look at Signor Mussolini. . . . [H]e wants to have a council of corporations, and that council of corporations is to succeed Parliament. I say, 'Hear, hear! More power to your elbow.' "[11]

Many Americans agreed, believing that Mussolini had found an effective cure for the economic crisis, though a brutal and distasteful one. Remarked *Fortune*: "No long-winded parliaments or congresses between idea and action. No ignorant masses to consult on complex economic questions. In the world Depression, marked by governmental wandering and uncertainty, Mussolini remains direct." Although the magazine doubted that the Western world was ready for fascism, it said that the Depression was testing a real alternative to democracy: "The answer is not yet in."[12]

A significant portion of the American press actively supported Mussolini. According to documents captured in Italy during World War II, the Italian ambassador to Washington surveyed American press from 1928 to 1931 and found that the newspapers most favorable to the regime belonged to *Il Gruppo Hearst*.[13]

HEARST, WANGER AND *GABRIEL*

William Randolph Hearst never advocated a fascist takeover of the United States. During the 1932 presidential campaign, he originally supported House Speaker John Nance Garner of Texas and then switched to Franklin Roosevelt. In his public writings, one searches in vain for any systematic political philosophy. Shallowness and inconsistency were his hallmarks.

But if Hearst was not wedded to the idea of fascism, he did carry on a serious flirtation. "Mussolini is a man I have always admired," Hearst wrote in 1928, "not only because of his astonishing ability, but because of his public service."[14] Hearst feared left-wing revolution in the United States and thought that Mussolini's system could supply a last-ditch defense against communism. "Fascism is definitely a movement to oppose and offset communism," he told his editors in 1934, "and so to prevent the least capable and least creditable class from getting control of the country. Fascism will only come into existence in the United States when such a movement becomes really necessary for the prevention of communism."[15]

Besides anticommunism, Hearst's other preoccupation was the movie career of his paramour Marion Davies. He ran a movie company, Cosmopolitan Productions, mainly to make films showcasing her talents. (Contrary to her fictional counterpart in *Citizen Kane*, Davies was a highly capable performer.) Early in 1933, however, producer Walter Wanger sought Hearst's financial backing for a different kind of picture, *Gabriel over the White House*.[16]

The story came from a recent novel by Thomas Tweed, a Briton who had extensive experience in his country's Liberal Party but who had never visited the United States. Tweed was a protégé of former Prime Minister David Lloyd George, who in turn was a close friend of Hearst.[17] Tweed had also drawn inspiration from an American businessman in London who had called for a benevolent, businesslike dictatorship in America.[18] Less than a month after Wanger had persuaded MGM's story editor to purchase Tweed's novel, Gregory La Cava received the assignment to direct, and screenwriter Carey Wilson had produced a screenplay. Wanger then took the script to Hearst, who took a literary interest in the project as well as a financial one. Writing in longhand on orange sheets of paper, he penned his own additions to the dialogue, including a climactic speech on world peace.

Hearst had known Wanger socially and was aware that they shared certain political views. Although Wanger was not really a fascist—he later made the antifascist movies *The President Vanishes* (1935) and *Blockade* (1938)—he admired Mussolini as much as Hearst did.[19] He had developed a deep affection for Italy while serving there during World War I, and he reportedly kept a picture of il Duce on his office door until the 1935 invasion of Ethiopia.[20] Even afterward, he would say: "Mussolini? He's marvelous! Plain! Simple! Sympathetic! Marvelous man! Knows everything!"[21]

Hearst and Wanger had plenty of company. Many people in Hollywood approved of Mussolini or harbored even stronger authoritarian sentiments. Harry Cohn of Columbia Pictures released a documentary on the dictator's life, and after visiting him in Rome, redecorated his own office to look like Mussolini's.[22] British-born actor Victor McLaglen (*The Informer*) helped organize the California Light Horse Regiment, a militia group with fascist overtones. In 1934, McLaglen led the regiment to Hearst's *Examiner* building in Los Angeles for "a goodwill serenade in honor of the newspaper."[23]

Although such attitudes scarcely commanded a majority in the early 1930s, neither did they dwell on Hollywood's lunatic fringe. When *Gabriel* started production, the motion picture community scarcely took notice. Its script underwent final revisions in early February, and Hearst reportedly contributed portions of the fictional president's speeches. In this era of rapid-fire moviemaking, principal photography took only a couple of weeks, so *Gabriel over the White House* was ready by the beginning of March. On seeing the picture at its Glendale premiere, Louis B. Mayer was upset, not because the movie implicitly advocated dictatorship, but because the sleazy, pre-conversion President Hammond was a blend of Warren Harding and Herbert Hoover, both of whom the Republican mogul had supported.[24] Mayer wanted to shelve the movie, but settled for some minor cuts.

Although some reviewers expressed shock at *Gabriel*'s themes, others were nonchalant. "It is a curious, somewhat fantastic, and often melodramatic story, but nevertheless one which at this time is very interesting," wrote Mordaunt Hall of the *New York Times*, who described the post-conversion President Hammond as tackling America's problems something after the fashion of Lincoln.[25] In *Commonweal*, Richard Dana Skinner labeled the movie as "propaganda akin to an underscored Hearst editorial." But he added that he did accept many parts of the propaganda itself: "If men are ever to be stirred to hot fury by the undeserved suffering of millions of their fellow human beings, now is the time when they should be stirred in every nerve and fiber."[26]

THE STORY

The picture's early sequences establish a tone of deep cynicism about the political and social system. At the end of an inaugural reception, President Hammond greets his young nephew, who announces to the other guests that his uncle will cure the Depression. Everyone laughs. Hammond looks at his toy gun and asks if he is going to be a soldier. "Noooo," the boy replies, "I'm going to be a *gangster*!"[27] As the guests are leaving, Hammond worries aloud about his campaign promises. Secretary of State Jasper Brooks (Arthur Byron), who had been his political angel, reassures him with a smirk: "You had to make some promises. By the time they realize you're not going to keep them, your term will be over."[28] Hammond thanks another politician for some unexpected votes from Alabama, and the pol replies, "Wait 'til you get the bill for them!" When his aide Hartley Beekman (Franchot Tone) earnestly expresses gratitude for a chance to serve the country, Hammond casually answers, "Yeah, oh, yeah."

Hammond puts his girlfriend, Pendy Molloy (Karen Morley), on the White House staff. Seeing Hammond holding Lincoln's quill pen, the idealistic Pendy reminds him that he could do great things. He suggests otherwise, offering an ominous explanation: "You see, Pendy, the party has a plan, and I'm just a member of the party." Earlier, Secretary of State Brooks told him that he would be "the best president the party ever had"—not the country, but the party. The film is implying that the forms of democracy have degenerated into a charade, and that hidden forces (the party) actually rule the country.

At a press conference, a reporter recites a litany of Depression woes and demands to know what Hammond will do about the collapse of American democracy. Hammond responds with trite remarks about the spirit of Valley Forge. Several other journalists ask about the million-man "Army of the Unemployed," an obvious analogue to the real-life Bonus March of a few months before. Hammond angrily says that he will refuse a meeting with the group's leader, John Bronson (David Landau). Just as Hoover denounced communists among the Bonus Marchers, Hammond calls Bronson a dangerous anarchist, threatening to have him arrested if he approaches the White House. Later, in what Robert McConnell calls "the film's most cinematically distinguished sequence,"[29] Bronson's heartfelt plea for justice is coming over the radio while Hammond completely ignores the speech and instead plays a game with his nephew.[30]

Up to this point, *Gabriel* is drawing a hopeless portrait of a callous governing party, an unseen opposition, an impotent press, and a doomed mass movement. (Everybody in 1933 knew what happened to the Bonus Marchers.) Hammond, however, is due for his transformation. His car crashes at high speed—the result of his own reckless driving—and his injuries put him into a coma. As he lies in his White House bedroom, a sweep of light and a blare of tinny music suggest a religious event. Hammond awakens from his coma a changed man. He drops his jovial informality and begins to address Pendy as "Miss Molloy," signaling the end of their romance. In contrast to previous sequences, director La Cava now uses harsh lighting to emphasize the shadows around Walter Huston's eyes, giving Judd Hammond an almost fanatical appearance.

Later, after Pendy sees the president reacting to the invisible angel, she says to Beekman: "[D]oes it seem too fanciful to believe that God might have sent the angel Gabriel to do for Judd Hammond what he did for Daniel?" Beekman says that Gabriel is a messenger of wrath. "Not always," she corrects him. "To some he was the angel of revelations, sent as a messenger of God to men." Beekman exclaims: "Gabriel over the White House!" The identity of the messenger shows serious interest on the Lord's part. In the Old Testament (Daniel 8:16–26 and 9:20–27), Gabriel interprets Daniel's vision of the ram and the goat as a prophecy of world history. In the New Testament, he announces the coming of John the Baptist (Luke 1:11–20) and Jesus (Luke 1:26–38).

The angel's visits and Hammond's abrupt adoption of chastity are consistent with the fascist ideal of the hero in history. "Only that magic flash of a moment of supreme intuition, that flash which renders for an instant man akin to God, can reveal the Truth," wrote fascist philosopher Mario Palmieri in 1936. "The supreme gifts of synthesis, intuition, revelation, are denied to us; they belong rightly to the hero and to none other." Palmieri added: "The life of the Fascist is a life of ascetic self-denial, heroic self-sacrifice, moral abnegation and religious enthusiasm."[31] The latter description fits President Hammond better than Mussolini.

Hammond's transformation has immediate political consequences; he calls an emergency Cabinet session to discuss the Army of the Unemployed. Just before the meeting, the department heads have an anxious discussion about the president's state of mind, which Secretary Brooks concludes by saying: "No matter what happens, the party comes first." After Hammond strides in, the Cabinet urges military action against the unemployed, who are heading for Washington. Hammond refuses, prompting a resignation threat from Brooks. The president shocks the Cabinet by accepting Brooks's resignation and coldly ordering him out of the room. The onetime get-along-go-along politician has now become an authority figure. "Gentlemen," he tells the startled pols, "I suggest you read the Constitution of the United States. You'll find the president has some power."

The secretary of war nevertheless makes plans to disperse the marchers when they reach Baltimore. Hammond tells him that U.S. troops are to help the marchers. "This is war," he says, "and the enemy is starvation." When Hammond visits the Army of the Unemployed at their Baltimore campground, he uses martial imagery to explain his bold plans for a massive public works employment program: "I propose therefore to create an army to be known as the Army of Construction. You'll be enlisted, subject to military discipline." As soon as he gets congressional approval, he tells them, he will open the first station in Baltimore, "and you shall be my first soldiers."

And you shall be my first soldiers. Hammond is addressing the men as supplicants who are about to trade their freedom for security. Hammond assures them that the government will muster them out as soon as the economy recovers, but he does not explain what will become of them if the hoped-for expansion should stall. Heedless of such concerns, the unemployed rally in support of Hammond, gathering outside the White House at night to sing "The Battle Hymn of the Republic." The lyrics underscore the apocalyptic dimension of Hammond's mission: "He hath loosed the fateful lightning of his terrible swift sword: His truth is marching on."

Hammond fires his entire Cabinet, which prompts a congressional revolt. Calling Hammond "a traitor to his party," one particularly bombastic senator calls for his impeachment. Silence falls upon the chamber when Hammond suddenly walks into the joint session and asks permission to speak. (Unlike *Mr. Smith Goes to Washington*, the film is rather hazy on congressional procedure.) He rails against the Congress, employing a fascist argument against democracy: "You have wasted precious days and weeks and years in futile discussion. We need action."

He requests money for his public works program. When the murmuring lawmakers appear to reject the idea, he ups the ante. One-man rule, which has been only an implicit theme in *Gabriel*, now takes an open bow, as Hammond asks Congress to adjourn while he wields emergency powers. An especially pompous senator accuses him of dictatorship and vows that Congress will never give up the government of the Framers. "You have given it up," Hammond replies, accusing the lawmakers of treason against democratic government. If his plans amount to dictatorship, he says, "then it is a dictatorship based on Jefferson's definition of democracy—a government for the greatest good of the greatest number." He closes by reminding Congress that he has the power to declare martial law.

These notions about law and history are pure fantasy. A president has no power to declare martial law in peacetime. Lincoln took unilateral action at the start of the Civil War, but he argued that he had no choice because Congress was not in session when rebellion threatened the nation's existence.[32] And Jefferson did not define democracy as "the greatest good for the greatest number" (an idea that came from the Utilitarians). He would have despised *Gabriel over the White House*. In writing about proposals to establish a "temporary" dictator in Virginia during the Revolution, Jefferson voiced outrage: "In God's name, from whence have they derived this power? Is it from our ancient laws? None such can be produced. Is it from any principle in our new constitution, expressed or implied? Every lineament of that expressed or implied, is in full opposition to it."[33]

One leader who did endorse a Hammond-like definition of democracy was the semi-tyrannical governor of Louisiana, Huey Long. He argued that his grip on the state only *looked* dictatorial: "A perfect democracy can come close to looking like a dictatorship, a democracy in which the people are so satisfied they have no complaint."[34]

In the film, Congress immediately accedes to Hammond's demands, and the United States becomes a dictatorship. In a radio address a short time later, he reports great progress against economic problems, and turns his attention to another plague facing the nation—racketeers. "I serve warning: These evil forces must be eliminated." He singles out the most notorious of the gangsters, Nick Diamond.

Earlier in the film, we see Diamond bribing a police inspector to purge the official files of his arrest record, which reveals his real name as Antone Brilawski. (The brief exchange, which reinforces the film's bleak view of America's condition, is typical of its period; films in the early 1930s often portrayed the police as ineffectual or worse.[35]) Believing that the march of the unemployed would be bad for his business, Diamond tries to buy them off by promising Bronson that he will see to their needs. After Bronson refuses, Diamond sends machine-gunners to assassinate him during the march. (Though most of the film is technically sound, this sequence is unintentionally funny. The fallen Bronson says: "Don't mind me, boys. Carry on to Washington." The demonstrators take him at his word and, without bothering to see whether he lives or dies, they all immediately march away, resuming their chorus of "John Brown's Body.")

C. Henry Gordon plays Diamond with a vague Eastern European accent, underscoring his status as an immigrant. This portrayal is not coincidental, since many Americans thought that immigrant communities constituted the breeding ground for crime waves.[36] Diamond wears elegant clothes, lives in a luxurious high-rise apartment, and has nothing but contempt for the American people ("just a bunch of boobs") and the president ("such a big shot"). In short, Diamond is the archetype of the enemy conjured up by various paranoid movements throughout history. As historian Richard Hofstadter put it: "The enemy is clearly delineated: he is a perfect model of malice, a kind of amoral superman: sinister, ubiquitous, powerful, cruel, sensual, luxury-loving."[37]

Hammond summons Diamond to the White House for an ultimatum: Go back to "your country" or else. (The notion of a president doing business with a gangster must have struck 1933 audiences as fanciful. John F. Kennedy was still in prep school.) Diamond strikes back by bombing a government liquor store (a Hammond initiative against the bootleg industry) and dispatching his hit squad to spray the White House lobby with bullets. The shooters miss Hammond but inflict nonfatal wounds on Pendy. This sequence probably seemed more realistic at the time than it does today. Zangara's attempt on FDR's life took place during *Gabriel*'s production. And although a carload of armed men probably could not have reached the White House door, security on the grounds was lax.

Fascism glorifies force, and the president's reaction to the attack would have done Mussolini proud. Looking for someone with reason to be ruthless (Beekman has fallen in love with Pendy), Hammond puts Beekman in charge of "the federal police," an Army unit that will shred the Bill of Rights in pursuit of Diamond and his kind. Beekman leads a group of armored cars to the gang's headquarters, where Diamond makes the mistake of ordering his men to fire. The bullets bounce off the armored cars, whose powerful guns destroy the building. Beekman arrests Diamond, informing him that he will face a court-martial instead of a civilian trial. Beekman also chairs that proceeding, which takes place in a modernistic courtroom that expresses the *futurismo* cultural motif of Italian fascism. Before pronouncing sentence, he tells Diamond: "We have in the White House a man who's enabled us to cut the red tape of legal procedures and get back to first principles." Immediately afterward, Diamond and his men face a firing squad on New York Harbor. As the moment of execution approaches, the camera dollies away from the criminals to the line of rifles, and in the background we see the Statue of Liberty. The symbol of immigration thus blesses the arbitrary killing of an evil immigrant.

Hammond now turns to the international stage. Insisting on payment of war debts, he tells a press conference that he is moving a scheduled summit from the White House to a private yacht. The new location will have a fine view of "a naval parade which—quite by coincidence, I assure you—will consist of the largest concentration of naval strength in the history of this nation."

Amid the display of might, Hammond warns the assembled heads of government that, unless they pay up, the United States will repudiate the naval limitations agreement that curbed the construction of warships.[38] The leaders quickly cave to Hammond's demand, but wonder how they can afford to comply. Hammond explains that they are all wasting too much money on armaments, and offers an unusual visual aid—the bombing of two unmanned battleships. The summit participants are awestruck, remember that the year is 1933, and Pearl Harbor is still eight years in the future. Hammond explains the point with a brief speech, one that Hearst added when Walter Wanger presented him with the original script. He says that the next war will be catastrophic, with "inconceivably devastating explosives" causing the slaughter of armies, navies and civilian populations. An international peace treaty, he suggests, will avert that disaster and allow countries to shift their resources to peaceful purposes, such as payment of debts to the United States. The next shot reveals a *Washington Post* headline: "WASHINGTON COVENANT TO BE SIGNED TODAY." The word "covenant" alludes to the Book of Daniel (9:27), where the angel Gabriel says that the Messiah "shall confirm the covenant with many for one week."

The film's final sequence depicts the ceremony, where Hammond uses Lincoln's quill pen to sign the treaty and then suddenly grows weak. His divinely appointed work complete, he dies.

In one respect, the subplot of the peace treaty clashes with the movie's fascist theme. Fascists had no use for utopian concepts of world peace. However, Hammond accomplishes his aims through intimidation, a method that fascists would applaud. Mussolini wrote that the "Fascist State is a will to power and to government" and that directly or indirectly leading other nations is "a manifestation of vitality."[39]

AFTER *GABRIEL*

Until the 20th Amendment, presidents took the oath of office on March 4, so Roosevelt's inaugural came after *Gabriel*'s Glendale premiere. In his inaugural address, Roosevelt used language with striking parallels to the rhetoric of the imaginary President Hammond:

[I]f we are to go forward, we must move as a trained and loyal army willing to sacrifice for the good of a common discipline, because without such discipline no progress is made, no leadership becomes effective. We are, I know, ready and willing to submit our lives and property to such discipline, because it makes possible a leadership which aims at a larger good. . . . The people of the United States have not failed. In their need they have registered a mandate that they want direct, vigorous action. They have asked for discipline and direction under leadership. They have made me the present instrument of their wishes. In the spirit of the gift I take it.[40]

As Garry Wills points out, the novel that inspired *Gabriel* contained descriptions of some of the steps that FDR would actually take: creation of a brain trust, establishment of public works programs, and even a plan to pack the Supreme Court.[41] FDR, of course, was not cribbing from either the book or the movie, like Hearst, Tweed and Wanger, he was drawing on ideas and images that were circulating in the general culture. As we have seen, that cultural atmosphere also included a curiosity about Mussolini. In 1933, Roosevelt wrote to his ambassador to Italy: "There seems to be no question but that he [Mussolini] is really interested in what we are doing and I am much interested and deeply impressed by what he has accomplished and by his evidenced honest purpose of restoring Italy and seeking to prevent general European trouble."[42]

Did the United States teeter on the verge of a fascist dictatorship under FDR? Not really. Congress did grant him extraordinary power, but nothing comparable to what we see in *Gabriel*. And even that power shrank as a result of hostile decisions from the Supreme Court, an institution that is notably absent from the movie. Just as important, FDR was no Judd Hammond. He saw himself a popularly elected Mr. Fixit, not a divinely called messiah.

What would have happened if Zangara's aim had been a shade more accurate and he had succeeded in killing FDR?[43] Under the conditions of the Depression, could the United States have gone the way of Italy or Germany? Although the constitutional system probably would have prevented a Huey Long from seizing dictatorial power, one cannot rule out the possibility. In that sense, *Gabriel over the White House* represents an improbable might-have-been, but not an impossible one.

One afterthought: Hammond's unconstitutional crimefighting methods still win applause in some circles. One prominent leader proposed cordoning off the Dallas ghetto, sending in the police to search every person and dwelling for drugs and guns—just "vacuum it up." Asked if such a sweep would not violate the Bill of Rights, he responded:

"Look, I'm sure 95 percent of the people who live there would support this."

For further reading on this leader and his ideas, you may consult a book titled *Citizen Perot*.[44]

NOTES

1. William Troy, "Fascism over Hollywood," *The Nation* (April 26, 1933), 482–83.

2. Benjamin Leontief Alpers, "Understanding Dictatorship and Defining Democracy in American Public Culture, 1930–1945" (Ph.D. diss., Princeton University, 1994), 35–39.

3. U.S. Department of Commerce, Bureau of the Census, *Historical Statistics of the United States, Colonial Times to 1970* (Washington, DC: Government Printing Office, 1975), 135, 225.

4. U.S. Department of Commerce, *Historical Statistics*, 49. See also Michael Barone, *Our Country: The Shaping of America from Roosevelt to Reagan* (New York: Free Press, 1990), 43–44.

5. U.S. Department of Commerce, *Historical Statistics*, 414; Joseph M. Bessette, "Homicide in the United States," *Bessette Quarterly Report on Crime and Justice, USA*, Summer 1995, 6.

6. Quoted in William Manchester, *The Glory and the Dream: A Narrative History of America 1932–1972* (New York: Bantam, 1975), 60.

7. Quoted in Arthur Schlesinger, *The Crisis of the Old Order 1919–1933* (Boston: Houghton Mifflin, 1957), 460.

8. Quoted in "Thomas Predicts Dictatorship Here," *New York Times*, February 7, 1933, 5.

9. Quoted in Schlesinger, Crisis, 268.

10. *Congressional Record*, 72d Cong, 1st sess, 1932, 75, pt. 9: 9644.

11. George Bernard Shaw, "Shaw Heaps Praise Upon the Dictators," *New York Times*, December 10, 1933, sec. XI, 2.

12. "Mussolini's Ships," *Fortune* (May 1932), 126.

13. John P. Diggins, *Mussolini and Fascism: The View from America* (Princeton, NJ: Princeton University Press, 1972), 48.

14. Ibid., 48.

15. Quoted in Raymond Gram Swing, *Forerunners of American Fascism* (Freeport, NY: Books for Libraries Press, 1969 [1935]), 148.

16. Bosley Crowther, *Hollywood Rajah* (New York: Henry Holt, 1960), 178–79.

17. Robert McConnell, "The Genesis and Ideology of *Gabriel over the White House*," in *Cinema Examined*, edited by Richard Dyer MacCann and Jack C. Ellis (New York: E. P. Dutton, 1982), 205–6.

18. Mordaunt Hall, "Gabriel over the White House," *New York Times*, April 9, 1933, ix, 3.

19. For background on other Wanger pictures, see Terry Christensen, *Reel Politics* (New York: Basil Blackwell, 1987), 35; James Combs, *American Political Movies* (New York: Garland, 1990), 29.

20. Diggins, *Mussolini and Fascism*, 243.

21. Quoted in Anthony Slide, "Hollywood's Fascist Follies," *Film Comment* (July/August 1991), 64. See also Matthew Bernstein, *Walter Wanger, Hollywood Independent* (Berkeley: University of California Press, 1994), 127.

22. Neal Gabler, *An Empire of Their Own: How the Jews Invented Hollywood* (New York: Doubleday/Anchor, 1989), 152.

23. Slide, "Hollywood's Fascist Follies," 63.

24. Jay Robert Nash and Stanley Ralph Ross, *Motion Picture Guide* (Chicago: Cinebooks, 1986), 964.

25. Mordaunt Hall, review of *Gabriel over the White House*, *New York Times*, April 1, 1933, 18.

26. Richard Dana Skinner, review of *Gabriel over the White House*, *The Commonwealth*, May 5, 1933, 20.

27. The screenplay has never been published. All quotations come from the author's transcription.

28. Coincidentally, this exchange foreshadows a scene in *Citizen Kane* in which Kane jokingly asks Bernstein: "You don't expect me to *keep* any of those promises, do you?"

29. McConnell, "Genesis and Ideology," 208.

30. In his radio speech, Bronson says that the Constitution grants "the rights of life, liberty, property, and the pursuit of happiness." There is, of course, no such phrase in the Constitution. The Declaration of Independence mentions life, liberty, and the pursuit of happiness, while the construction life, liberty, and property comes from John Locke.

31. Mario Palmieri, excerpts from "The Philosophy of Fascism," in *Communism, Fascism, and Democracy*, edited by Carl Cohen (New York: Random House, 1962), 373–74.

32. Richard M. Pious, *The American Presidency* (New York: Basic, 1979), 57–58.

33. Thomas Jefferson, *Notes on the State of Virginia*, edited by William Peden (New York: Norton, 1982 [1787]), 127.

34. Quoted in T. Harry Williams, *Huey Long* (New York: Random House/Vintage, 1981 [1969]), 762.

35. Andrew Bergman, *We're in the Money: Depression America and Its Films* (New York: New York University Press, 1971), 13.

36. Despite some notorious criminals with overseas roots, immigrants tended to commit less crime than natives of the same social and economic background. Julian L. Simon, *The Economic Consequences of Immigration* (Cambridge, MA: Basil Blackwell, 1989), 102–3.

37. Richard Hofstadter, *The Paranoid Style in American Politics and Other Essays* (New York: Alfred A. Knopf, 1965), 31–32.

38. The Five-Power Naval Limitation Treaty (1922) set strict limits on warships for the United States, Britain, France, Italy and Japan. The agreement fell apart in 1936 when the other nations rejected Japan's demands for an increase in its limit.

39. Benito Mussolini, "The Doctrine of Fascism," in Cohen, *Communism, Fascism, and Democracy*, 363–64.

40. *Inaugural Addresses of the Presidents of the United States* (Washington, DC: Government Printing Office, 1989), 272, 273.

41. Garry Wills, *Reagan's America: Innocents at Home* (Garden City, NY: Doubleday, 1987), 67.

42. Franklin Roosevelt letter to Breckinridge Long, in *FDR: His Personal Letters 1928–1945*, Vol. I, edited by Elliott Roosevelt (New York: Duell, Sloan, and Pearce, 1950), 351–52.

43. Science fiction writer Philip K. Dick suggested this scenario in *The Man in the High Castle* (New York: Ace, 1988 [1962]).

44. Gerald Posner, *Citizen Perot: His Life and Times* (New York: Random House, 1996), 228–29.

Chapter Five

Antifascism in *Citizen Kane*

John J. Pitney, Jr.

"I don't think any word can explain a man's life," says the reporter (William Alland) at the end of *Citizen Kane*. "No, I guess Rosebud is just a piece in a jigsaw puzzle, a missing piece."[1] The line is fitting, since *Citizen Kane* deals with many themes: love, loss, longing, and greed, to name a few. Antifascism is a piece in this puzzle, albeit one that recent analyses have often overlooked. It is easy to miss the film's political message, whereas *Gabriel over the White House* displays its political message with all the gaudiness of a Hearst editorial, *Citizen Kane* takes a subtle approach.

Each picture reflects the politics of its time. When *Citizen Kane* opened in 1941, only eight years had passed since *Gabriel over the White House*, yet it played to a very different America. In 1933, the country faced an ever-worsening domestic disaster that threatened to spawn dictatorship or violent revolution. In 1941, things were picking up, at least on the domestic scene. The unemployment rate had dropped to single digits for the first time since the start of the Depression. Repeal of Prohibition had curbed gangland mayhem, and the murder rate stood one-third lower than it had been in 1933.[2] Roosevelt's policies had helped restore faith in government, while his political coalition had captured and tamed many radical activists who had once seemed so frightening.

In 1933, Mussolini had substantial support in the United States. Hitler had just taken power in Germany, and although few Americans expressed admiration for him, fewer still regarded him as a clear and present danger. In 1941, Americans saw both men as evil incarnate. Most of Europe lay under Nazi rule, and there seemed to be no limits to the

Orson Welles and Joseph Cotten in *Citizen Kane*. Courtesy of the Academy of Motion Picture Arts and Sciences.

dictators' expansionist designs. Fascism was no longer an "alternative." It was a menace.

Accordingly, antifascism was a growth stock, especially in the public opinion-conscious motion picture industry. As early as 1936, a wide range of movie figures had formed the Hollywood Anti-Nazi League, in which members of the Communist Party played a prominent role.[3] Movies with antifascist themes became more common. Walter Wanger, who had made the profascist *Gabriel* in 1933, produced Alfred Hitchcock's antifascist *Foreign Correspondent* (1940). The film ends with Joel McCrea broadcasting from a London air raid, urging Americans to rearm and to "hang on to your lights! They're the only lights left in the world."[4]

ORSON WELLES

Just as antifascist ferment was building in the mid-1930s, Orson Welles began his career on the New York stage. Welles had a deep interest in politics. His first script dealt with the life of John Brown, while the first play he directed professionally was the all-black *Macbeth* for the WPA's Federal Theater Project. He followed up with the highly controversial *The Cradle Will Rock*, a labor opera written by Marcus Blitzstein, an active communist.[5] The government tried to shut it down, but Welles then led the company and the audience to another theater, where they performed it in defiance of Washington.

In 1937, he reached his Broadway peak with a modern-dress production of *Julius Caesar*. In the Welles version of Shakespeare, Caesar was the dictator; Brutus, the liberal; Cassius, the revolutionary; and the citizens of Rome, the pliable masses.[6] Joseph Holland, who looked like Mussolini, played Caesar; and his first gesture was a fascist salute that the others returned. According to John Houseman, his then-friend and producer, the use of modern dress was an essential element in Welles's conception of *Julius Caesar* as a political melodrama with clear contemporary parallels. In his memoirs, Houseman explained the context:

All over the Western world sophisticated democratic structures were breaking down. First in Italy, then in Germany, dictatorships had taken over; the issues of political violence and the duty of the individual in the face of tyranny had become urgent and inescapable. To emphasize the similarity between the last days of the Roman republic and the political climate of Europe in the mid-thirties, our Roman aristocrats wore military uniforms with black belts that suggested but did not exactly reproduce the current fashion of the Fascist ruling class; our crowd wore the dark, nondescript clothes of the big-city proletariat.[7]

Welles also became a presence on national radio. In 1938, his broadcast of *The War of the Worlds* scared much of its audience into believing that the United States was under attack from Martians. At the time, many observers read the Welles-induced panic as a sign of how the mass media could manipulate the masses.

In 1939, RKO studio President George Schaefer brought Welles to Hollywood. On arriving in the movie colony, Welles planned to film Joseph Conrad's *Heart of Darkness*, a fitting choice in light of Welles's concern about the dangers of political power. "*Heart of Darkness* was a kind of parable of fascism," Welles later told Peter Bogdanovich. "Remember the time I was working on that, 1939–1940. War hadn't started, and fascism was the big issue of the time. It was a very clear parable."[8] When that project ran into trouble, he began work on an adaptation of *The Smiler with a Knife*, a contemporary political thriller about a fascist organization secretly attempting to establish a dictatorship.[9]

Welles then moved to the project that would change film history, *Citizen Kane*. Welles began with the notion of telling a story from several different viewpoints. He also wanted to build the plot around a major public figure, and after reflecting on the power of the mass media, he decided that the central character should be a press lord.[10] During conversations with screenwriter Herman Mankiewicz, Welles developed the character into a man who bore a striking resemblance to William Randolph Hearst. Mankiewicz set out to write the first draft of a screenplay, with the aid of John Houseman, who helped him maintain literary focus and physical sobriety.[11] Mankiewicz was personally acquainted with Hearst, and he drew on firsthand knowledge for *American*, the draft screenplay that became *Citizen Kane*. There is evidence, however, that he also consulted *Imperial Hearst*, a 1936 biography by Ferdinand Lundberg.[12] Noticing the similarities between his book and the *Kane* story, Lundberg sued for copyright infringement and settled with RKO for $15,000 plus court costs.[13]

The influence of *Imperial Hearst* is significant, since Lundberg called Hearst "the most influential American fascist."[14] He explained:

Hearst's personal editorials in all his papers have deplored both communism and fascism as abhorrent, un-Jeffersonian forms of regimentation. Hearst's Jeffersonianism is one of the most effective political blinds behind which . . . to deceive the American population. [Recall Hammond's invocation of Jefferson in *Gabriel*.] But in action, Hearst praises Italy and Germany, the outstanding fascist states, approves violent assaults on organized labor and farmers, terrorization of teachers, reduction of school budgets, creation of concentration camps for radicals, and the like. Hearst has become fascist in deed, even though he is still afraid to endorse fascism explicitly.[15]

World War II started three years after Lundberg's book, and its out-break made antifascism all the more urgent. As we shall see shortly, direct and indirect references to World War II appear throughout the film. Welles and Mankiewicz worked on the *Kane* script during the spring of 1940, when Hitler was completing his conquest of Western Europe. Production extended from June 29 through October 23 (a very long shooting schedule for the era), a period that included the Battle of Britain. The last day of production coincided with Hitler's meeting with another fascist dictator, Francisco Franco.[16]

THE STORY

All movie buffs know the plot of *Citizen Kane*, so it is unnecessary to recount it in detail. In the following, I concentrate on those elements of the film that express the theme of antifascism. Often, the idea shows up in unexpected places.

The first, almost subliminal, mention of fascism comes early, when the "News on the March" newsreel rapidly displays a series of Kane's obit-uaries. For one split second, we see the headline of the *Chicago Globe*:

DEATH CALLS PUBLISHER CHARLES KANE
POLICIES SWAYED WORLD
Stormy Career Ends for US Fascist No. 1

In the same sequence, Walter Parks Thatcher (George Coulouris) tells a congressional committee that Kane is nothing but a communist. That month at a Union Square labor rally, a speaker voices a different opinion: "The words 'Charles Foster Kane' are a menace to every working man in this land. He is today what he always has been and always will be: a fascist." A title card offers Kane's own rejoinder: "I am, have been, and will be only one thing—an American."

In this way, Welles signals that he will not paint Kane as an overt authoritarian. Welles is being true to Hearst, who did not adhere to any systematic ideology. Yet tyranny can wear homespun garments. Many a dictator or proto-dictator has denied bad motives and pledged allegiance to democratic ideals (again, think of Judd Hammond and his Hearst-written dialogue in Gabriel). If Kane had somehow achieved political power, the film implies, he might have become a menace to liberty.

The newsreel narration provides one clue to this message when it re-fers to Kane's collection of paintings, statues, and stones from other pal-aces as the loot of the world. In the 1990s, this phrase sounds quaintly bombastic. In 1941, however, it had sinister overtones, because the world's most notorious "collector" at the time was Adolf Hitler. Two years earlier, Hitler had set out to assemble the world's greatest art collection, through confiscation or forced sale.[17] He started with Austria and Czechoslovakia, and when World War II began, his looters followed closely behind the German army. Hitler cared more for acquisition than appreciation, he lost interest in a masterpiece once it fell into his hands.[18] Hearst (like the imaginary Kane) shared this characteristic, although he gained his artworks through legitimate means, usually paying inflated prices.[19]

An even subtler reference to the forces of evil comes when the narration mentions his race for governor, with "the White House seemingly the next easy step in a lightning political career." The use of the word "lightning" as an adjective had long denoted great swiftness, but during the early days of World War II, it also summoned up thoughts of the Germans. In its coverage of the invasion of Poland in 1939, *Time* had introduced Americans to a new word: *Blitzkrieg,* "lightning war."[20]

If the newsreel sequence hints at Kane's fascist tendencies, it shows clearly that Kane is naive about real fascist leaders.[21] The narration says that there was no public man whom Kane did not support or denounce. As we see Kane posing on a balcony with Hitler, the narration adds: "Often support, then denounce." In 1934, Hearst did meet with Hitler, who assured him that the persecution of the Jews was temporary and that National Socialism was really democratic. At the time, American newspapers quoted Hearst as saying: "If Hitler succeeds in pointing the way of peace and order . . . he will have accomplished a measure of good not only for his own people but for all of humanity."[22] The papers also featured a photograph of Hearst with Dr. Alfred Rosenberg and other Nazis. Hearst pleaded misquotation, but the photograph left a different impression in the minds of many Americans.

In the newsreel, a reporter asks an aging Kane about the chances of war. Kane replies: "I talked with the responsible leaders of the Great Powers—England, France, Germany and Italy." (Note the application of the term "responsible leaders" to Hitler and Mussolini.) "They are too intelligent to embark on a project which would mean the end of civilization as we now know it. You can take my word for it, there will be no war," Kane says. For most of the 1930s, Hearst did not believe that war would break out. He helped write the sequence in *Gabriel over the White House* in which foreign leaders agree to a global peace treaty as soon as the American president makes them understand the destructiveness of modern combat. By the time of *Citizen Kane*'s premiere, however, World War II had been in progress for a year and a half, and Pearl Harbor was only a few months away.

The newsreel sequence provides a frame of reference for all that follows. When we first see Kane as a youthful, handsome and apparently high-minded newspaper publisher, we have already glimpsed his heart of darkness. Thatcher (George Coulouris) confronts young Kane over his campaign against the Public Transit Company. Kane says that he takes pleasure in keeping "money-mad pirates" from robbing hardworking people. "You see, I have money and property," he explains to Thatcher. "If I don't look after the interests of the underprivileged, maybe somebody else will—maybe somebody without any money or property. [Thatcher mutters, "Yes, yes, yes."] And that would be too bad."

This sequence takes place in 1898. In that year, the Russian Revolution still lay nineteen years ahead, but Americans were already worrying about anarchism, socialism and other forms of radicalism.[23] Many of them thought that extreme, perhaps authoritarian, measures would be necessary to stop the leftist tide. During World War I, such sentiments would mingle with martial fervor to produce severe government crackdowns on left-wing activists.

A charismatic figure such as Charles Foster Kane would have been well suited to take political advantage of this atmosphere. The film shows Kane to be casual about abusing the power that he already has. In the first memory of Bernstein (Everett Sloan), Kane orders the *Inquirer*'s old editor to dig out more information about an apparent murder. The paper's best reporter is to pretend that he is a detective from "the Central Office" and tell the suspect that if he doesn't produce the victim at once, the *Inquirer* will have him arrested. If the suspect, a Mr. Silverstone, asks to see a badge, "your man is to get indignant and call Mr. Silverstone an anarchist. Loudly, so the neighbors can hear." Here, Kane is both charming and chilling. To get what he wants, he is perfectly happy to employ deception and political intimidation.

We can see through Kane's "Declaration of Principles" as soon as he writes it. He promises to "tell all the news honestly" but we have previously seen him issuing monumental lies ("Galleons of Spain off Jersey Coast"). He says that his paper will provide New Yorkers "with a fighting and tireless champion of their rights as citizens and as human beings," but he has just sent a reporter to browbeat Mr. Silverstone. Jed Leland (Joseph Cotten) is appropriately skeptical when he calls the Declaration an important document, like "my first report card at school." Kane's reaction appears awkward and forced. Welles told Peter Bogdanovich that the expression was intentional: "[I]t's not supposed to be a real smile, but the smile of somebody deeply embarrassed, being caught out."[24]

While Kane is reading his Declaration aloud, Bernstein warns him: "You don't want to make any promises, Mr. Kane, you don't want to keep." The film jumps six years ahead, to a party celebrating the *Inquirer*'s acquisition of its rival paper's staff. Bernstein jokingly gets Kane to promise that he will buy more European artworks. To laughter, Kane agrees, and then adds with a smile: "Mr. Bernstein, . . . you don't expect me to keep any of those promises, do you?" Kane is reacting to Bernstein's joke, but the proximity of the two sequences clearly implies that he is not going to keep his Declaration promises, either.

Much later in the story, after Kane breaks with Leland, an envelope arrives for him. Kane opens it, to find that Leland has sent him back the Declaration. Susan Alexander, Kane's second wife, asks him what it is, and he replies: "An antique."

Kane's faithlessness links him to the fascist leaders of the twentieth century, who were audacious promise-breakers. (In 1940, Charlie Chaplin's *The Great Dictator* portrayed a Hitler figure, Adenoid Hynkel, as ruling under the sign of the "Double Cross.") Hitler tricked Chamberlain into believing that the Munich agreement was "peace for our time," and 1941 moviegoers could vividly recall the newsreels of the British leader holding up the worthless document—an "antique," so to speak. Mussolini and other fascists revered Machiavelli, who taught that "those princes who have done great things have held good faith of little account." Machiavelli said, "A wise lord, cannot, nor ought he to, keep faith when such observance may be turned against him, and when the reasons that caused him to pledge it exist no longer."[25]

Kane unwittingly illustrates this precept when telling Leland and Bernstein why he has to publish the Declaration: "I've got to make the *New York Inquirer* as important to New York as the gas in that light"— and then he turns off the light.

Kane is a controller as well as a deceiver. Leland asks Bernstein if the new staff members were just as devoted to the rival's policy as they are to Kane's. Bernstein says, "Sure, they're just like anybody else. They've got work to do, they do it." Kane is already the dictator of his realm, and his minions will be following orders. Still, Leland wonders whether the new staff will change Kane without his knowing it. (His comment raises questions that the rest of the film does not answer, since we see no more of the new *Inquirer* staff.)

The newsreel narration calls Kane a "molder of mass opinion," implying that powerful individuals can shape the thoughts of the masses. The film reiterates the point when depicting the decay of Kane's first marriage. Emily (Ruth Warrick) says, "Really, Charles, people will think . . ." Kane cuts her off by saying, "What I tell them to think." Later, he upbraids his second wife's opera teacher, who fears that her incompetence will make him a laughingstock: "You're concerned with what people will think, Signor Matisti? I may be able to enlighten you a bit. I'm something of an authority about what people will think."

During this period in history, most intellectuals saw public opinion as soft clay in the hands of propagandists, whose power could lead to fascist control. In 1940, Hadley Cantril published *The Invasion from Mars: A Study in the Psychology of Panic*, which analyzed public reaction to Welles's *War of the Worlds* broadcast. Cantril drew a dark conclusion from the apparent suggestibility of so many listeners: "The whole tactics of Hitler show the importance he places on providing directed relief to bewildered souls. If they are not already sufficiently bewildered, bewilderment can be manufactured by sufficient propaganda."[26]

Writing in the following year, Robert Strausz-Hupe made a similar point: "The key to Nazi-Fascist writing on any and all subjects is to be found in Hitler's evaluation of mass psychology and mass susceptibility to propagandistic treatment."[27] Strausz-Hupe added: "As examples of this 'emotional impact,' one need only cite the success of Hitler's speeches in producing mass hysteria and—closer to home—the astonishing panic caused by Orsen [sic] Welles' famous broadcast, *The War of the Worlds*, in the winter of 1938."[28] Such fears may have been overblown, but the impact of *War of the Worlds* reinforced Welles's belief in the power and danger of propaganda.

That belief had wide currency in Hollywood. Another classic film of 1941, Frank Capra's *Meet John Doe*, also linked newspapers, propaganda and fascism. In this movie, sinister newspaper magnate D. B. Norton (Edward Arnold) uses a naive former baseball player (Gary Cooper) as his front man in a plot to win the presidency and rule the country with an iron hand. When John Doe finally recognizes the plot and tries to break away, Norton instantly turns public opinion against him.

Whereas *Meet John Doe* is an all-American story, though a dark one, *Citizen Kane* has European overtones. Kane's first meeting with Susan ends with her singing a line from *The Barber of Seville* that translates from the Italian: "I have sworn it, I will conquer." Immediately, the film cuts to Kane's campaign for governor. While Kane is haranguing a massive indoor rally about his selfless concern for the workingman and the slum child, the images suggest something different. Behind him is a group of well-dressed, rich-looking middle-aged men, not a slum child in the bunch. The huge, ugly picture of Kane hanging in the background tells the story of an egomaniac who is no longer the handsome rake who penned a Declaration of Principles. The long shot of the rally, with the triangle of light over the dais and the symmetrical ranks of supporters sitting in semi-darkness, clearly suggests the Nuremberg rallies.[29] In his stage production of *Julius Caesar*, Welles used similar lighting effects to evoke Hitler and Mussolini.[30]

During his speech, Kane uses broad and overdramatic arm gestures, much like the European dictators. This element of the performance establishes a contrast between Kane and Welles's ideal democratic leader, Franklin D. Roosevelt. (Roosevelt did not use arm gestures in his public speeches, because he could not. The paralysis of his legs meant that he could maintain his balance only by tightly gripping the podium.)

Kane says that every poll shows that he is going to win, so he can now afford to make promises. Welles has already put us on guard against Kane's promises, so when he repeats his pledge to protect the interests of the workingman and the slum child, we know that he is also protecting the interests of the frock coats around him. In making yet another promise, he adopts an angry, vengeful tone: "My first official act as governor will be to appoint a special district attorney to arrange for the indictment, prosecution, and conviction of Boss Jim W. Gettys."

At this point, Kane may superficially sound like a crusader, but he is really saying that he will act like a fascist: A new dictator usually starts by putting the old regime behind bars. After the rally, a nameless politician says of Gettys: "He isn't just scared anymore, he's sick." Kane answers: "I think it's beginning to dawn on Jim Gettys that I mean what I say."

Gettys has been watching Kane from a vantage point high above the floor. In the next sequence, the confrontation in Susan Alexander's apartment, Gettys suggests that he understands the gravity of Kane's threat: "Mrs. Kane, I'm fighting for my life, not just my political life, my life." Gettys is blackmailing Kane not just to win the election but to prevent his imprisonment, which could mean death.

Gettys differs radically from Nick Diamond, the villain of *Gabriel over the White House*. Diamond, born Antone Brilawski, speaks with a refined European accent. Gettys's name resonates with American history (Gettysburg), and Ray Collins plays him with a working-class inflection.[31] Diamond contemptuously mocks the president ("such a big shot") whereas Gettys resorts to brutal tactics out of genuine fear. Diamond represents "the enemy," whose wickedness and foreignness justify the authoritarian measures that the president uses against him. Gettys is not a good guy, but he is probably not worse than Kane. In telling Mrs. Kane the terms of his blackmail, Gettys says: "It's more of a chance than he'd give me."

Kane refuses the deal, and the ensuing scandal wrecks his campaign for governor. After all the campaign workers have gone home on election night, Leland walks in on a lonely Kane, who complains that the people would prefer Gettys to him. Leland says: "You talk about the people as though you owned them. As though they belong to you. As long as I can remember you've talked about giving the people their rights as if you could make them a present of liberty, as a reward for services rendered."

"As though they belong to you." In *Gabriel*, President Hammond tells the Army of the Unemployed all that he will do for them, including the establishment of a construction army—"and you shall be *my* first soldiers" (emphasis added). In a fascist regime, the government does not exist to serve the people; rather, the people exist to serve the state. In this view, "rights" are not inalienable claims, but indulgences that the state can grant or withhold at will. According to fascist philosopher

Mario Palmieri: "Liberty, therefore, cannot be concerned with the individual's claims, but must find its maximum concern in the fullest expression of the nation's life."[32]

Leland continues:

> You remember the working man? . . . He's turning into something called organized labor. You're not going to like that one little bit when you find out it means your workingman expects something as his right and not your gift. Charlie, when your precious underprivileged really get together—oh boy, that's going to add up to something bigger than your privilege and then I don't know what you'll do. Sail away to a desert island, probably, and lord it over the monkeys.

A fascist government, of course, makes no room for an independent labor movement, which is also why we see no union leaders in *Gabriel*. In 1941, unions were much on America's mind. Since passage of the Wagner Act six years earlier, union membership had more than doubled, and the newspapers were filled with stories of strikes and other labor activity. To liberals such as Welles and Mankiewicz, this activity was an essential bulwark of liberty. In contrasting democracy and fascism, liberal commentators invariably pointed to Americans' freedom of collective bargaining. As one liberal scholar said in 1935: "[S]uch danger as we may face from the Fascist tendencies of the Hearsts . . . the merchants and manufacturers associations, and the better America federations has its origins in the potential adaptation of the Fascist technique to the repression of labor organization and the right to strike."[33]

After Kane loses his bid to govern the state, Kane focuses more on controlling his environment. In addition to gathering artworks from Europe, Kane drives his second wife (Susan Alexander, played by Dorothy Comingore) to pursue an opera career, even after the effort brings her pain and humiliation. She attempts suicide, telling him: "You don't know what it means to feel that the whole audience doesn't want you." He says: "That's when you've got to fight them." His obsession with culture and struggle calls to mind Mussolini's statement that fascism "conceives of life as a struggle, considering that it behooves man to conquer for himself that life truly worthy of him. . . . Hence the high value of culture in all its forms (art, religion, science)."[34] In this case, Kane's pursuit of culture nearly kills Susan.

Reluctantly accepting her decision to stop singing, he builds his Xanadu. The aging Leland sums up Kane's motivation: "He was disappointed in the world, so he built one of his own, an absolute monarchy."[35] And he rules it as a petty dictator. When he says that he is going to "invite" his hangers-on to an Everglades picnic, Susan answers: "Invite everybody! Order everybody, you mean, and make them sleep in tents."

In the end, Kane has nothing of value. Susan leaves him, and his only son is long gone, having died in a 1918 car accident. The first draft of the script, titled *American*, was even bleaker. In that version of the story, Kane's son grows up but suffers fatal wounds when he takes part in a fascist raid on a Washington armory.[36]

Why does Kane fail? Although he has dangerous, fascistic tendencies, he also has characteristics that undercut his drive for power. "He married for love," says Leland. "Love . . . that's why he did everything. That's why he went into politics. It seems we weren't enough. He wanted the voters to love him, too." A true authoritarian leader, as Machiavelli taught, must care more about being feared than being loved. In *Gabriel over the White House*, Judd Hammond can become an effective dictator precisely because he sets aside all his personal attachments, giving up his mistress and turning his back on his onetime political supporters. When addressing Congress or the world leaders, he does not court their affection; instead, he intimidates them with the threat of extreme action.

Furthermore, Kane lacks the kind of vision that drives charismatic dictators. Says Leland: "I don't suppose anybody ever had so many opinions. But he never believed in anything except Charlie Kane. He never had a conviction except Charlie Kane in his life. I suppose he died without one. That must have been pretty unpleasant." Judd Hammond, by contrast, is literally on a mission from God. When he dies, he knows that he has accomplished that mission.

AFTER *KANE*

If *Gabriel* provided Hearst with a sense of fatherly pride, *Kane* prompted his vendetta against Welles. Although his empire had dwindled since the Depression, he still had enough power to hurt Welles's career. Among other things, his newspapers refused to accept ads for the movie. His friend Louis B. Mayer offered to pay George Schaefer, the president of RKO, $800,000 if he would destroy the negative and all the prints.[37] (Ironically, this was the same man who had held up the release of Hearst's *Gabriel* because of its negative connotations about Warren Harding and Herbert Hoover.)

Welles overcame the pressure and managed to get *Kane* to the theaters, where it proved a critical success, contrary to later myth. In the following years, he used his high public profile for political activities that went well beyond inserting social messages into movie scripts. Because he was an active supporter of many liberal or leftist causes, the FBI opened a file on Welles in 1941, and later placed him on its Security Index of people whom the government should round up in case of national security emergency.[38] For a brief time, Welles became a semi-serious political figure. He campaigned extensively for Roosevelt in 1944, then launched a daily political column for the *New York Post*. He even considered a campaign for the U.S. Senate in 1946, but Democratic political figure Alan Cranston talked him out of it.[39]

Welles's financial and artistic problems soon put an end to his political ambitions, but he remained a resolute liberal and antifascist. One sign of his political convictions was speech he invented for his character Harry Lime in *The Third Man* (1949): "In Italy for thirty years under the Borgias they had warfare, terror, murder, bloodshed—they produced Michelangelo, Leonardo da Vinci and the Renaissance. In Switzerland, they had brotherly love, five hundred years of democracy and peace, and what did that produce? The cuckoo clock."[40] Lime's lines embody an old justification for fascism: that democracies are stagnant and sterile, while dictatorships are creative and virile. Welles put these words (including the reference to Italy) in the mouth of a beguiling yet despicable character, who meets a violent death in a Vienna sewer.

In 1958 came *Touch of Evil*, which pits an honest Mexican detective (Charlton Heston) against an evil American police chief (Welles). In response to critics who called it a hymn to fascism and decadence, Welles said it was "if anything *too clearly antifascist*. . . . They didn't understand that I was *against* the decadence" (emphasis in the original). Bogdanovich quoted an exchange in which one character remarks that it is tough to be a policeman and Heston's character replies: "It's supposed to be tough—a policeman's job is only easy in a police state." Welles explained the line: "Yes, I decided that, since I was doing a melodrama, I'd do one about good and evil, and it's a quite simple statement of what I considered to be good and evil. Spelled right out for everybody."[41]

In *Citizen Kane*, a greatly superior movie, the antifascist theme is not spelled out for everybody, but it is just as powerful.

NOTES

1. These and all subsequent quotations come from the RKO cutting continuity of *Citizen Kane*, in *The Citizen Kane Book* (Boston: Little, Brown, 1971), 305–423.

2. U.S. Department of Commerce, Bureau of the Census, *Historical Statistics of the United States, Colonial Times to 1970*, Vol. I (Washington, DC: Government Printing Office, 1975), 135, 414.

3. Ronald Brownstein, *The Power and the Glitter* (New York: Vintage, 1992), 59–60.

4. Matthew Bernstein, *Walter Wanger, Hollywood Independent* (Berkeley: University of California Press, 1994), 162.

5. Stuart Klawans, review of *Orson Welles: The Road to Xanadu, the Nation* (January 8, 1996), 28.

6. Richard France, *The Theatre of Orson Welles* (Lewisberg, PA: Bucknell University Press, 1977), 106.

7. John Houseman, *Run-Through: A Memoir* (New York: Simon and Schuster, 1972), 298.

8. Orson Welles and Peter Bogdanovich, *This Is Orson Welles* (New York: HarperCollins/HarperPerennial, 1993), 32–33.

9. Robert L. Carringer, *The Making of Citizen Kane*, rev. ed. (Berkeley: University of California Press, 1996), 13–14.

10. Welles statement in Laura Mulvey, *Citizen Kane* (London: British Film Institute, 1992), 80–83. See also Welles and Bogdanovich, *This Is Orson Welles*, 52–53.

11. Carringer, *The Making of Citizen Kane*, 17. There is great controversy as to whether Welles or Mankiewicz deserves primary credit for the story, but that debate will not concern us here.

12. Ferdinand Lundberg, *Imperial Hearst: A Social Biography* (New York: Equinox Cooperative Press, 1936). For a comparison of this book and the script, see Carringer, *The Making of Citizen Kane*, 21–23.

13. Pauline Kael, "Raising Kane," in *The Citizen Kane Book* edited by Pauline Kael (Boston: Little, Brown, 1971), 81–82.

14. Lundberg, *Imperial Hearst*, 343.

15. Ibid., 354.

16. Martin Gilbert, *The Second World War: A Complete History* (New York: Henry Hold, 1991), 133–34.

17. David Roxan and Ken Wanstall, *The Rape of Art: The Story of Hitler's Plunder of the Great Masterpieces of Europe* (New York: Coward-McCann, 1964), 20–21.

18. Ibid., 11.

19. W. A. Swanberg, *Citizen Hearst* (New York: Scribner/Collier, 1986 [1961]), 551.

20. Quoted in William Manchester, *The Glory and the Dream: A Narrative History of America 1932–1972* (New York: Bantam, 1975), 203.

21. Sarah Street, "Citizen Kane," *History Today* (March 1996), 50.

22. Quoted in Swanberg, *Citizen Hearst*, 525.

23. In the presidential campaign of 1896, Republicans said that anarchists had infiltrated the Democratic Party, which had issued "a declaration of war on civilization." See Robert H. Wiebe, *The Search for Order 1877–1920* (New York: Hill and Wang, 1967), 103.

24. Welles and Bogdanovich, *This Is Orson Welles*, 50.

25. Niccolo Machiavelli, "Concerning the Way in Which Princes Should Keep Faith" (from *The Prince*), *Communism, Fascism, and Democracy*, ed. Carl Cohen (New York: Random House, 1962), 270.

26. Hadley Cantril, *The Invasion from Mars: A Study in the Psychology of Panic* (Princeton, NJ: Princeton University Press, 1940), 203.

27. Robert Strausz-Hupe, *Axis America: Hitler Plans Our Future* (New York: G. P. Putnam's Sons, 1941), 255.

28. Ibid., 239. He erred about the date of the broadcast, which took place on Halloween.

29. James Naremore, *The Magic World of Orson Welles*, rev. ed. (Dallas: Southern Methodist University Press, 1989), 70.

30. Peter Bogdanovich, "The Kane Mutiny," *Esquire* (October 1972), 104.

31. Welles took Gettys's name from a relative of one of his teachers at the Todd School. See Welles and Bogdanovich, *This Is Orson Welles*, 63.

32. Mario Palmieri, "Fascism and Liberty," in *Communism, Fascism, and Democracy*, ed. Carl Cohen (New York: Random House, 1962), 375.

33. H. Arthur Steiner, "Fascism in America?" *American Political Science Review* 29 (October 1935), 827.

34. Benito Mussolini, "The Doctrine of Fascism," in *Communism, Fascism, and Democracy*, ed. Carl Cohen (New York: Random House, 1962), 350.

35. Robert Paul Lamb, "*Citizen Kane* and the Quest for Kingship," *Journal of American Studies* 19 (August 1985), 269.

36. Carringer, *The Making of Citizen Kane*, 21.

37. Bosley Crowther, *Hollywood Rajah* (New York: Henry Holt, 1960), 258.

38. Jon Wiener, "Hoover, Hearst, and Citizen Welles," *The Nation* (May 27, 1996), 20.

39. Brownstein, *The Power and the Glitter*, 105.

40. Graham Greene and Carol Reed, *The Third Man* (New York: Simon and Schuster, 1968). For Welles's authorship of the line, see Naremore, *The Magic World of Orson Welles*, 174–75.

41. Welles and Bogdanovich, *This Is Orson Welles*, 299.

Paul Henreid, Ingrid Bergman, Claude Rains and Humphrey Bogart in *Casablanca*. Courtesy of the Academy of Motion Picture Arts and Sciences.

Chapter Six

Internationalism in *Casablanca*

Craig R. Smith

World War I not only marked a turning point in history, it fractured any consensus Americans might have enjoyed regarding America's role in the world. America's easy victory in the Spanish-American War, its quick expansion into the Pacific and the Caribbean, and the success of President Theodore Roosevelt in dealing with the Russo-Japanese War gave Americans a sense that they had a major role to play on the world's stage. While President Woodrow Wilson did what he could to keep the United States out of the Great War, he was eventually snared by his own moralistic hubris. Almost unanimously, Congress declared war in April 1917.

America's participation in the war brought victory to the Allies, but political fault lines were apparent before the ink was dry on the Versailles Treaty, a treaty the Senate would not ratify because of its requirement that the United States join a new League of Nations. Wilson's position that a force of united nations could keep the peace would echo through the ages and find resonance in the Dumbarton Oaks Charter following World War II. But in 1918 and following, Wilson's call was challenged by many different voices. Irish- and German-Americans resented America's alliance with England. They joined pacifists and xenophobes, mostly concentrated in the Midwest, to provide support for Republicans to recapture the Senate in the elections of 1918. That support was buttressed by many Americans who opposed the Wilson administration's use of suppression to silence its opponents. The "Red Scare," a new set of alien and sedition acts, and the creation of the Creel Committee to censor motions pictures rankled civil libertarians. When Wilson snubbed Henry Cabot Lodge, the new head of the Foreign Relations

Committee, by not inviting him to the peace talks in Versailles, he created an animosity that would return to haunt him. At Versailles, Wilson
made other mistakes. He abandoned any claims for territory by the
United States but allowed England, France and Italy to carve up German
possessions abroad and to emasculate German economic potential at
home. He even gave up on his pledge to end secret diplomacy, which
caused the young Walter Lippman to quit as an aide and return to America to become a journalist. When the treaty came to the Senate for ratification, Lodge had enough votes to stop it. He gave a magnificent
speech on the floor of the Senate outlining the dangers of America's
involvement in world affairs and proving that joining the League of
Nations would lead to a loss of America's sovereignty. Wilson refused
to negotiate and the treaty was defeated.

In the 1920 election, Republicans realized that Americans had had
enough of foreign adventures. They called for a "return to normalcy,"
and won in a landslide. The desire for America to turn inward was
reinforced by the sight of the walking wounded returning from war,
those who had suffered through mustard gas, trench warfare and U-boat
attacks. It was an ugly, technological war without morality that led to a
"lost generation" of Americans filled with cynicism.

Over the next two decades, the forces of isolation and noninvolvement
prevailed. America wouldn't raise a finger to protect the royalists against
the forces of fascism in Spain or to protect Ethiopia from Italy's attack.
Japan's invasion of Manchuria and China went unchallenged by America
until President Franklin Roosevelt ordered an oil embargo of Japan, joining members of the League of Nations. Charles Lindbergh became the
leading spokesperson for the America First movement, which opposed
the entangling policies of Roosevelt who was desperately trying to save
Britain as it stood alone against Hitler's sweeping victories of 1939 and
1940.

The isolationist position was blown to as many bits as the American
fleet when the Japanese bombed Pearl Harbor on December 7, 1941. But
had that event not occurred, America might not have entered the war.
And though it did occur, Americans still needed to be mobilized to fight
in Europe. To unite the country, more than a sea change in public opinion was needed; it was time to examine our values again. The motion
picture industry played no small part in that effort.

After the war, Wilson's dream of a League of Nations was reborn as
the United Nations. America took up its burden to play peacemaker in
the world, first with the Marshall Plan in Europe, then with its entry into
Korea and Vietnam. The question was not whether we should intervene
in the foreign affairs of other nations, but under what circumstances. The
advocates were divided into those who believed our role was to enforce
"human rights" wherever they were violated and those who believed

that our role was to protect "vital national interests." The former found leaders in presidents such as John Kennedy and Jimmy Carter. Kennedy would "pay any price, bear any burden" to ensure the march of democracy; he was the first president to commit combat troops to Vietnam. The "vital interests" school found leaders in Presidents Richard Nixon, Ronald Reagan and George Bush. Reagan kicked the Communists out of Grenada and Bush protected our oil supply from the Middle East.

By 1940, when *Casablanca* was being put together, two schools of thought had emerged with regard to foreign policy: isolation and intervention. The isolationists consisted of the cynics who had learned their lesson in World War I, and were distrustful of any European promises about being high-minded. The isolationists also included noninterventionists, America-Firsters, pacifists, and many Irish- and German-Americans. The interventionists included the high-minded idealists who still dreamed of "making the world safe for democracy" by ending the totalitarian regimes of German, Italy and Japan. Other interventionists, such as Republican nominee Wendell Willkie, believed it was in America's economic and security interests to enter the war.

It was in this context that *Casablanca* was made. Thus, it should come as no surprise that the script and the characters represent variations on these political themes. As we shall see, they provide the tensions and dialectics as well as the commitments that drive the story and make it compelling. Ultimately, of course, the film endorses the view that cries for intervention on behalf of democratic self-determination. As the story progresses, it also develops a parallel between love and politics that leads to subliminal reinforcements of message. But its success in delivering that message requires a close look at how characterization advanced ideology.

IDENTIFICATION

Characters draw us into films because they are vehicles of identification. Successful films have characters who appeal to large segments of the audience. For example, while viewing the cult classic *Bonnie and Clyde*, women seeking adventure may identify with the impulsive and poetic Bonnie Parker. Young men who are tentative about their sexual prowess or ready to defy authority may identify with the impotent but heroic Clyde Barrow. The supporting characters function to seduce other audience members into the film. Blanch, the preacher's daughter, appeals to the puritanical and rule-bound woman who finally finds her passions. Buck Barrow, Clyde's older brother, is a man's man, the guy who keeps everybody on track.

Because characters attract audiences, one of the chief tasks of a cinema critic who wants to determine how a film works is to analyze the various kinds of identification being used by the filmmaker. Just as important is the political ideology being advanced by the identification and symbolic action of the film. For example, once the audience has identified with the characters in *Bonnie and Clyde*, the characters function to encourage the audience members to take chances and break rules because such actions lead to self-discovery and true love.

Casablanca is no different: Identification advances ideology. *Casablanca* is driven by "dialectical tensions," open oppositions, that arise from these identifications. In fact, *Casablanca* succeeds as good entertainment and effective propaganda because of its unique combination of identification, ideology and dialectic. This film is worthy of analysis not only because it won the Academy Award for best picture,[1] but because when the American Film Institute did its exhaustive survey to determine the greatest films of all time, *Casablanca* was ranked third, behind *Gone with the Wind* and *Citizen Kane*. Furthermore, it is worthy of our attention because of the message it advances.

From the title sequence, the audience realizes it is watching a political polemic because the opening appears to be a newsreel revealing a tense political context. The film was rushed into release[2] just after the Allies invaded North Africa, pushing Morocco into the headlines on November 8, 1942, the first victory over the Nazis since the beginning of the war. Both Howard Barnes in his review for the *New York Times* and Bosley Crowther in his for the *New York Tribune* called the film "topical." The New York *Morning Telegraph* called it a "crackling, timely melodrama." The New York *Mirror* claimed the movie translated "today's headlines into arresting drama."[3] Furthermore, Roosevelt met with Prime Minister Churchill in Casablanca only two months after the film was released. Casablanca, which means "white house" in Spanish, soon had some critics arguing that Rick Blaine symbolized Roosevelt and Victor Laszlo symbolized Churchill.

CENSORSHIP AND THE MAKING OF *CASABLANCA*

Before this study establishes a more sensible view of the film's ideology, it is important to get some facts clear and to understand how history constrained the script in such a way that it became a propaganda piece by the time of its release. First, there were several factors at work that no one could have anticipated. Following Pearl Harbor, the Roosevelt administration established the Office of War Information with a Bureau of Motion Pictures to encourage Hollywood to make films that supported the war effort. Each producer was asked, "Will this picture help win the war?" *Casablanca* was reviewed by the bureau, which found the film to be a very good picture about the enemy, and one that supported the spirit of the underground movement.

The coercion of the government was nothing compared to the coercion Hollywood brought on itself. As part of the war effort, the industry put Joseph I. Breen in charge of the Motion Picture Producers and Distributors Association. Censorship was nothing new to Hollywood. The new medium was barely commercially viable when in 1915 the Supreme Court ruled that films were subject to the prior restraint of state censorship boards.[4] The court argued that as a matter of "common sense" the First Amendment was not designed for movies. The Trading with the Enemy Act of 1917 allowed President Wilson to create the Committee on Public Information, known as the Creel Committee after its head, George Creel, a former muckraker who had supported Wilson in 1912 and 1916. The committee was charged with uniting a divided public behind the war effort by putting out "information" and "correcting" disinformation.[5] Faced with the surprising growth of the motion picture industry, Creel initiated a policy of "benign censorship." A devout Catholic, Breen took up where Creel left off, imposing a new code, which commanded that "the sanctity of the institution of marriage and the home shall be upheld. Pictures should not infer that low forms of sex relationship are the accepted or common thing. . . . Adultery . . . must not be explicitly treated, or justified, or presented attractively." The Production Code Administration was formed in 1934. Based on this code, Breen condemned parts of the script of *Casablanca* and ensured that when the plane left the runway in the final scene, Ilsa would be on it with her husband, not on the ground with her lover.

The script is based on the play, *Everyone Comes to Rick's* by Murray Burnett, who in 1938 personally witnessed the horrors of fascism. While vacationing in the south of France, Burnett spoke with refugees making the circuitous journey to freedom. It usually began in Paris, headed into southern Vichy France, continued to Oran in North Africa through Casablanca to neutral Lisbon, Portugal, where flights to America were easier to secure. These shifts required letters of transit, which were very difficult to obtain. In 1940, Burnett co-wrote a play with Joan Allison about what he had seen and heard.

Howard Koch, who had gained some fame for *The Sea Hawk* and *The Letter*, was given the job of writing the film script. Though he worked with at least five other contributors,[6] he shaped the main arguments of the film. That's an important fact, given Koch's leftist tendencies. He was blacklisted after the war. Little did he know that the script would be changed so often it became almost extemporaneous at moments. The cast was asked to stand by to film a second ending once the first one was complete. Thus, while the dialogue reflects much of the Burnett and Allison play, the changes the screenwriters made were crucial to the texture of the film. For example, "Of all the cafes in all the towns in the world, she walks into my cafe," became "Of all the gin joints in all the towns in all the world, she walks into mine." Happily, "Here's good luck to you," became "Here's looking at you, kid."

Two weeks before filming was to start, only one-quarter of the script had been finished; on the day shooting began it was only half complete.[7] There is an internal joke in the script that alludes to this problem. Ilsa says, "Can I tell you a story? I don't know the finish yet." Rick responds, "Well, go on, tell it. Maybe one will come to you as you go along."[8] Even the title was changed. Julius and Philip Epstein's plot outline was based on *Everyone Comes to Rick's*, the Bennett and Allison play about a cafe on the Riviera.[9]

Hal Wallis first saw the plot outline four days after Pearl Harbor; he became the producer. He loved the idea of *Casablanca* not only because of its propaganda value but because its setting matched that of *Algiers*, his 1938 box-office success staring Hedy Lamar and Charles Boyer. The studio head was Jack Warner, perhaps FDR's biggest fan in Hollywood; that fact, too, helped determine the final outcome of the script. Warner became a lieutenant colonel in World War II. Michael Steiner, who wrote the score, used "As Time Goes By," "Perfidia," "Deutschland Uber Alles" and "La Marseillaise" to underscore the love and ideological themes.[10] The last two of these tunes established the political battle lines.

Michael Curtiz, Wallis's close friend, became the director of what would become his forty-third film.[11] Owen Marks, the editor, followed their instructions as he cut the film to a very tight 102 minutes. It was released on Warner's B list on Thanksgiving Day, November 27, 1942, becoming an A picture only after it won the Academy Award for Best Picture.

These behind-the-scenes machinations fail to ruin the timeless sentiment. The first song we hear, "It Had To Be You," takes us back in time but also foreshadows Ilsa's arrival. "As Time Goes By," originally written for a Broadway show in 1931, not only sets a mood but establishes the important temporal theme about waiting. Against this backdrop romantics identify with Ilsa, cynics with Rick and patriots with Victor. Our darker natures are seduced by the Nazis and their Vichy puppets. In an ironic subtext, it should be noted that many of the stars of the film were refugees from fascism, including Paul Henreid, Peter Lorre, Marcel Dalio, S. Z. Sakall and even Conrad Veidt, the chief villain. Veidt hated the Nazis and as an established actor in England was able to save Henreid from being sent to an internment camp when the war broke out. Soon Henreid left England for the American stage and then Hollywood. When America entered the war, Henreid agreed to star in *Casablanca* after first turning it down. He wished to underline his antifascist credentials. Their appearance in the film reinforced the message in a subtle way.

IDEOLOGICAL CHARACTERS

All of the characters shroud themselves in mystery and reveal their depths slowly. For example, at the beginning of the flashback to Paris, Rick asks Ilsa, "Who are you really? And what were you before? What did you do and what did you think?" She retains a sense of mystery by refusing to answer him, but only a few moments later she asks him, "A franc for your thoughts." Later Ilsa confirms, "We knew very little about each other when we were in love in Paris."

Each of the major characters represents a different ideology and symbolizes a different segment of the story. In this way they create dialectical tensions or identificational commitments that swirl around the parallel planes of love and politics. Victor Laszlo, played by Paul Henreid, a guy who knows how to light a cigarette, is the sincere Pharisee.[12] He claims, "Each of us has destiny, for good or for evil." He publishes propaganda against the Nazis; he sings the "Marseillaise" wearing his patriotism on his sleeve. He is a Czechoslovak who has escaped from a concentration camp. For Victor, ideology is more important than romance; he is committed politically, which causes deep divisions with the fascists and minor alienation from their fellow travelers and cynics such as Rick. He espouses the ideology of Western democracy, particularly freedom as opposed to authoritarian fascism. He is the voice of late European consciousness seeking to end the decadence and cynicism of the 1920s and the existentialism of the 1930s. Yet, it is precisely because he is so committed to his political agenda that Ilsa loves him and Rick eventually trusts him. Victor's commitment to political solutions reveals a character to whom others can commit themselves on other planes.

What may first strike contemporary audiences about Ilsa Lund, the Norwegian, played by Swedish actress Ingrid Bergman, is that she is so untouched by modern political feminist ideology.[13] Her eyes fill with tears more often than Demi Moore's do in *Ghost*; Ilsa remains the voice of innocence while being pushed around by history. Her inability to decide between Victor and Rick creates a terrific tension that is resolved only when Rick makes her decision for her at the climax of the film.[14] "You said I was to do the thinking for both of us," says Rick at the end of the film. This was not a part for Katharine Hepburn or Barbara Stanwyck.

Ilsa commits on the romantic plane of the movie and is one of the least political characters in the film. While she clearly disdains the Nazis, her attitude toward them is built more on fear than on loathing. And while Victor wants to make the world right again, Ilsa at first wants only to escape to America and a little later to find true love. In short, while Victor is the heart of the political drama, Ilsa is the heart of the romantic drama.

The bridge between the two is Rick Blaine, played by the versatile Humphrey Bogart, who inadvertently established this persona with his masterful performance as the private eye in *The Maltese Falcon*, also produced by Wallis. We should not forget that both Sam Spade and Rick Blaine are self-sufficient guys who can take care of themselves. They are a step ahead of everybody else and they are in control, much like America in 1940.

As *Casablanca* begins, Rick runs a swank bar called Rick's Cafe Americain, better known as Rick's Place. We first see him sitting alone playing chess, a symbolic representation of world politics, the black pieces of the Nazi Reich versus the white pieces of the Allies.[15] The political plane of the film is front and center, as Rick sometimes protects persons of dubious reputation and only hints at his decency by protecting his devoted employees. Rick ran guns to Ethiopia in its losing effort against Italy and was disappointed again in the Spanish Civil War where he fought on the losing Loyalist side against Generalissimo Franco, who had the backing of the forces of fascism. Having learned his lesson, Rick will no longer risk everything to save outsiders, saying: "I stick my neck out for nobody."[16] To which Renault replies, "A wise foreign policy." When Rick hears about two Germans being killed, he responds, "They got a lucky break. Yesterday they were just two German clerks; today they're the honored dead."[17] Like isolationist America, Rick isn't willing to take chances until he has no choice, a theme to which we shall return.

But no sooner have we learned from the dialogue that Rick is a coldhearted cynic than we learn in his next exchange that he has his ideals. He will not sell his cafe to Ferrari at any price because Ferrari takes advantage of refugees. Rick can't be bought; he thereby demonstrates the higher moral position with which many American identified. It becomes a recurring theme throughout the film and helped to rationalize America's entry into the European theater, which only a few years earlier had been seen as decadent.

Almost immediately after the exchange with Ferrari, Rick enters a third dialogue, which reinforces his schizophrenic persona and disdain for women. The conversation brings the issue of romance to the fore, but in a negative way. There is no sense of commitment here, only alienation. This time his victim is Yvonne, a woman with whom he is having an affair. She says, "Where were you last night?" He responds, "That's so long ago, I don't remember." She says, "Will I see you tonight?" He says, "I never make plans that far ahead." Thus, at the outset of the film, we learn that Rick does not like to make commitments. He is a man who will not be controlled, but we have seen a hint of his principle. This alternating attitude toward morality is reinforced when Renault says to Rick a few minutes later, "I suspect that under that cynical shell you're at heart a sentimentalist."[18] We soon learn that the root of Rick's cynicism is the loss of his love, Ilsa, an allegory for America's loss of innocence in World War I and the Depression. When she appears, Rick is thrown into a drunken funk in which he retrieves his memory of the affair, and the political plane is abandoned for the romantic as Rick stares at his drink.

The long flashback to a happier time begins, the time to which we all hope to return after the war. We learn from Sam that before the fall of France, Rick was blacklisted by the Nazis and had a price on his head. Thus, the script establishes a tension between the known and unknown in a character, and another tension, between Rick's sentiment and his cynical self-preservation, which is maintained until the last few moments of the film.[19] It helps us believe that Rick might ally himself with Renault to keep Victor in jail so that Rick can escape with Ilsa. His cynicism is crucial to maintaining the mystery of the story until the end.

Louis Renault, played superbly by Claude Rains, leads one of the best casts of character actors ever assembled. Performing in his eighth film under Curtiz's direction, Rains captures the essence of Renault, who claims to "blow with the wind," having "no conviction" of his own. He calls his heart his least vulnerable spot. Renault begins by playing the Vichy dupe of the Nazis, who seems to do their bidding in order to survive. He even provides "[a] little demonstration of the efficiency of my administration" when he orders arrests in Rick's Cafe.

As the film progresses, we see glimpses of revulsion and a certain impish quality begin to develop. These highlight Renault's redeeming qualities, while appealing to the resistance in all of us. For example, when he first meets the Nazi officers who have come to town, he says, "Unoccupied France welcomes you to Casablanca." A few sentences later, he tells Strasser, "You may find the climate of Casablanca a trifle warm," meaning that there are underground operations at work. The irony of the statements is not missed by Strasser who is put on his guard, making the political game all the more interesting. When Strasser refers to blundering Americans, Renault says, "I was with them when they 'blundered' into Berlin in 1918," thereby insulting Strasser while establishing his allegiance to the Allied cause and resurfacing memories of World War I. Thus, it makes sense that Rick will present Renault with his match at both verbal and political dueling. It is only at the end of the film that Renault joins Rick in an enlightened cynicism and survivalist philosophy that leads to the beginning of a beautiful friendship. It is fitting that they walk off into the night fog together, having cleansed Casablanca of the very bad and the very good. Thus, even in the case of Renault, characterization operates in the realms of the political and of the romantic. The question until the end of the film is whether Renault is capable of moral commitment.

S. K. Sakall as Carl, the Old World, German waiter, balances the wicked Nazis with his lovable characteristics.[20] Yes, his character says, there are good Germans in the world too. Peter Lorre as Guillermo Ugarte, the petty operator who attempts to get away near the beginning, gives us a sense of the tense political atmosphere when he brings his purloined passes to Rick.[21] Conrad Veidt as Strasser is the suave Nazi rat who sets Renault into action. Sydney Greenstreet as Ugarte's partner, Ferrari, runs a rival cafe, The Blue Parrot. And in case one misses who the evil Ferrari is, Rick dubs him a "fat hypocrite" about half way through the film. Ferrari lives off the fat of the land and the misfortune of others. Leonid Kinskey provides comic relief as the bartender Sasha. Finally, no one can forget Dooley Wilson as Sam, who actually could not play the piano.[22]

IDEOLOGICAL RELATIONSHIPS

The relationships among these characters advance ideologies; though they come from different countries, they are in the same place and share similar problems. This overarching theme of one-worldism is supported by several subthemes. One of the first to appear is tolerance because Sam, who is black, brings a sense of racism to the film. The first song he plays is "Shine," the lyrics of which include "Just because my hair is curly, just because my teeth are pearly." Rick takes care of Sam and confides in him. Sam reciprocates. He tries to fend Ilsa off, knowing she will cause Rick pain. Later when Rick asks Sam to play the painful theme song, Sam pretends he doesn't know it. In Paris, it was Sam who pulled Rick on the train to escape the Nazis when Ilsa failed to show at the station.

The relationship of Rick and Renault serves as a metaphor for American involvement in the war effort. The first time we see them together is outside Rick's Cafe, where they have a pleasant and intimate conversation in the open night air. Back inside the cafe in his first conversation with Ilsa, Renault describes Rick this way: "[H]e's the kind of a man that, well, if I were a woman and I were not around, I should be in love with Rick. But what a fool I am talking to a beautiful woman about another man."

We need to note that Rick intervenes to prevent Annina from having to sleep with Captain Louis Renault, Prefect of Police. Was his motive pure or self-interest? Finally, the film ends with these lines: Renault says, "And that ten thousand should pay our expenses." Rick responds, "*Our* expenses!" Renault assures him, "Uh huh." Rick concedes, "Louis, I think this is the beginning of a beautiful friendship." Thus, Rick has left Ilsa, the symbol of Europe, to the tender loving care of Victor, the embodiment of patriotism and high-minded values, while Rick has committed himself to a friendship with Renault.

Finally there is the love between Rick and his other employees, who come from diverse backgrounds, some of them not popular in America at the time. Carl is German; Sasha, who kisses Rick with joy at one point, is Russian; Carmina is Spanish; the doorman, Abdul is Muslim. When Rick sells his cafe to Ferrari near the end of the film, he makes sure each employee is taken care of in the sale agreement.[23] Is this an argument for one world, for a United Nations? All doubts are removed in the "Marseillaise" scene, in which everybody unites against the Nazis and forces them to sit down when Rick gives the band leader the cue to play the anthem. The room rings with "Vive la France! Vive la democracie!"[24]

DIALECTICAL TENSIONS

Of course, it is not through the characters alone that we see the dialectical tensions that reveal the ideology endorsed in the film. From the beginning, these tensions are thrust in our face, whether they are between the real and the ideal, patriotism and cynicism, or reason and feeling. To put it another way, the dialectical tensions are complicated by the way they are developed on the political and romantic planes of the film. At first, the political is featured as in a newsreel, as the film opens with a map of the world in December 1941, then narrows in on Europe and North Africa. Casablanca, a notoriously corrupt city through which Europeans were trying to escape tyranny, becomes a character itself, a place with which we can identify. The camera pans the turrets and rooftops of Casablanca, then sinks to police headquarters.[25] We know right away we are not in an occidental world. Instead we are an Islamic world of bazaars and deals, and a world of moral nihilism. Rick observes that "everybody in Casablanca has problems." Strasser sees that "in Casablanca human life is cheap." Renault claims that "nobody is supposed to sleep well in Casablanca."

Rick's Cafe is divided into the outer bar, into which is wedged a small band, and the inner casino, where money is lost and plots are hatched. The claustrophobia intensifies the desperation of those trying to escape. Furthermore, we are in a world where papers matter; if you don't have them you can be incarcerated or, worse, sent back to where you came from. And if you try to escape, you'll be shot. The locals are out to make a buck; their Vichy governors are two-faced, dipping into the black market when it suits their purposes and punishing those who participate in it when they need to make a show. They are condemned within the first few moments of the film when the police shoot a civilian who tries to escape because he has no papers. He dies beneath a poster of Marshal Philippe Petain, the World War I hero who has become the Vichy puppet of the Nazis. The contrast between the "go-along-to-get-along" Vichy group and the idealistic French patriots represented in the inscription "Liberte, Egalite, Fraternite"—ironically, inscribed over headquarters of

Renault's corrupt police operation—reinforces the dialectic between the real and the ideal in the political realm.

Those who make it to Lisbon are transferred on to the New World, but those who fight their way to Casablanca must wait and wait "as time goes by."[26] The theme is repeated in various guises throughout the film; for example, Strasser says, "Every French province in Africa is honeycombed with traitors waiting their chance, waiting, perhaps, for a leader."[27] The refugees, particularly Annina and Jan, are torn between the ideal waiting for them in America and the real price they have to pay to get there. Until saved by Rick's generosity, Annina considers sleeping with Renault in order to get an exit visa. The scene foreshadows Ilsa's offer to sleep with Rick in order to get the papers for Victor. She also embraces the notion of "better the real body in bed than the dead ideal" when she sleeps with Rick, believing that Victor has been killed in a concentration camp.

Another dialectical tension runs between cynicism and patriotism in politics. We have seen it in the persona of Rick, but it is made more explicit in the tension between Victor and the Nazis. The Nazis, who are evil and rule-bound, balance the patriots, who, like Victor Laszlo, are purely good and of high moral character. Strasser offers Laszlo an exit visa in exchange for the names of various agents. Laszlo says that if they couldn't get that information from him when he was in a concentration camp, they aren't going to get it now. He thereby transcends the real world with his idealism, a trick he repeats throughout the film. The most stirring moment occurs when Laszlo leads the French in the singing of the "Marseillaise" to drown out the Germans, who had been singing "Wacht am Rhein" (Watch on the Rhine).[28]

Laszlo's approach to life sharply contrasts with the cynical and worldly approach of Rick and Renault who rationalize their existence in the amoral cesspool of Casablanca. By coping, they create oases of comfort for themselves as long as the outside world does not intrude. Unfortunately for Renault, the Nazi Strasser is too big a fish to ignore. Unfortunately for Rick, Ilsa is too painful a memory to ignore. The world does intrude on both the political and romantic plane, and each character will be tested in his own way in the dialectical cauldron created by the invasion of the truly evil and the truly good into Casablanca. As Martin Heidegger repeatedly reminded us, the world seeps into our illusions no matter how well they are constructed.

The tension between Ilsa and Rick is important to the development of romantic commitment as a theme. Our curiosity about their relationship keeps us interested in the film. When Ilsa enters the cafe, we know nothing of the couple's history. She spots Sam, who first lies about Rick's whereabouts, then tells her to leave him alone. She overrides his reticence with a request: "Play it, Sam. Play 'As Time Goes By.'" Sam resists, but she hums her siren song and begs, "Sing it, Sam." And so he does. It brings an angry Rick out of the gambling room who is stunned to find Ilsa in his cafe. Is he still in love with her? Will he fall for her again? What happened to break them up when the Nazis marched into Paris? After she leaves, Rick commands Sam to "play it" and is transported back to the magic prewar days in Paris. The light and the daytime give us a much-needed relief from the enclosed world of Casablanca.

The dynamic between Rick and Ilsa is soon complicated by a love triangle that plays the virtue of Laszlo against the passion of Rick. The triangular tension is supported by the psyche of each of these three characters. Sigmund Freud would tell us that Victor is the narcissist; Rick is the dominant anaclitic, one who takes care of others; and Ilsa is the submissive anaclitic, one who wants to be taken care of. Since we all at various times love idealized versions of ourselves, wish to take care of others, and wish to be taken care of, the love triangle reinforces the other strains of identification woven into the plot. The love triangle parallels the political theme of the French slogan "Liberte, Egalite, Fraternite." Victor represents liberty, Ilsa represents equality, at least among the men in her life, and Rick represents fraternity.

The love triangle reinforces identification in another way that advances the film's theme of commitment as opposed to alienation: Each lover has his or her perfect love despoiled. Ilsa did not wait for Victor; she did not show up for Rick; and she loses her true love in the end. While Ilsa and Victor fly off to freedom, we wonder how soon they will be filing for divorce, given what they know about one another. At one point, we are led to believe that Rick has cynically manipulated the situation to win Ilsa's hand. Renault confirms this deal when he says, "Love, it seems, has triumphed over virtue." But Rick, who continues to run the show, reverses his field at the end. It is better to sacrifice your lover for a good cause than to keep her and have to live with your decision. Rick does not believe there is anything like living happily ever after. Maybe nobility is more important than love. To put it another way, Rick chooses a love that transcends passion, which satisfies the audience emotionally by relieving Rick's disillusionment over Ilsa's innocent mistake. Thus, she retains her innocence and he retains his self-sufficient manhood and integrity.

This last theme certainly would resonate with feelings about European wars in the United States. Because of certain films and various forms of propaganda, many contemporary Americans mistakenly believe that Americans universally supported World War I. But that was not the case. As we have seen, Irish-Americans hated President Wilson for supporting England. German-Americans also despised his siding with the Allies. While Wilson came back with nothing to show for his efforts except some reparation payments, the French, Italians and English divided the spoils of war including German holdings around the world. When it was over, it did not seem to most Americans that it was the war to make the world safe for democracy; rather it was, as Senator Henry Cabot Lodge characterized it, the same old European game that could be traced back to the so-called Holy Alliance that took over Europe after the fall of Napoleon.[29] The 1994 Tristar release *Legends of the Fall* presents a realistic picture of the war and the reaction of many Americans to it. As men came home from the battle missing legs, arms, and lungs, Americans realized that this was an ugly modern war.[30] It created a lost generation.

From the late 1930s to Pearl Harbor, politicians like Burton Wheeler and national heroes like Charles Lindbergh were successful in rallying isolationist sentiment around the America First theme. Just as Rick had learned his lesson in the Spanish Civil War, America had learned its lesson in World War I. Just as Rick had been betrayed at the train station in Paris by Ilsa, so America, embodied by Wilson, had been betrayed at the bargaining table in Versailles. In this way, the film teaches us to be careful of the idealists like Laszlo and the innocents like Ilsa; they can hurt you if you are not careful. The parallel is to be wary of the European allies no matter how idealistic or romantic they sound because they will pull you into affairs that will tear you apart. Thus, FDR, like Wilson before him, promised in his presidential campaign to keep us out of the war, and said America would not get involved until absolutely forced to.

Rick symbolizes this American consciousness when he says, "I bet they're asleep in New York. I'll bet they're asleep all over America." When America did get involved, like Rick, America was good, but it was not naive, as in World War I. This ambiguity over entering the war is symbolized in various ways throughout the film. One of the most telling moments occurs when a French officer and a German officer get in a fight over Yvonne, whom Rick has spurned. He quickly steps in between them and breaks up the fight, exercising total control over the situation. He says, "I don't like disturbances in my place. Either lay off politics or get out." In this moment, he has sounded the neutralist and isolationist cry.

But like the love theme, the political theme is also resolved to the audience's satisfaction because the isolationists who identify with Rick are not evil, they are merely mistaken, just as Rick was in his love affair. There comes a time when one must intervene, no matter how self-sufficient one is. Rick achieves this moment of transcendence near the end of the film when he kills Strasser and frees Victor. At that moment, we realize that, like his love for Ilsa, Rick's commitment to the Allies was never in question. It was just a matter of when the commitment would begin and at what level of intensity. Intervention requires moral commitment; moral commitment often requires self-sacrifice. Thus, Rick, like a good Platonist, abandons passion for a higher good.

AESTHETIC QUALITY

This film has significant dialectical tensions that have been built on characters with whom we can identify on two separate planes, the political and the romantic. But it is also a stylistic and symbolic masterpiece. The script possesses remarkable balance not only because of the dialectical tensions, but because of the refrains that call us back again and again to the core of the story. For example, early on there is a sinister reference to "the customary round up of refugees." And at the end, the ominous line is turned to irony when Renault says he will solve the problem of explaining Strasser's killing by rounding up "the usual suspects." Using lines like these at the opening and ending of a film gives it a unity of style while satisfying our expectations. Another example occurs when Rick continues to show his love for Ilsa with the line, "Here's looking at you, kid," which also serves to round out scene after scene with a wonderful continuity. One of the most interesting symbolic ties among the three main characters is that they each say the words "play it" at some point in the film. Ilsa tells Sam to "play it," meaning "As Time Goes By." Soon after Rick makes the same request, not to remind him of something pleasant, but to remind him of his painful lost love. Finally, in one of the most important scenes in the film, Victor says, "Play the 'Marseillaise,' play it."

Symbolism is used to reinforce the various ideological themes. Near the opening of the film, a plane comes in for a landing and the refugees in the street watch with hope that they will be able to be on board when it leaves. The plane represents transcendence and hope. A little later Rick's face is illuminated by the light of the revolving beacon at the airport, one of the few non-claustrophobic moments in the film, and a plane flies overhead, symbolizing freedom. The scene foreshadows the end of the film where Rick is left on the ground as the plane with Ilsa aboard flies away. But the beacon also symbolizes the end of waiting, an escape and the hope of the American dream, which Victor Laszlo, the Leuchtags and other refugees continually seek. When Rick and Ilsa reconcile, they stand near the window, and the beacon sweeps light over them, blessing their reunion. Rick's back room is used to symbolize the fact that life is a gamble; we place our bets and take our chances.

There are what critic Kenneth Burke would call incidental symbols that help to weave the plot and characters. Glasses of alcohol are spilled at crucial moments to signify an end to something. In Paris, Rick wears a daisy in his lapel to signify that this is a happy time. At the end of the film, Victor Laszlo wears a white hat; he is the good guy.

CONCLUSION

The rich texture of the film, its style, its symbolism, and its dialectical tensions raise important political and romantic questions that are resolved only at the end of the film. Are people more important than causes? Is it better to die fighting for freedom than to live in corruption? Is love more important than nobility? Perhaps the answers can be found in Rick's speech to Ilsa near the end of the film: "Look, I'm no good at being noble, but it doesn't take much to see that the problems of three little people don't amount to a hill of beans in this crazy world. Someday you'll understand that." We don't admire people who take advantage of others, even if they are in love. We do admire the noble character who gives up his or her love because nobility makes the world a better place for the rest of us.

Is Casablanca a place to stay or a way station on the road to freedom and self-discovery? There are only four ways out of Casablanca: back from where you came, death, forward to another Casablanca for which you must pay dearly, or traveling on to your destiny, which requires that you acquire the magic key (a letter of transport) that is guarded by Renault. As the characters jockey for ways out of Casablanca, they learn a good deal about themselves and how much they are willing to sacrifice for another person and/or for the cause. The theme of the need for self-sacrifice in the world culminates with Rick's ultimate sacrifice of his love for Ilsa and his putting his life on the line for her and Victor's escape.

Perhaps these are existential questions that we should be asking ourselves every day. Perhaps that is why this film has such enduring quality. It transcends its time and place by appealing to universal values that lie beyond the ideology of the film. While it endorses uniting to defeat evil, while it begs for involvement and one-worldism, it also attracts us to higher values by reinforcing them with people with whom we can identify. Rick begins as a mercenary; Victor is a patriot. But by the end of the film, both are more noble versions of ourselves; they allow us for a few hours to leave our mundane and perhaps corrupt existences behind and become the heroes we wish we could be. Ilsa is a more romantic version of ourselves; she allows us to leave our mundane and less romantic lives and become the lovers we wish we could be. In that sense, *Casablanca* is like Plato's world, an idealized and transcendent version of this one. It provides a universal *telos* that refreshes us each time we touch upon it. For this enduring quality and the ideological themes it advances, it has become a film classic.

NOTES

1. It also won Oscars for its screenplay and director. The film was one of the top-grossing films of the season and won numerous other awards.

2. In 1942 there were 20,000 theaters in America, twice as many as exist today. Charles Francisco, *You Must Remember This . . . The Filming of Casablanca* (Englewood Cliffs, NJ: Prentice Hall, 1980), 12.

3. As cited in Howard Koch, *The 50th Anniversary Edition of Casablanca: Script and Legend* (Woodstock, NY: Overlook, 1992), 274, 277.

4. *Mutual Film Corporation vs. Industrial Communication of Ohio*, 236 U.S. 230 (1915); *Mutual Film Corporation of Missouri vs. Hodges*, 236 U.S. 248 (1915).

5. George Creel, *How We Advertised America: The First Telling of the Amazing Story of the Committee on Public Information That Carried the Gospel of Americanism to Every Corner of the Globe* (New York: Harper and Brothers, 1920). See also Cedric Larson and James R. Mock, "The Lost Files of the Creel Committee of 1917–19," *Public Opinion Quarterly* 3 (1939), 5–29; Thomas A. Hollihan, "Propagandizing in the Interest of War: A Rhetorical Study of the Committee on Public Information," *Southern Speech Communication Journal* 49 (Spring 1984), particularly 240–46.

6. Koch, *50th Anniversary Edition*, 10.

7. Ibid., 17.

8. Umberto Eco, "Casablanca: Cult Movies and Intertextual Collage," in Koch, *50th Anniversary Edition*, 257, holds the unstable script responsible for the fact that each time Laszlo orders a drink, it is something different.

9. This screenplay was fished out of a stack of manuscripts by reader Stephen Karnot at the time the Japanese attacked Pearl Harbor; Francisco, *You Must Remember This*, 28. Burnett and Allison were paid $20,000 for the play, the highest amount to that date for an unproduced play, but an amount far below what the movie would reap; Francisco, *You Must Remember This*, 34.

10. He did not like "As Time Goes By" and wanted it cut from the film; Francisco, *You Must Remember This*, 185. Unfortunately for Steiner, and fortunately for the movie, he did not see the rough cut until it was too late to change it. Bergman could not reshoot her scenes because her hair had been cut so she could play Maria in *For Whom the Bell Tolls*. Steiner had scored *Gone with the Wind* and *Now, Voyager*; thus he had enormous credibility. But it was too late, so he did use "As Time Goes By" to create a wonderful score.

11. Koch claims that three directors turned the project down before it was offered to Curtiz. But Francisco claims that Curtiz was Wallis's only choice. Curtiz was Hungarian, like many others in the cast, and had a strong sympathy for the plight of refugees.

12. Wallis had produced Henreid's star vehicle, *Now, Voyager*. Henreid was from Austrian nobility and had studied under the great Max Reinhardt.

13. She was Wallis's first choice for the part and had to be borrowed from David O. Selznick's studio. Francisco, *You Must Remember This*, 88. Bergman had made her debut in 1940 in *Intermezzo*.

14. That's why it is consistent in terms of character and ideology to pack Ilsa and Victor off on the same plane at the end of the movie. In her autobiography,

Bergman wrote that Bogart was aloof and hard to relate to. No doubt she preferred rushing off with Henreid.

15. In the next-to-last version of the screenplay, he was playing solitaire, which was meant to reinforce his loneliness and isolation.

16. A line he repeats in the early part of the film. Near the climax, Rick says to Ilsa, "I'm not fighting for anything anymore, except myself."

17. He and Ugarte are seated at a chess table with the pieces configured as if the game has been underway for a while.

18. He later calls Rick a romantic and Laszlo praises Rick for fighting for the underdog.

19. Rick shows his good side and his cynical side repeatedly. When Annina asks Rick if she should sleep with Renault in order to get a pass to America, he tells her to go back to Bulgaria. But a few moments later he allows her naive husband Jan to win at roulette so he can buy them passes.

20. Sakall was Hungarian, like many others in the cast. He had only recently learned to speak English. See Francisco, *You Must Remember This*, 133.

21. Lorre is yet another Hungarian in the cast, and another alumnus of *The Maltese Falcon*. He had studied with Freud and Adler and helped to develop psychodrama. See Francisco, *You Must Remember This*, 124.

22. Koch, *50th Anniversary Edition*, 8.

23. Earlier, Rick had refused to allow Sam to work for Ferrari.

24. The scene was written by Murray Burnett in 1940 and survived in the movie's script. In fact, the scene was heightened to make Laszlo even more attractive, thereby further justifying Ilsa's being torn between him and Rick.

25. The scene was shot in Burbank, as was most of the movie. But clips of Paris and other stock footage created the illusion of being in Casablanca.

26. Strasser, for example, says to Victor Laszlo, "Don't be in such a hurry. You have all the time in the world. You may be in Casablanca indefinitely."

27. This technique of advancing the same principle in various guises is analyzed by Kenneth Burke in *Counter-statement* (New York: Harcourt Brace, 1931).

28. In one scene, Ilsa amuses herself by looking at a tablecloth priced at 700 francs. When Rick arrives and explains that she is being cheated, the merchant changes the price to 200 francs. That's the real world. Everything changes, values are not real.

29. The script plays to these nationalist tensions in at least two places: Carl is a sympathetic, Old World, lovable German waiter; the Leuchtags who are escaping speak nothing but English, "so we should feel at home ven ve get to America." Carl and the Leuchtags toast, "To America." They balance the Nazis.

30. Director Michael Curtiz had fought in World War I in the Austro-Hungarian army.

Chapter Seven

Isolationism in *All Quiet on the Western Front*

Herbert E. Gooch III

August 27, 1928: Twelve nations, including the great European powers and the United States, signed the Pact of Paris outlawing resort to war in international relations—excepting only in case of self-defense.[1] But one nation's defensive resort might look suspiciously like aggression to another, and there was neither a superior authority to judge nor a mechanism to implement sanctions against an aggressor. The pact would prove to have, as one contemporary judged it, the ultimate effect of an "international kiss."

Throughout the same month, in Germany, the prestigious publishing house of Ullstein set the galley proofs for serial publication of the work of an unknown young veteran, a magazine writer, former school teacher and race-car driver named Erich Maria Remarque.[2] Loosely based on his wartime experiences, it purported to be a realistic account of war from the viewpoint of the common soldier. Remarque's preface (which also appeared in the original and restored movie versions after the title and credits) stated: "This book is to be neither an accusation nor a confession, and least of all an adventure, for death is not an adventure to those who stand face to face with it. It will try simply to tell of a generation who, even though they may have escaped its shells, were destroyed by the war."[3]

The Paris Pact looked forward to a future of world peace; the German novel looked back to the effects of world war. The former was symbolic of a view of international relations that, though not exclusively American (it was the initiative of U.S. Secretary of State Frank B. Kellogg and French Foreign Minister Aristide Briand), is critical to understanding a set of assumptions about democracy and war, violence and the inter-

Lew Ayres in the final scene of *All Quiet on the Western Front.* Courtesy of the Academy of Motion Picture Arts and Sciences.

national arena that is distinctive to the United States and popularly labeled isolationism. The latter quickly found its way to the best-seller list in America and, by spring 1930, an American movie version was in theaters to become one of the most popular and surprising movie hits of the 1930s.

Hollywood cinema has been notorious for shying away from political "message" films, yet this movie was clearly pacifist, was advertised as a political statement, reveled in political controversy—and proved immensely popular. What were the relationships between novel and movie, movie-making and audience, American political beliefs and historical moment that might explain that popularity? How this movie came about, and its link to American isolationist attitudes and beliefs regarding foreign affairs are explored to help understand the movie's reception.

NOVEL AND MOVIE

All Quiet on the Western Front (Im Westen Nichts Neues) was an immediate best-seller, published in book form in January 1929. By the end of the year, it had sold seven million copies and been translated into twenty languages. In the spring, Remarque was approached by Carl ("Uncle Carl") Laemmle, a German by birth, and one of the eccentric, ruthless and highly successful founders of Hollywood, Universal Studios in particular.[4] Laemmle purchased the film rights as part of a complicated strategic move to advance Universal (the only major studio without an Oscar) and his family into a position of prestige and greater prominence in Hollywood, while producing a "blockbuster" film to ensure the studio's financial success. The previous summer, he had turned over management of the multi million-dollar enterprise to his twenty-one-year-old son "Junior," who was the main producer of *All Quiet.*

Prospects for the movie's success seemed dubious. It was based on a best-selling novel, but Hollywood had a stable overflowing with movie flops made from best-selling novels. It had a novice studio head as producer, a director unproven in the genre of serious war films, and an investment so large that it gambled the fate of the entire Universal studio on a single movie. Moreover, it challenged common-sense advice in Hollywood about how to make a successful movie by offering an unhappy ending, no love interest, a hero and his buddies who all die, no major stars in the leading roles to carry the film, and a didactic "political" message about the misadventures of soldiers, soldiers on the losing side, soldiers who were the enemy just a few years before!

Production began to great fanfare. The Laemmle production and advertising strategy was to build upon the popularity of the novel and its subject matter as a "realistic" portrayal of war. Thus a point was made to begin production on November 11, 1929, Armistice Day, and the attention to realistic detail was heavily advertised. For example, real German and French uniforms were imported, battle scenes were staged over twenty acres on Irvine Ranch (near the present campus of University of California Irvine), an entire village with thirty-five sets was constructed, only to be blown apart on cue, real drill instructors drilled over 2,000 troops, and thousands of tons of explosives and real howitzers were used.

The Laemmles built systematically upon the mood of disillusionment fashionable in the reassessment of World War I a decade after its conclusion. A cycle of war movies had begun by the mid-1920s. The top-grossing silent movie was King Vidor's *The Big Parade* (1925), famous for John Gilbert, an American "doughboy," showing a French girl (Renee Adoree) how to chew gum. The great success of the Broadway play *What Price Glory?* (1925) led to a relatively successful, explicitly antiwar movie version (1927). The hiring of its playwright, Sherwood Anderson, as the screenwriter to adapt *All Quiet*, and one of its stars, Louis Wolheim, to play Kat ensured an antiwar identification for the movie.

Cost was to be no object in faithfully rendering the novel and re-enacting the experience of war. Calculated at costing between $1.2 and $1.45 million, it was one of the most expensive movies Hollywood had produced to date. The director, Lewis Milestone, was a second but highly recommended choice because of his wartime experience in film work for the Signal Corps and his Oscar credit for his war comedy *Two Arabian Knights* (1927).[5] A young but recognized cinematographer, Arthur Edeson, who had experience in Western and outdoor action cinematography and camera sound work, was hired. The main characters of Paul and his buddies were selected from fresh faces rather than established stars to ensure that the war, not a particular character, remained the central focus.[6]

CONTENT AND TIMING

The novel told the story of seven youthful school mates from their initial, naive and idealistic patriotic enlistment to their progressive disillusionment, cynicism and, finally, death. The point of view of the novel is through the eyes of Paul Baumer, the surrogate for Remarque, who notes with lyric precision the dirty, ugly business of warfare, and its immense physical and psychic toll. The sole redeeming element amid the horror and brutality of war in the trenches lay in comradeship with Kat (Louis Wolheim), the veteran, tough, scavenging NCO who takes Paul and his friends under his wing to teach them survival. When Kat dies, the last link between Paul and the world of family, society, country and emotion is extinguished. Emotionally and symbolically, Kat's death is the focal point of the novel in finally cutting off Paul (and by extension his generation) from the possibility of sharing feeling and communication. Paul's death later is literally "nichts neues" (nothing of news) to report on the Western Front that day; he has already died with Kat.

The powerful emotional effect of the novel derives from its propensity toward understatement, most graphically exemplified in the ending paragraphs, where the point of view shifts abruptly from Paul's perception of the world to an omnipresent, third person reporting about fighting on the front. Paul is reported dead, and the novel quotes simply the official wording:

> He fell in October 1918, on a day that was so quiet and still on the whole front that the army report confined itself to the single sentence: All quiet on the Western Front.
> He had fallen forward and lay on the earth as though sleeping. Turning him over one saw that he could not have suffered long; his face had an expression of calm, as though almost glad the end had come.[7]

The ending has a stunning affect. It leaves the reader less emotionally charged with anger, less outraged at the fate of Paul and his comrades than drained, devoid of emotion. As J. Glenn Gray has noted of war, "Just as creation raises us above the level of the animal, destruction forces us below it by eliminating communication," so Remarque brilliantly captures the effect of war in dissolving the possibility of meaning.[8] His point is that war not only cuts off human beings from civil society, but destroys the emotional and cognitive capacity to share meaning even on the most primitive levels. He is writing about the alienation of his generation, a generation whose capacity to feel, relate and find meaning in everyday participation in ordinary life was crushed by the experience of war.

Remarque's view of war is only one of many possible interpretations, but certainly one that is politically meaningful. He went to great lengths, however, to disavow a political message. He did not identify himself with a specific political ideology or party, or a specific literary circle, although clearly his orientation was leftist and he wrote in a style and from a viewpoint of social realism, from the perspective of what Hans Fallada would later characterize as the *kleine Mann*, the forgotten, marginal, working-class "little man" in society.[9] Note that he was writing in 1928, a time when a defeated Germany had weathered political disruption from violence on the Left (Spartacists, 1920) and on the Right (the Kapp Putsch, 1923, which landed Hitler in prison where he wrote *Mein Kampf*). By this time, Germany was on the mend, thanks to the Dawes Plan (1923) and the Young Reparations Plan (1927). Remarque, after drifting about after the war for several years, had settled into regular employment and was experiencing a rising standard of living, a situation reflected generally in the rising economic conditions and political stability of Germany at the end of the 1920s.

He said of the novel that "it wrote itself" in just eight weeks, and thought of it more as a kind of exorcism of the demons haunting him since the war than as a political tract. He wrote of the experience of war as a source of psychic alienation, not political inspiration or explanation. Given its subject matter, its denunciation by various conservative elements in society (e.g., military, patriotic and veterans groups, church and family groups) was expected. But it was also suspect and attacked, even while praised for the antiwar and antipatriotic message, by groups on the extreme Left on the grounds that it lacked a clear exposition of the causes of war or prescription for its elimination. The political extremes criticized the novel and later the movie, as being either too political (the position of the Right) or not political enough (the position of the Left) while Remarque appears to have thought of himself as writing about a state of affairs that transcended politics altogether: the spiritual death of a generation.

Timing is critical, and undoubtedly the magnitude of the novel's popular reception had to do with the arrival of a period of social, economic and political recovery a decade after Armistice. The war was far away enough to become a memory that could be edited to popular understanding, rather than a raw experience whose sheer facticity overwhelmed the capacity to put it into perspective. The novel not only touched on a concern and resonated with the emotional and intellectual temper of the time, but also helped form it. The movie shared and reinforced this capacity. Where the novel was read by millions, the movie was seen by tens of millions. Where the novel had a primary impact in forming opinion in the reading public, the movie reached out to the great masses composing public opinion at its most extensive, encompassing and elemental.

Timing was also important in another way specific to the great popularity of the movie, a point commentators have uniformly overlooked. What is most often mentioned by way of explaining its popularity is the connection to the growing strength of isolationist and antiwar sentiments. The production schedule inadvertently corresponded with the onset of the Great Depression: Black Tuesday, the first plummeting of the market, was October 24, 1929, and *All Quiet* started filming less than two weeks later. By the time of its release in late April 1930, the tremendous reception quite likely was linked to the growing sense of confusion, desperation and anxiety brought on by deepening effects of the Depression. By 1932 the market was valued at 80 percent below its 1929 high, and twelve million people were out of work. This sense was also conveyed effectively in depicting war as an experience of constant fright, anxiety and bewilderment, of being at the whim of implacable, inexorable, impersonal forces beyond one's control.[10] Like the novel, the movie exudes a pervasive sense of spectacular waste and loss, not only of life but of control. Both the novel and the movie are iconoclastic and speak to a sense of disillusionment, to the suspicion that the possibility of order, values and relationship has been swept away.

The movie's timing was also important because 1927 had witnessed the first hit of the "talkies," *The Jazz Singer* with Al Jolson. Hollywood was slow to change over from the silents, but by 1930 over half of the motion picture theaters in America were wired for sound. These represented the largest and most lucrative exhibition outlets, however. Still very expensive to produce and exhibit, it was clear the wave of the future would be in sound, and therefore *All Quiet* was shot in two versions, sound and silent. The cinematographer, Arthur Edeson, had experience with new camera and sound equipment, which made him attractive to the Laemmles. George Cukor was hired as a dialogue coach for the movie (and he in turn recommended the young Lew Ayres, who spelled his name Louis Ayres). *All Quiet* appeared at a time of change and experimentation, the juncture between the passing of silents and the coming of sound into movies. Milestone, at only thirty-three years of age, was willing to experiment, to adapt to new uses of dialogue and try camera techniques little used before, such as Edeson's use of the soaring and tracking crane shots, and the rapid montage effects used to film the battle scenes. But what is perhaps most striking was his use of sound effects to heighten the sensation of battle, and the use of music to produce extraordinary effects.[11] Part of the movie's success stems from the scale of the effects and their skillful application, and the artistic interweaving of special effects and music in ways that were fresh, even startling to most audiences in 1930.

The special effects used to create the impression of "realism" focus on action photography. Some of the most influential and famous scenes in the movie are those of the night photography of artillery explosions, and the magnificent montage of battle, with first one side advancing and being mowed down by the rat-tat-tat of machine-gun fire, and then the other. After showing graphic carnage on both sides charging and retreating (including a set of disembodied hands left clinging to barbed wire), the original trenches are reoccupied, with no gain to either side, only mutual losses. A twenty-five-ton crane was used to shoot these sequences, characterized not only by montage, but by the soaring, sweeping and tracking shots of soldiers in the trenches. These shots of war have rarely been exceeded in their capacity to evoke the terror, confusion and frenzied excitement of battle.[12]

The most memorable scenes are those least, strictly speaking, "realistic": The battle scenes were greatly influenced by D. W. Griffith and the

Russian montage effects of Sergei Eisenstein and Dziga Vertov. The ending in particular owes more to German expressionism and symbolism than to realism. Three other striking examples are found in (1) the use of a pair of boots passed on to each soldier as another dies to show the systematic, inexorable progress of death without having to film each death scene in detail; (2) filming Paul and his friend in the reflection of a mirror as they see a poster model of a young woman, underscoring a double alienation from ordinary and natural life—the woman is only a representation, but they are filmed only as a reflection of themselves as well; and (3) the use, in the love scene where Paul and two comrades meet some young French girls, of a phonograph needle, having played the record and with no one to lift the needle, endlessly scratching the disk—a symbol of the sterility of the affair, and the scene of Paul and a French girl in bed, filmed as an image of shadows on a wall above the bed with voice-overs in different, mutually incomprehensible languages—symbolizing the lack of understanding and ability to form love at any deeper level than physical attachment.

NOVEL AND MOVIE

There are three major departures from the approach of the novel by the movie: in plot, point of view, and ending. In the novel, there is repeated use of flashbacks and interior monologues in which Paul expresses his reactions to his surroundings. The movie reorders the incidents recorded in the book into a linear progress, starting with the boys in the classroom, enlisting, going through basic training, their first encounter with the front, and the ebb and flow of battle.[13] Scenes, like characters, are embellished, added or deleted to make the movie more comprehensible. For instance, a neat symmetry is established by having Paul toward the end of the movie revisit his old classroom where his bitter monologue against war and patriotism is a response to the schoolmaster's Latin translation of how fitting and noble death is.

This sequencing, Paul's return, and his speech are not in the novel.

> I heard you in there reciting that same old stuff—making Iron Men, more young heroes! You think it's still beautiful and sweet to die for your country, don't you? Well, we used to think you knew but the first bombardment taught us better. It is dirty and painful to die for your country. When it comes to dying for your country, it's better not to die at all.[14]

The point of view throughout the novel is through Paul's eyes, and the ending is abrupt and stunning in shifting to an impersonal, omnipresent point of view. Movies have almost uniformly found that filming literally from the point of view of the protagonist is tedious to audiences.

The audience wants to *see* Paul, and that dictates that the story be told by the camera outside the characters. This poses a number of difficulties in transferring what is read on the page to what is seen on the screen. A major aspect of these difficulties can be illustrated by the decision of how to depict Paul's death on the screen.

The original screenplay attempted to do this by shifting to a typed epilogue over the concluding shot of Paul in death. This would have the benefit of reminding the reader how faithful the movie is to the book, and put a "closing cover" on the movie to match the book and the preface. But this version of the ending clearly did not work in audience previews. In February 1930, only weeks before its Hollywood premiere, preview responses revealed two major flaws: Zasu Pitts played Paul's mother, but had recently gained fame as a leading comedienne, and the audience was clearly unprepared to accept her in the role of a caring, despairing, tragic mother. Her scenes were cut, Beryl Mercer was recruited to play the mother and the scenes were quickly reshot.

The other flaw was the ending. Audiences simply did not like it and Milestone and company did not know what to do about it. Within two weeks of the premiere, Karl Freund, a Czech immigre cinematographer trained at Universum Film Aktiengesellschoft (UFA) in German expressionism, came up with a brilliant suggestion (Edeson had already gone on location for another film). Picking up on the homecoming in which the camera catches the butterfly collection mounted on Paul's bedroom wall, Freund and Milestone invented the famous scene in which Paul is killed while reaching out for a butterfly. Time was short, and so Milestone used his own hand in the shot. There is the sound of a winsome harmonica, Paul sees a butterfly and moves toward it as a French sniper takes aim. Tension is built as the camera cuts between Paul's outstretched hand and the sniper's finger tightening on the trigger; with the sound of a single bullet, the hand twitches, then relaxes into death. There is a quick cut to the final scene, a grim epilogue. The screen is filled with endless burial crosses dotting black hills. Superimposed on this image, Paul and his classmates, as part of an endless column of troops, march away, each turning back to look hauntingly at the audience, a generation staring back from a premature grave.

HISTORICAL CONTEXT

Commentators today look at the film in terms of its future rather than its present in 1930. Isolationism had been growing in the United States in reaction against a long cycle of political activism and reform chiefly characterized domestically by Progressivism, first under Theodore Roosevelt (1901–1908), then Woodrow Wilson (1912–1920), and internationally by an activist, interventionist stance toward Latin America and the Pacific (1890s into the 1920s). The 1920s had been a period of rapid economic growth, especially in consumer durables, resulting in a nearly 40 percent increase in the per capita standard of living in a single decade. World War I and the decade of the 1920s had elevated America to a preeminent position economically, but the will to become further engaged and lead in international political affairs was not asserted. Although Wilson had proposed the League of Nations, the U.S. Senate rejected the principle of collective security and "foreign entanglement" in the League in voting against treaty ratification. The United States never joined the League. The war had been sold as a moral crusade, as "the war to end all wars" and "the war to make the world safe for democracy." In its aftermath, the country turned bitterly against further involvement abroad and negotiations over the Treaty of Versailles seemed to make a mockery of Wilson's high idealism.

Added to the disillusionment over Versailles were uncertain economic times, a "Red Scare" of subversives and Wilson's physical deterioration (which left the country without strong leadership for a year and a half). Public sentiment shifted toward cynical detachment from political idealism and a withdrawal from domestic political reform and international leadership. The Republicans came into power starting in 1920, and stressed less government, fewer programs, lower taxes and less regulation of business. Immigration was severely curtailed with the National Immigration Quotas Act of 1925. The Ku Klux Klan enjoyed a resurgence, expanding with strong political membership in the Midwest, and added Catholics and other ethnic and religious minorities to its demonology. The two most famous political trials of the decade (Scopes in 1925, concerning the issue of teaching science and religious fundamentalism; and Sacco-Vanzetti in 1927, dealing with political radicalism associated with immigrants) indicated the rise and force of religious fundamentalism and reassertion of nativist, anti-foreign opinion.

The 1920s were prosperous times in which the United States was resentful of, but not threatened by, the great European powers. The continuing issue of unpaid foreign war debts, with some $10 billion in loans owed to the United States, reinforced American resentment against the Europeans. This was reflected in the reassertion of an isolationist stance in foreign policy. But with the coming of the Depression in the 1930s, the situation changed, bringing a hardening and deepening of the isolationist impulse, and its articulation as a political doctrine with the organization of interest groups and factions within the two major parties. *All Quiet* came out just as the change was beginning, and it probably benefited by its sense of social and personal anxiety, confusion and loss of control (albeit in terms of war rather than peacetime economic conditions) that resonated with many viewers. The isolationist impulse in 1930 was not yet as powerful or as partisan as it would become later when it was fueled by economic weakness and uncertainty, and the rise of new international threats. By the end of the decade a more direct link was forged between isolationism and antiwar doctrines, welded finally by the outbreak of another world war in 1939.

The impulse in 1930 was based more on resentment than fear. The key international response to the Depression was to cut America off from other countries with the Smoot-Hawley Tariffs (1930), to dismiss rather than engage the European powers. The Depression deepened, and a turning point came in 1933 with the ascension of Hitler and Roosevelt to power in their countries. There is a tendency to see *All Quiet* as quintessentially an antiwar film, and to account for its popularity as the expression of a single, dominant popular sentiment against war. But that is to exaggerate a single aspect of the film to explain its popularity. It derives from a tendency to interpret the movie's significance retrospectively in light of its later contribution to and the growing importance of isolationism in the 1930s. In this decade isolationism became a hardened article of faith coupled with antiwar propaganda for many, and an ideological weapon wielded by politicians against one another.

The movie version did develop the political implications of the novel to make more explicit a political message. But the motivation was less one of political persuasion than commercial calculation—the belief that Sherwood Anderson might do a better, more "serious" screenplay, and the hope that in stressing a political message a more prestigious reputation would accrue to the movie. It was only after the movie had proved a hit that Universal was willing to emphasize its political side and play on the controversy to promote the movie as a major event.

ROOTS OF ISOLATIONISM

Americans tend to reject Karl von Clausewitz's famous maxim about war being an extension of politics, preferring instead to imagine war as an aberration, the opposite rather than the extension of political life. They believe this despite their reliance on war for their own liberty (Revolutionary War), expansion of their polity (Mexican-American and Spanish-American Wars), preservation of their union (Civil War), and their participation in the great (the two World Wars) and small (Philippine and Vietnam wars) wars of this century.

The persistence of this belief despite evidence to the contrary owes much to American ideas about and attitudes toward political life. Because America was founded as a set of colonies, Americans developed a view of themselves as participating in a "New World" in contrast to the "Old." There was a sense of hope and, for many, a sense of religious mission to be found as a "shining city upon a hill."[15] The American Revolution reinforced this sense of uniqueness and special destiny, identifying the latter with the establishment of democracy. In this respect, the most influential political philosopher in the development of American political thought was John Locke, through his *Two Treatises on Civil Government* (1690).

Americans are the heirs of Locke in their fundamental assumption of a benign state of nature that underlies civil society. Governments are metaphorically "contracted" among people to create sovereigns who govern by the consent of the governed. The state of nature is inconvenient, therefore as individuals exercising reason and self-interest, people create societies. Locke's metaphor of the social contract has the decided advantages of justifying a widening democratic participation, and providing an ultimate recourse to revolution conceived of as a right to cancel a sovereign's contract to rule for abuse of authority or nonperformance.

The social contract metaphor inclines Americans to view nondemocratic states as corrupt, deficient or not fully legitimate societies. In alignment with this sense of uniqueness and destiny, it predisposes Americans to moralize about politics, leading to a deeply ambivalent attitude toward political life in general and foreign affairs in particular. There is the suspicion that involvement in politics may only frustrate or corrupt, and a tendency for Americans to see their country as a moral agency imperiled by acting in the international arena. The effect is to pose alternative strategic visions of what the United States might do to operate in that arena. On the one hand, America might be seen as having the right and duty to impose its will on others out of a need for defense or an enlightened desire to improve others; this is the interventionist role of the crusader. On the other hand, Americans might be seen as leading by example, to avoid the risk of corruption and frustration by not intervening, but to serve instead as a moral example with minimal political contact with others—the isolationist role of the monk.

It is difficult to imagine a state that does not want to imagine itself as a moral agency of high ideals. However, in the case of America, its conception of itself as possessed of a unique moral destiny was reinforced by the ideological conception of Lockean democracy and by the fortunes of geography—the possession of enormous continental resources, weak neighbors and wide oceans, which permitted it the luxury of dealing with the great powers at a distance. American foreign policy over the last 200 years reveals a pattern of alternating roles. For instance, in the twentieth century, phases of interventionism dominated foreign policy from the 1890s through the 1910s, and from the 1940s through the 1960s. Isolationism dominated the 1920s and 1930s, and it has been increasingly characteristic of post-Vietnam foreign policy.

The social contract metaphor operates in another way to shape American perception of politics and foreign relations. There is an assumption that a "natural" condition of harmony underlies domestic and international order. The American view of the international arena follows

Locke's view of the state of nature in stark contrast to Hobbes's famous depiction of the state of nature as the "war of every man against every other" (*Leviathan*, 1651). War is imagined as a distinctly civic condition, however corrupt, something not "natural" but artificially constructed by human agency. Americans start their understanding of foreign relations by assuming war is not the primary or desired condition of natural society, or a legitimate civil association, but rather an alternative to it, an "unnatural" occurrence. In contrasting American attitudes regarding the permanency of foreign relations "entanglements," Michael Wood notes that

Europeans are born entangled, and harbor only the most diffident and complicated dreams of escape from others. Americans, on the other hand are the children of Rousseau [and Locke for that matter since they shared a benign view of the state of nature in contrast with Hobbes] to a greater extent than we shall ever chart, and they start from isolation as a primary or desired condition. This doesn't make Americans isolationists [only], since most are ready to trade in their isolation when the time seems right for them. But it does tinge all their relations with others—other nations, other people—with a shade of reluctance.[16]

For the politically radical, democratic new United States, a foreign policy of isolationism was recommended by force of circumstances. In his farewell speech (1796), Washington warned his countrymen to stay clear of permanent alliances, and in terms of the European great powers, this view held sway until the aftermath of World War II with the signing of the Rio Pact (1947) and the birth of NATO (1949). For the most part protected from the great European powers by an Atlantic moat, and surrounded by weaker neighbors, the United States could afford to practice isolation or intervention at its own will. Wood adds that understanding this posture of moral and physical superiority "is at the heart of an American puzzle about our relations with others, for both generosity and selfishness are unilateralist, isolationist attitudes, depending only on our will and our condescension, on our acceptance or refusal of community. We are benign or indifferent gods, ready to do business with humanity only on our terms."[17]

WAR AND ISOLATIONISM

Both the novel and the movie version of *All Quiet* appeared amid a cycle of isolationism allied to a conservative thrust in politics, itself in opposition to a prior cycle of Progressive reformism. Disgust with the Versailles negotiations and resentment over foreign war debts were catalysts in forming the mood toward conservatism in domestic affairs and isolationism in foreign affairs. Through the 1930s, the Depression deepened, then slowly moderated. But while the domestic policy and political mood shifted toward the liberalism of the New Deal, the isolationist impulse only grew. Restoration of hope fueled the domestic shift in domestic affairs, while growing fear reinforced the isolationist impulse as Europe and the Pacific moved toward conflict. To the initial reputation of *All Quiet* as an antiwar statement about a past war was gradually added its reputation as an isolationist film, for it dramatically illustrated the horror and insanity of war and seemed to underline the futility and likely consequences of foreign entanglements. In 1939 a version was recut and distributed to build isolationist sentiment against American involvement in Europe.

The antiwar message implicit in the novel was made explicit in the movie by Sherwood's added dialogue, by graphically showing the consequences and experience of war, and by subtly transferring the focus of the denouement from the death of Kat to Paul's death. In the novel, Kat's death is emphasized; the last possible link to human community is symbolically sundered, underscoring the significance of the novel as explaining the spiritual death of a generation in the trenches of the Western front. In the movie, Paul's death is emphasized, underscoring the waste and inhumanity of war.

The overwhelming success of the movie unexpectedly served to form public opinion and mood against war, thereby illustrating a possible consequence of foreign involvement. But its appeal was not solely in terms of its antiwar message. Political meanings aside, the movie appealed emotionally, visually and aesthetically to tremendous numbers of people who were undoubtedly not politically attuned or mindful of the intellectual and political implications of the movie. Still, in providing such a graphic interpretation of war, the movie helped form public perception of the meaning of war.

The movie *All Quiet* was not intended to promote isolationism, but calculated to take advantage of sentiments favoring isolationism. It was intended primarily to be a "realistic" portrait of war and to be faithful to the novel not as a political statement, but as part of a market strategy to create a "prestige" film and make money for Universal Studios. The movie version reshaped the novel toward being a political commentary not only on World War I, but on all war, and thereby very clearly carried an antiwar message. A detailed analysis of how this was accomplished and of the possible explanations for the immense popularity of the movie reveals that Universal began to stress the political message only after the movie had been released. Moreover, a variety of factors explains how it was received and why it has remained a popular classic of moviemaking, perhaps even in spite of its political message.

RECEPTION OF THE MOVIE

The movie premiered to standing-room-only audiences and quickly established attendance records across the country and internationally, at least where it was not banned. It won the Photoplay Award for Best Picture, and Oscars for Best Picture and Best Director for 1930. In addition, it won Oscar nominations for Best Writing Achievement and Best Cinematography. At the Oscar ceremonies there was talk of the possibility of the author winning the Nobel Prize for literature. The Laemmles' gamble seemed to have paid off handsomely.

In national and foreign distribution it encountered censorship problems, only some of which stemmed from its overtly antiwar message. Criticism was most often directed at the attacks on patriotism, revered institutions such as the military, churches, and hospitals, and (most frequently) at the depiction of filth, gore, low language and rough behavior of the soldiers. The film was frequently cut to fit local censorship requirements.[18]

Abroad it was banned or highly censored in most countries. In Germany, its premiere corresponded with the rise of the National Socialists. Hitler's Propaganda Minister Joseph Goebbels personally directed a mass protest at its first showings to stop further release. A national board of censors reviewed it subsequently, and with restrictions and censored cuts, allowed it to be shown for two years until it was banned in 1932. With Hitler's ascension to power in January 1933, movie and novel were officially anathema, and the book was publicly burned. Remarque went into exile, first to France and then Hollywood and New York, and eventually back to Europe. He was internationally recognized as a novelist as well as a Hollywood screenwriter, and carried on a lengthy, well-publicized affair with Marlene Dietrich before marrying Paulette Goddard.

All Quiet was re-released and re-edited repeatedly, and a profusion of versions flooded the marketplace. Soon after its release, having won many rewards and having been the subject of great controversy, Universal substituted for the original preface from the novel introducing the film, a list of its awards and critical praise it had garnered in an obvious attempt to capitalize on its fame and the controversy surrounding it. The original versions in fact were lost, probably cut and recut so many times that there exists no definitive print of what appeared on screens at its April 1930 premiere. A highly truncated version, blatantly designed to promote isolationism and antiwar sentiment, was released briefly in 1939. In 1979, it was remade for television, directed by Delbert Mann on location in Germany, with Ernest Borgnine as Kat and Richard Thomas as Paul. Although it followed the book with greater fidelity, it was generally deemed inferior to the 1930 version. In 1983, after four years of work, a German television editor put together a restored 139-minute version close to the original sound release. As Modris Eksteins notes, "While eleven minutes short of the 150 minutes Milestone claimed he made, this may be the closest we will get to the original creation."[19]

CONTROVERSY AND CONTEXT

The movie opened to controversy, and was designed to court it and capitalize on it commercially. The Laemmles had chosen Sherwood Anderson, a famous and committed antiwar writer (the author of the popular pacifist play, later movie, *What Price Glory?*) to develop the screenplay. They initially promoted it primarily as a realistic depiction of war and a faithful rendition of the novel, although they clearly intended it to be taken also as a serious statement of antiwar art comparable to the novel and meriting the favorable reception the novel had received in intellectual circles as serious literature. What they might not have expected was the magnitude and extent of the reception to the specifically antiwar message of the film. The movie trade journal *Variety* noted: "Here exhibited is war as it is, butchery. The League of Nations could make no better investment than to buy up the master print, reproduce it in every language to be shown to every nation every year until the word war is taken out of the dictionaries."[20]

In retrospect, the antiwar motif of the movie stands out as not only reflecting popular sentiment, but in helping to form it. Millions saw the movie and critics often pointed out its highly effective political message and the audiences' response. Lew Ayres credits his involvement in the movie with turning him into a passionate, lifelong antiwar activist. Like many others, he attributed the crystallizing of antiwar sentiment for his generation (he was twenty-one when filming started in 1930 for *All Quiet*) to this film. A 1939 version of the movie was cut to propagandize the case for remaining out of World War II, and widely shown across the nation.

While it's quite accurate to characterize *All Quiet* as an antiwar film, such a characterization is incomplete and misleading in several respects. There is no way to prove that it was the antiwar message alone, or even centrally, that attracted the vast numbers in America and around the world who viewed the film. War movies were a "hot" item in the late 1920s and early 1930s. If the antiwar theme alone was primarily responsible for the popularity of *All Quiet*, it would be difficult to explain the popularity of so many war movies that did not carry this explicit message, such as *The Big Parade* (1925), the highest grossing silent. *Wings* (1927) and *Dawn Patrol* (1930) were also immensely popular.

All Quiet came in the midst of a cycle of war films,[21] and to some extent its success as an antiwar film might be attributed to the novelty of cutting against the cycle—its novelty and shock effect within the popular war genre, rather than its specific political message, may explain its popularity. In this regard, bear in mind the pre-release publicity and the opening months of release underscored a claim to being a "realistic" portrait of war and the faithful rendering of a popular novel, and avoided mention of any antiwar message. Although it may have been fashionable to be disillusioned with war, undoubtedly the vast number of Americans who had supported and served in a recent victory would not be attracted to a story whose thesis was that their victory was senseless and they were wrong to have participated. The American reception might have been very different if Paul and his comrades had been depicted as members of the victorious American Expeditionary Force rather than the defeated Wehrmacht. Paul's speech proclaiming that when it comes to dying for your country, "it is better not to die at all" was decidedly more palatable coming from a German than from an American character.

An additional reason for its popularity relates not to the message at all, but rather to the effect the movie had as spectacle and its aesthetic attraction. Given the anticipation generated by spending so much to film such a popular and influential novel, and the controversy surrounding both novel and movie, the exhibition of the movie was in itself a spectacle, a "happening" that promoted itself as a historic event. Moreover, the movie's technical effects were spectacular and the skillful use of lighting, camera technique and sound were outstanding. (*All Quiet* received an Oscar nomination for Best Cinematography.) Sixty-five years after its premiere, the movie still moves and thrills audiences. *All Quiet* remains internationally acclaimed as a classic not only in respect of its cultural and political significance in its own time, but even more for its lasting aesthetic qualities.

NOTES

1. The number would grow to twenty-three states. This development at the state level was matched by local efforts in schools and universities throughout the world from the late 1920s through the 1930s to renounce warfare.

2. For Remarque's biography, and literary and cultural analyses of his life and work, see C. R. Baker and R. W. Last, *Erich Maria Remarque* (Lanham, MD: Barnes & Noble Books-Imports, 1979); A. F. Bance, "*Im Westen nichts Neues*: A Bestseller in Cultural Context," *Modern Language Review* 72 (April 1977), 359–73; Arnold Berson, "Erich Maria Remarque," *Films in Review* 45 (September/October 1994), 28–35; Richard Arthur Firda, *All Quiet on the Western Front: Literary Analysis and Cultural Context* (New York: Twayne, 1993); R. Schumacher, "Remarque's Abyss of Time: *Im Westen nichts Neues*," in *Focus on Robert Graves and his Contemporaries*, edited by J. W. Presley, 1 (Winter 1990–1991), 24–36; B. A. Rowley, "Jour-

nalism Into Fiction: *Im Westen nichts Neues,"* in *The First World War in Fiction,* edited by Holger Michael Klein (London: Macmillan, 1976); Harley U. Taylor Jr., *Erich Maria Remarque: A Literary and Film Biography* (New York: Peter Lang, 1989); and M. P. A. Travers, *German Novels on the First World War and Their Ideological Implications, 1918–1933* (Stuttgart: H-D Heinz, 1982).

3. Erich Maria Remarque, *All Quiet on the Western Front,* translated by A. W. Wheen (Boston: Little, Brown, 1929).

4. On Laemmle and Universal Studios, see John Drinkwater, *The Life and Adventures of Carl Laemmle* (New York: William Heinemann, 1931); I. G. Edmonds, *Big U: Universal in the Silent Days* (New York: A. S. Barnes, 1977); and Clive Hirschorn, *The Universal Story* (New York: Crown, 1983).

5. On the making of the film, see John Whiteclay Chalmers II, *"All Quiet on the Western Front* (1930): The Antiwar Film and the Image of the First World War,"* Historical Journal of Film, Radio and Television* 14 (1994), 4; Ivan Butler, *The War Film* (South Brunswick and New York: A. S. Barnes, 1974); Modris Eksteins, *Rites of Spring: The Great War and the Birth of the Modern Age* (New York: Doubleday, 1990); Modris Eksteins, *"All Quiet on the Western Front* and the Fate of a War,"* Journal of Contemporary History* 15:20 (2) (April 1980), 345–66; Modris Eksteins, "War, Memory and Politics: The Fate of the Film *All Quiet on the Western Front,"* Central European History* 13 (March 1980), 60–82; Modris Eksteins, "All Quiet on the Western Front," *History Today* 45 (November 1995), 29–35; Michael Isenberg, *Interpreting Film: Studies in the Historical Reception of American Cinema* 99:2 (April 1993), 296; Michael T. Isenberg, *War on Film: The American Cinema and World War I, 1914–1941* (Rutherford, NJ: Fairleigh Dickinson University Press, 1981); Michael T. Isenberg, "An Ambiguous Pacifism: A Retrospective on World War Films, 1930–1938," *Journal of Popular Films and Television* 4:2 (1975), 98–115; Michael T. Isenberg, "The Great War Viewed from the Twenties: *The Big Parade* (1925)" in *American History/American Film: Interpreting the Hollywood Image,* edited by John E. O'Connor and Martin A. Jackson (New York: Frederick Ungar, 1979) 17–38; G. T. Mitchell, "Making *All Quiet on the Western Front," American Cinematographer* 66 (September 1985), 34–43; P. A. Soderbergh, "Aux Armes! The Rise of the Hollywood War Film, 1916–1930," *South Atlantic Quarterly,* 65:4 (1964), 509–22; and J. M. Winter, *The Experience of World War I* (New York: Oxford University Press, 1991).

6. The only recognized members of the cast were Zasu Pitts, who played Paul's mother (and whose scenes were later deleted), Wolheim for his prior theater work, and Paul Griffith, who played a French soldier Paul stabs and then must spend the night with as he dies. Due to a throat condition, Griffith's career more or less ended with the advent of sound and he played (reputedly gratis) the *poilu* dying in silence. Lew Ayres was suggested by George Cukor, who had seen him in Ayres's only prior movie work as a young lover of Greta Garbo in *The Kiss* (1928).

7. On its cutting and the issue of domestic and international censorship, see Eksteins, "War, Memory and Politics," 60–82; Eksteins, "All Quiet on the Western Front," 29–35; and Jerrold Simmons, "Film and International Politics: Banning of *All Quiet on the Western Front* in Germany and Austria, 1930–31," *The Historian: A Journal of History* 52:1 (November 1989), 40–46.

8. Eksteins, "All Quiet," 35.

9. Hans Fallada, *Little Man, What Now?*, translated by Eric Sutton (New York: Frederick Ungar, 1933).

10. Thomas Hobbes, *Leviathan* (1651).

11. J. Glenn Gray, *The Warriors: Reflections on Men in Battle* (New York: Harper & Row, 1970), 56.

12. On the making of the film, see Butler, *The War Film* Chalmers, "*All Quiet on the Western Front* (1930): The Antiwar Film," 4; Eksteins, "War, Memory and Politics," 60–82; Eksteins, "*All Quiet on the Western Front* and the Fate of a War," 345–66; Eksteins, *Rites of Spring*; Isenberg, "Ambiguous Pacifism," 98–115; Isenberg, "The Great War"; Isenberg, *War on Film*; Isenberg, "Interpreting Film," 296; Mitchell, "Making *All Quiet on the Western Front*"; Soderberg, "Aux Armes! The Rise of the Hollywood War Film, 1916–1930," 509–22; D. J. Wenden, "Images of War 1930 and 1988: *All Quiet on the Western Front* and *Journey's End*: Preliminary Notes for a Comparative Study," *Film Historia* 3:1–2 (1993), 33–37; and Winter (1991).

13. For the imperatives of plot linearity in the "Hollywood style" of movie-making, see David Bordwell and Kristin Thompson, *Film Art: An Introduction* (Reading, MA.: Addison-Wesley, 1970).

14. Peter Guttmacher, *Legendary War Movies* (New York: Metrobooks, 1996), 109.

15. Gov. John Winthrop of the Massachusetts Bay Colony, 1621.

16. Michael Wood, *American in the Movies: Or, "Santa Maria," It had Slipped My Mind* (New York: Basic Books, 1975), 39.

17. Ibid., 30.

18. On its cutting and the issue of domestic and international censorship, see Eksteins, "War, Memory and Politics: The Fate of the Film *All Quiet on the Western Front*," 60–82; Eksteins, "All Quiet on the Western Front," 29–35; and Simmons "Film and International Politics," 40–46.

19. Eksteins, "All Quiet on the Western Front," 35.

20. *Variety* (May 7, 1930), as quoted in Andrew Kelly, "*All Quiet on the Western Front*: Brutal Cutting, Stupid Censors and Bigoted Politicos, 1930–1984," *Historical Journal of Film, Radio, and Television* 9:2 (1989), 135–50.

21. For the cycle and analysis of the *genre*, see Chalmers "All Quiet on the Western Front (1930)," 4; Eksteins "War, Memory and Politics: The Fate of the Film *All Quiet on the Western Front*," 60–82; Paul Fussell, *The Great War and Modern Memory* (New York: Oxford University Press, 1975); Guttmacher, *Legendary War Movies*; Robert Hughes, *Film: Book 2, Films of War and Peace* (New York, 1962); Isenberg, "The Great War"; Soderbergh "Aux Armes," 509–22; Joe Edwin Vines, *Wings vs. All Quiet on the Western Front: Two Views of War on Film*, unpublished master's thesis, University of Georgia, 1981; and Winter *Experience of WWI*.

Ditch-digging scene in *Our Daily Bread*. Courtesy of the Academy of Motion Picture Arts and Sciences.

Chapter Eight

Communism in *Our Daily Bread*

Beverly Merrill Kelley

Our Daily Bread was intended as the second installment in a proposed film trilogy documenting the depths of the Depression. Beaten down by unemployment, Mary (Karen Morley) and John Sims (Tom Keene) are offered a dilapidated farmhouse on a worn-out piece of land by Mary's uncle. They consider the offer an answer to prayer despite the fact that John knows little about agriculture. A deluge of dropouts looking for work, the makings of a society in microcosm, floods the Sims homestead. The residents of the loosely organized collective sweat from dawn to dusk to eke out three squares a day. John Sims grows restless and increasingly depressed in his leadership role. A slattern named Sally (Barbara Pepper) seduces John into deserting Mary and the rest of the farm workers. The wheat, which the commune hopes to harvest, withers during an endless drought. As John and Sally make their escape, John is halted by a vision that leads to the gurgling of a hidden stream. He hustles back to the farm with a plan to divert the waterway into irrigating the thirsty crops. Men form a human chain as they dig furiously, shoring up the aqueduct's banks with their own bodies when the water bolts downhill. The jubilant homesteaders cartwheel through the mud as the harvest is saved.

Veteran writer, producer and director King Vidor would never find himself on anyone's auteur agenda. If one of the *Cahiers du Cinema* crowd, who seem to cherish directoral consistency above all, stumbled across Vidor's work, he'd be dumbstruck. Unlike the directors examined in previous chapters, who were easily linked to a specific ideology, Vidor spent his life championing political diversity. Liberals swarmed to the socially conscious Vidor while conservatives just as enthusiastically claimed him as a fellow *Saturday Evening Post* populist.

Vidor was able to wrap his mind around cerebral complexity to such a degree that within a fifteen-year span, during which a modicum of microchange might well be expected, he was able to embrace the communal solution explored in *Our Daily Bread* (1934) with the same ferocity as Ayn Rand's slap in the face to collectivism in *The Fountainhead* (1949), a film explored in Chapter 9. Even Vidor biographers Raymond Durgnat and Scott Simmon, who have scrutinized Vidor's life nuance by nuance, found the democratic humanism of *Our Daily Bread* juxtaposed against the Objectivist polemic exhibited in Vidor's *noir*-era adaptation of Ayn Rand more than a little jarring.[1] Communism provides a political lens through which one might survey these two films, although at times, one might find the images a bit blurred.

The difficulty in surveying these two movies in terms of ideological opposition rests with the alien nature of communism not only to the American mentality, but also to the American experience. With the exception of *Mission to Moscow*, a film made to celebrate America's alliance with Russia, there simply were no American films embracing the communist ideology. In fact, the 1947 House Committee on Un-American Activities (HUAC) and its successors failed to establish that the party line had ever been interjected into a Hollywood vehicle. Communism, especially sung to Lenin's tune of violent revolution and the creation of an elite advance guard, remained a tough sell in the United States. Even the scientific socialism proposed by Marx was unpalatable to this country. Vidor drew on strains of American rural populist principles in fantasizing his version of a socialist utopia, which seemed to resonate with Depression-era moviegoers. That a single director's cinematic output during the 1930s and 1940s was able to encompass the contradictory creeds in which the American public seemed awash still surprises film critics.

KING VIDOR

King Vidor's expressed dream, making films about wheat, steel and war, augmented his ability to traverse genres. Influenced by both D. W. Griffith's realism (also reminiscent of documentarian Robert Flaherty) as well as Sergei Eisenstein's technique in employing montage juxtaposition, Vidor comes closer than any other director to reconciling these cinematic opposites. Hollywood considered him its resident intellectual, yet Vidor was equally well known for his sensuous, often erotic explorations into the moral failings of his protagonists. Exploring conflicting forces fascinated Vidor, who often featured an individual noisily challenging the mores of duty and responsibility while evading the more difficult challenge of remaining honest and true to oneself.

Vidor made more than one pilgrimage to the psychoanalyst's couch, seeking the answer to the question, "Are we entitled to all we can get out of life?" He usually opted for the gusto, with three marriages,[2] a body of fifty-six movies spanning both silent and sound cinema, a mid-life switch to academia where he shared his expertise on film with the nation's youth, five Academy Award nominations for direction (*The Crowd* in 1927, *Hallelujah* in 1929, *The Champ* in 1931, *The Citadel* in 1938 and *War and Peace* in 1956) and an honorary Oscar bestowed "for his incomparable achievements as a cinematic creator and innovator" in 1978.

King Wallace Vidor was born on February 8, 1894, in Galveston, Texas, named for his mother's favorite brother. He died of heart failure on November 1, 1982, in Paso Robles, California. He became infatuated with film as a schoolboy, taking tickets and substituting as a projectionist in Galveston's first nickelodeon in 1909. Vidor shot local events for national newsreel companies before starting the Hotex Motion Picture Company in Houston in 1914. To finance his move to Hollywood, he attempted to persuade Ford Motors into forking over funds for his footage of the trip west, shot from the window of his Model T. After a variety of production jobs, he settled down at Universal as a writer (pseudonym Charles K. Wallis) on a short detailing the reform work of a Boys Town-type judge (William Brown) from Salt Lake City. Backed by nine Christian Science doctors, Vidor produced a series of ten inspirational two-reelers in 1918, followed by an extremely successful feature, *The Turn in the Road*, the following year.

Modeled after the studio started by Charlie Chaplin, Mack Sennett and D. W. Griffith, "Vidor Village" produced eight pictures before folding in 1927. Meanwhile, Vidor went to work for Metro and Goldwyn studios. The 1924 merger vaulted him to senior director status and presented him with the opportunity to direct the most profitable silent, *The Big Parade* (1925), a critical and popular success that made John Gilbert a star, catapulted MGM to a top-ranked studio and conferred unrestricted creative control on Vidor.

Vidor used *The Big Parade* to explore one of his favorite characters, Everyman, the promising precursor to John in *Our Daily Bread*. Vidor's record as a bankable director allowed him to make another unusual city parable with a similar theme, *The Crowd* (1928), the predecessor of *Our Daily Bread*. Although a financial failure, the film corroborated Vidor's now global reputation as an uncompromising advocate for social issues. Influenced by Fritz Lang's *Metropolis*, Vidor presented us with a prophetic pre-Depression protagonist who detests his job, chafes at marital

routine, wrestles with mediocrity and fails because of his own feckless-
ness despite the prosperity all about him.

Two critical milestones, *Hallelujah* (1929), a breakthrough musical with
an African-American cast, and *Street Scene* (1930), an adaptation of Elmer
Rice's socially conscious drama, preceded Vidor's story of a Depression-
motivated agricultural commune, *Our Daily Bread*. Vidor is clearly in-
debted to Soviet montage filmmakers such as Sergei Eisenstein and Victor Turin[3] for the film's structure and, at least according to William
Randolph Hearst, beholden to Soviet political ideology for its substance.
Colin Shindler in *Hollywood in Crisis* contends, in addition to Hearst,
"The Hollywood studios, however, saw the script in its simplest terms
as pure Communist propaganda, which is why Vidor experienced such
difficulty in acquiring financial backing for the film."[4]

THE PRODUCTION OF *OUR DAILY BREAD*

As a director who favored fables about the farming community, Vidor
felt so compelled to translate this story to the screen that he left the
cocoon-like security of the studio system to gamble his own cash in a
fight against formula with Vidor-owned and operated Viking Productions. His consciousness had been raised by reading about various Hoov-
ervilles dotting the landscape as well as consequent hunger marches,
overturned milk trucks and tillers of the soil banding together to block
the sale of farms in foreclosure. Newspaper headlines prompted him to
wonder "how I could corral this nationwide unrest and tragedy into a
film. I wanted to take my two protagonists out of *The Crowd* and follow
them through the struggles of a typical young American couple in this
most difficult period."[5]

He serendipitously discovered a *Reader's Digest* article written by a
college professor teaching economics during the worst of all possible
times. Malcolm McDermott claimed that turning to cooperatives and limiting the use of money might provide an alternative to unemployment
unrest. Vidor especially remembers the article's mention of "barter theaters" in the South, which allowed the exchange of turnips for tickets.
Although the article was only a few pages long, Vidor bought the rights
because the piece was "a good examination of the economics of the
time."[6] Most likely it was a June 1932 item, "An Agricultural Army,"
which describes the fortunes of a city couple attempting an *Our Daily
Bread* experiment, that provided the film's genesis.[7]

Vidor spent four months scripting *Our Daily Bread* with the assistance
of his wife, Elizabeth Hill, who often served as his co-writer. While Joseph Mankiewicz received writing credit for the picture, Vidor minimized Mankiewicz's contribution, leaving open the questions of who

really wrote *Our Daily Bread* and why Vidor allowed Mankiewicz's name to remain in the credits. Vidor attributed the need for another writer to

> a hangover from theater. It was called dialogue writing, not script writing. If someone read the script, and they could not think of anything else to say, they would comment that the dialogue might be improved. That's what Mankiewicz did. It became a regular cliché to tell someone that the dialogue could be improved. . . . [W]e weren't enthused about everything he wrote. We might have kept a few lines.[8]

The first individual to whom Vidor took the script was Irving Thalberg, who considered Vidor's *The Big Parade* one of his favorites. Thalberg gave Vidor positive feedback but refused to approve the film for MGM, which was committed, at that time, to the glamour cycle of Depression films. Furthermore, Thalberg classified the project as too obscure to appeal to a mass audience. Vidor then turned to Charlie Chaplin, who, responding to the highly sentimental and perhaps leftist theme, agreed to release the feature through United Artists.

Vidor's remaining challenge was coming up with the currency to finance the production. Unwilling to cut the eye-popping foreclosure scene, which was predictably controversial with the bankers whose support he sought, Vidor was forced to pledge his assets as collateral in a dubious deal with a motion picture loan shark. According to Vidor, the film ran roughly $125,000 to produce (Hollywood budgets in 1934 averaged between $300,000 and $500,000) despite money-saving schemes such as shooting the last week (the ditch-digging montage) without sound. While Vidor claims to have made back enough money to cover the loan, his memory appears somewhat selective in that regard.[9]

Vidor originally invited James Murray (*The Crowd*) to play the lead, but Murray rejected Vidor's stipulation that he lay off the booze so Vidor substituted a lookalike, Tom Keene, to play John Sims. Keene affected a high energy demeanor, punctuated his dialogue with expletives such as "There's a humdinger!" to indicate the character's quick enthusiasm and affected a lunkish stroll to demonstrate his equally speedy discouragement. Karen Morley, who played Pendy in *Gabriel over the White House*, portrayed Mary Sims. She was the only marquee name in the lot and the only member of the cast later blacklisted as a communist. Vidor chose John T. Qualen, a regular in Vidor films, to play Chris, whose Swedish accent appears not only unintentionally comical, but politically incorrect by today's standards. Barbara Pepper, who played the blonde Theda Bara character, was forced on Vidor by a financial backer.

Budgetary considerations limited salaries of cast members to subsistence wages. The going rate for character actors was actually three to four times higher than Vidor could afford, so he turned to recruits from the unemployment lines in Los Angeles for casting purposes. Interiors were shot at the Goldwyn Studios on Santa Monica Boulevard and the exteriors at a heavily shrubbed Tarzana golf course that had gone bankrupt. There was a small house on the property but no source of water. With the entire cast living full time in trailers on the set, it was hardly surprising that they came under the picture's spell. The tight living quarters forced the actors to become closely connected with each other and seemed to spur them into a genuine enthusiasm for the film, a necessity in light of the herculean effort required for the last act.

In the final sequence of *Our Daily Bread*, a dramatic struggle of man against nature, the amateur farmers feverishly dig a long downhill channel to order to divert water to the parched corn. This melodramatic climax warranted mention in every review of the film. Vidor recalls in his autobiography, "I decided to treat the work of building this ditch in a manner I imagined a choreographer would use in plotting out the movements of a ballet."[10] The effort took ten days to stage and film.

Vidor strove to personally involve the audience in the finale, intending to leave them physically exhausted and emotionally depleted via a physical and musical catharsis. He controlled the mounting excitement by manipulating the tempo of sound and action. Vidor was an amateur musician, specializing in the banjo and guitar. While admittedly influenced by the Russian documentary *Turksib*, which used only a bass fiddle and a flute for the music, Vidor reached back into his memory of silent music from *Three Wise Fools* (1923) and the death march in *The Big Parade* in choosing to couple a metronome and a bass drum playing in four-four rhythm. By undercranking (decreasing the camera speed, which in turn increases the apparent tempo of the action) he was able to accelerate the contrapuntal action of the picks and shovels decades before George Lucas perfected his warp-speed editing techniques. Vidor reflects in his autobiography: "Digging a long ditch in straight, pictorial action without the use of rhythmic design to integrate it could have been boring, and it would have been impractical to use more than a few cuts in the finished picture. Unified into a musical pattern, however, the episode held an emotional interest for the full eight hundred feet of its length."[11]

COMMUNISM AS POLITICAL IDEOLOGY

Communism in the broadest sense becomes an umbrella term for economic and/or political systems ranging from the communist industrial and urban ideal to the socialist utopian community proposed by Vidor in *Our Daily Bread*. A definition unifying various points along the socialist-communist continuum must, by necessity, focus on the use of community-owned property, if not necessarily the common ownership of it, for the production of goods or services.

Equality through communism, a hardly novel yet highly seductive dogma, can be discovered in Plato's *Republic* as well as Sir Thomas More's *Utopia*. The early Christians, the Anabaptists of the Middle Ages as well as early experimental communities enduring less than a few decades such as New Harmony, Indiana (organized by "the father of English socialism" Robert Owen, 1771–1856), or Brook Farm, Massachusetts (based on the principles of French social reformer Francois Marie Charles Fourier, 1772–1837), are examples of communist utopias. American utopian populations proved riveting to Karl Marx, who worked as a foreign correspondent for the *New York Daily Tribune*. He failed to note that communes don't last, faltering because the seeds of self-destruction are sown along with its egalitarian ideals.

Marx co-opted the term "communist"[12] to differentiate his doctrine of scientific socialism from that of the cooperative principles of the utopian socialists. The enticement of both, however, rests on the philosophical promise of human freedom fully realized in the absence of both the constraints and wants inherent in a consumer society. Once scarcity has been abolished, the constraints to human wants remain merely artificial, imposed by the wealthy. "From each according to his abilities to each according to his needs" evolved from Karl Marx's *Critique of the Gotha Program* (1875) and was later adopted by the communist movement as a slogan.[13] In practice, however, the effect is to discourage ability while encouraging need. Over time, totalitarian practices result in the underdevelopment of technology as well as decreased worker productivity, an effective recipe for economic disaster.

It was Lenin who stressed the necessity of violent revolution guided by a highly trained and disciplined "vanguard" party[14] in order to overthrow capitalism and allow the state to control the means of production. Marx's contribution included both a systematic theory depicting society as moving inevitably toward communism and a political ideology crying out for revolution. The overlay of a seemingly scientific veneer rendered Marx's romantic and moral vision all the more beguiling.

On the whole, however, *The Communist Manifesto* (1848) views history as a series of class struggles, with social and political life controlled by the economic elite (bourgeoisie or capitalists), who dominate the workers (proletariat) by using the government (the state) and religion to suppress revolt against subsistence living conditions. To crush all opposition during the period before a classless "brotherhood of workers" living in peace and prosperity is achieved, Lenin added that a temporary proletarian communist-led dictatorship would be essential to organizing and completing the revolution. The success of the Marxist-Leninist ideologies was evidenced by communist dominion of more than one-third of the world's population by the latter half of the twentieth century.

On November 7, 1917, the Bolsheviks under Lenin seized power from the Social Democrats who had previously toppled the czar, promising peace and bread for Russia, land for the peasants, and power to the Soviets, subsequently kicking off the communist era. Most Americans were initially rocked by the loss of their Russian military ally. Lenin's Decree on Peace provoked President Woodrow Wilson to continue America's cooperation in a war effort that had amounted to a mere six-month investment at that point. Wilson's response, the "Fourteen Points" speech of January 8, 1918, cemented his doctrine of liberal internationalism, which would underpin foreign policy goals pursued during the rest of this century.

To those who rejected Wilson's internationalist League of Nations, Trotsky and Lenin provided a revolutionary alternative with the Comintern, whose mission statement insisted that the first duty of communists and fellow travelers was to empower the Soviet Union and extend communism. On August 20, 1918, Lenin wrote the first of his letters to American labor, calling for a working-class revolt. As if in response, a series of strikes ensued that winter in the United States.

Over the next decade or so, the Bolshevik victors were wildly embraced by liberal American intellectuals and radicals. Middle-class reformers, pacifists, socialists, anarchists and violent revolutionaries united against anti-union industrialists who, according to the working class, were in league with government and the courts. Ministers, rabbis and priests sharing a commitment to social justice were lured by the communist ideology as well.

Yet by the 1930s, the Soviets no longer enjoyed the initial idealistic ardor that successfully romanced many of the early supporters. The vicissitudes of communist fortune commenced with the popular front, Stalin's foreign-policy directive based on a broad collaboration between left-wing and bourgeois parties, which condemned fascism. Stalin figured he could bring together a support base by condemning the socialists and other liberals as the prime enemy. Popular-front governments garnered strength in France and Spain from 1936 to 1938. Communists abroad, particularly those laboring in the Hollywood vineyards, enthusiastically embraced the antifascist struggle as well.

By 1938, with the West rerouting the Nazi offensive and the surrender of Czechoslovakia opening the door to the eastern front, Stalin sent his foreign ministers into a clandestine huddle. They produced a major policy reversal: the Nazi-Soviet Nonaggression Pact. In return for half of Poland, implements of war, economic aid and free rein to gobble up eastern Poland and Finland, Hitler got the go-ahead to invade the East and take western Poland. Overnight, communists worldwide were asked to shift gears, redirecting their antipathy from the fascists toward socialists and democracies.

With Hitler's betrayal of Stalin in the summer of 1941 and the subsequent invasion of the Soviet Union, another Soviet foreign-policy reversal ensued. The Nazis once again were portrayed as the enemy, allowing the Soviets to forge alliances with the democracies and everyone else. Pearl Harbor helped hasten this turnaround by dragging the United States into the war.

In the first part of 1945, just after Roosevelt's death, Harry Truman, who as vice president was kept out of the loop regarding the billion-dollar Manhattan Project, took a hard line against the Soviets. In 1946, Churchill's "Iron Curtain" speech, delivered in Fulton, Missouri, coupled with Truman's offer (Truman Doctrine) to pick up the economic and military bills of all who might oppose communism internationally, codified the Cold War.

By 1947, Soviet foreign policy shifted to the anti-United States direction. Relations between the former allies reached a nadir with the 1948 communist takeover of Czechoslovakia. The HUAC, active during the late 1930s although not specifically anticommunist, was launched in earnest in 1948, with hearings bulls-eying Hollywood. That year the United States initiated the Marshall Plan, which extended $17 billion in loans and grants to rebuild Europe and included a sufficient number of strings to ensure the Soviets would refuse the loot. Two years later, an obscure junior senator from Wisconsin, Joseph Raymond McCarthy, won the national limelight by baldly asserting during a speech in Wheeling, West Virginia, that 205 communists had infiltrated the State Department.

VIDOR'S EXPLORATION OF THE COLLECTIVE

Vidor's gentle flirtation with communist ideals was not evident in *The Crowd*. The main characters in *Our Daily Bread*, John (Tom Keene) and Mary (Karen Morley) Sims, made their initial appearance in the considerably darker, urban film in 1928. Vidor considered *Our Daily Bread* a sequel only in the sense that the couple, without progeny, was transplanted from a rat race in the 1920s to a rural repose in the 1930s.

Not only does *Our Daily Bread* score higher than Michael Curtiz's *Mission to Moscow* with respect to its production but it also captures the romantic idealism of universal equality as well as the clarion call for community that initially drew adherents to communism. "It glorifies the earth, and growing things in general. It glorifies helping each other. It gets away from all the complications of money exchange, middlemen and competition. Those values are just as valid today," wrote Vidor to explain the appeal of *Our Daily Bread*.[15] The romance of rural community was not a uniquely American phenomenon.

For most Russians, the real revolution occurred in 1929, when communal farms, averaging a few thousand acres each and considered the collective property of the farmers residing there, punctuated Soviet real estate. The Bolsheviks knew nothing about the smell of freshly plowed earth and the sense of community that flourished in rural areas. By denying the individual and overemphasizing community, the concept of the cooperative becomes skewed. Ultimately, collectivization exacted a crushing cost. The bucolic countryside was ravaged by a bloody, village class war in which the most capable farmers were slain, but not before slaughtering most of their livestock. In 1932, after agricultural chaos and two summers of bad weather, a famine in southeast Russia took the lives of an estimated two million to three million persons.[16]

Yet even before agrarian communism's failings became common knowledge, Americans continued to balance communism's promise of justice for all with a tendency toward self-reliance. As Raymond Durgnat and Scott Simmon point out, instead of Vidor persuasively promoting "some sort of 'anti-trust' control of the banks by the government, *Our Daily Bread* offered the poor man's self-help—a voluntary, corporate, morally inspired form of rugged individualism."[17]

Communists position themselves to play on existing internal unrest. Since our law permits communists to form their own political parties or, at least, what amounted to front organizations, anticommunist leftists could be discovered working alongside communists for economic reform in this country.

Even before massive unemployment hit, American agriculture failed to pay a living wage; industry provided much heftier paychecks. In the early part of the century, Progressives had enacted child labor laws and other protections; however, unemployment insurance was not yet a reality. The concept would never have occurred to business owners, who were focused on reinvesting profit, which they could realize only by keeping wages as low as possible.

By 1935, however, national legislation (the Wagner Act) recognized labor's right to organize and gave federal protection to workers. For the first time in American history, the power and prestige of the American government were marshaled on the side of the employee. Communists exploited this opportunity in their efforts to unionize the mass of unorganized industrial personnel previously ignored by the American Federation of Labor's craft unions. The infiltration of the Congress of Industrial Organizations by the communists was not a very well-kept secret. In creating the CIO, however, the communists helped eliminate the inequities that had given them any edge with American workers, leading to a massive failure to win over the logical target of their efforts. Communism, in any of its incarnations, was rejected as democratic ideals were buttressed by a recovering economic system.

However, in 1929, Americans learned first-hand the reality of a free enterprise system run amok and the limitations of laissez-faire capitalism. Herbert Hoover dealt with the Depression by adopting a noninterventionist economic policy in the private sector and by maintaining that relief from the Depression was just around an ever-receding corner, a viewpoint contradicted by people's personal experience on a daily basis, and which led to a crisis of confidence. Stock values driven into the economic stratosphere by unrestrained speculation fell by 40 percent. In thirty-six months, 5,000 American banks closed, national income dwindled from $85 billion to $37 billion and the industrial stock index plummeted from 252 to 61,[18] with multiplier effects rippling from this country to the rest of the world.

Once the economy tanked and unemployment became a way of life, the collapse of capitalism was seen by many as setting the stage for an imminent collapse of democracy. Joblessness overwhelmed the American psyche. With the disappearance of wages and farm income hitting bottom, the decline in mass purchasing power forced men in the prime of life, as well as newly minted machines, to remain idle. Millions like John and Mary Sims found themselves without financial resources or dependent on the pittance offered by charities, the dole, relief or outright begging. Spiritually crushed by a sense of uselessness, demoralized by fruitless job searches, disgusted by the waste of skills and experience, Americans were receptive to new disturbing political ideas. Communists could legitimately point to social and economic evils to open the American psyche to alternative doctrine.

What communists failed to take into account was the possibility of reform, that working conditions and unemployment in the United States might improve without the necessity of violence or revolution. American workers not only exercised a voting role in government but, as stockholders, were free to enter the arena of capitalism themselves. While claiming to be creating a classless society, the communist leadership itself acted within a rigid class structure, permitting the party elite a better standard of living than the workers they supposedly served.

In one scene in *Our Daily Bread*, the politician (Henry Burroughs) insists: "We don't have to have a democracy, we have to have a sacred covenant."

The undertaker (Addison Richards) responds, "Ah, it was that kind of talk that got us here in the first place." This has been interpreted as evidence that Vidor believed our democratic institutions were in serious trouble. In all probability, the exchange was probably more of a comment on the economy than on the government. There is ample evidence that

Vidor supported Roosevelt's pragmatic and eclectic New Deal solutions. The last-ditch effort to rescue the corn crop is an allegory of private enterprise, which possesses both the means and motivation to pull its adherents up by their bootstraps.

MARX MEETS HOLLYWOOD

Too ambiguous to be seen as a piece of communist propaganda by even the communists, *Our Daily Bread* failed to win first prize at the 1935 Soviet International Exposition on Film, yet it did merit a second place plaque, bestowed in the futile hope that Vidor might try harder with his next effort. In spite of its only slightly leftist slant, Vidor's script met with considerable resistance from the heads of major studios, who looked askance at narratives about collectives, apparently allergic to fables leaning too far to the left. The *Los Angeles Times* refused the advertising layout for *Our Daily Bread*, due to its presumed radical orientation.

Liberal Hollywood woke up to ideological politics in 1934 when Democrats nominated Upton Sinclair for governor. As part of his EPIC (End Poverty in California) campaign, Sinclair announced his intention of taxing the movie industry, an act provoking conservative studio executives into threatening mass migration to Florida as well as shooting phony and propagandistic newsreels for the Republican incumbent, Governor Frank Merriam. By soliciting half a million dollars in contributions from studio employees in order to "save California from Russianization," moguls angered personnel already involved in unionization efforts, consolidating the Left in Hollywood and opening the door for communists to capture the attention of left-leaning thinkers. These activists coalesced into the Hollywood Anti-Nazi League, the Motion Picture Artists' Committee, and the Motion Picture Democratic Committee, known as "the popular front," which busied itself through 1938 with fund-raising efforts geared toward electing a socialist governor. These organizations, with many others, would be designated "communist front organizations" and their members attacked as "fellow travelers" a decade later. But that year, the House Un-American Activities Committee was chaired by Representative Martin Dies, a Texas Democrat described as "impetuous, eager, suspicious of immigrants and intellectuals, hostile to virtually all forms of social change, and inordinately fond of publicity."[19] Although considerably less effectual than the leaders of the late 1940s reincarnation of HUAC, Dies's erratic shotgun approach was a significant hazard to the Hollywood popular front.[20]

Card-carrying members of the Communist Party in Hollywood were estimated at no more than a few hundred. The least powerful members of the creative community, the writers (such as Sidney Buchman, who wrote the screenplay for *Mr. Smith Goes to Washington*), constituted the biggest bloc. Unfortunately, Hollywood society members, inside and outside the studio, remained unimpressed with employees they considered one step up from silent film scenarists or title writers. Screenwriters were relegated to dining in the commissary with technicians and punching a clock during a five-and-a-half-day week in which they were expected to turn in eleven pages of script. Harry Cohn of Columbia was said to have bellowed out of his window in the general vicinity of the Writers' Building if he heard the clacking of typewriters begin to diminish.[21] Humiliating treatment, however, translated into more money and lots of free time between contracts, which the writers used to indulge a privileged passion for largely left-wing politics.

It is easy to see why communists targeted Tinseltown. Washington politicians had yet to realize how useful Hollywood money and celebrity might prove to election efforts; no gleaning at the grass roots could surpass the local movie theater in reaching the public. By 1946, one-third of the American public attended a movie every week.[22]

Entertainment industry workers in the 1930s were modestly political with the possible exception of management (excluding the "Combining Good Citizenship with Good Picturemaking" Warner Bros.), which became hysterically anticommunist. The creative community's receptivity to communism is most often attributed to the largely liberal attitudes held by most artists. Hollywood's rank and file might have been drawn to communism's ideological simplicity and romantic idealism. Disenchanted by elitist excesses or afraid that the country was permanently mired in desperate times, entertainment industry workers were not unlike the movie-goer sitting in the third row at the neighborhood Bijou. For the most part, the scriptwriters were most impressed with the communist's self-confident explanation of events in the weekly newsreels. Their Marxist-Leninist view provided a comprehensible pattern to what seemed an incomprehensible blur projected on a global screen at breakneck speed. Ronald Brownstein comments: "Communism seemed to offer not only passion but also order. Its certitude, as much as its fervor, allowed the Communist party to put down deep roots in the film community."[23]

The politically savvy American Communist Party exercised patience in pushing its ideology. The enemy that ultimately united the Right and the Left proved to be Hitler. Benefiting from an alliance against the fascist menace, the sedulous strategizing of the communists paid off in converts. Their only apparent mistake was discounting the homage paid by Hollywood liberals to Roosevelt, especially in light of the New Deal projects specifically aimed at the creative community. Jack and Harry Warner organized a Los Angeles Coliseum rally featuring box-office stars and studio executives in support of FDR's first bid for the White House. Gore Vidal wrote, "It is worth at least a doctoral thesis for some scholar to count how often in films of the 1930s and 1940s a portrait of Franklin Roosevelt can be found, usually hanging on a post-office wall."[24] *Our Daily Bread* remained no exception.

In fact, Vidor's script could have been culled from the meetings of the Subsistence Homestead Division set up by the Roosevelt administration's National Industrial Recovery Act of 1933. Vidor wrote in an October 1934 letter to White House assistant Stephen Early that *Our Daily Bread* was consistent with Roosevelt's policy on subsistence farming although the final cut of the film backed away from the government's making any contribution to the Sims commune.[25] An unpublished seventy-five-page treatment by "Karl Wallis," abandoned by Vidor for unknown reasons, originally located *Our Daily Bread* in Washington with a Capraesque hero named Hank lobbying for the passage of an "Agricultural Army" bill to aid the unemployed. The unmitigated success of Hanktown, an experimental Virginia co-op, made the bill much more appetizing to a majority of trough-fed Senators. Ironically, it was a Republican president, Herbert Hoover, whose tireless faith in self-help co-ops led him to offer Federal Farm Board[26] loans to boost wheat yields, which ultimately caused commodity prices to plummet.

Variety mentioned Vidor in the same breath as Walter Pitkin (Clearing House for Hope) and Upton Sinclair (EPIC).[27] The liberal press championed *Our Daily Bread* and critics merely substituted "sociological" for "socialistic," in what amounted to a raft of rave reviews. The film won recognition as a crucial document of leftist Depression-era ideology and garnered the League of Nation's award for "contribution to humanity." The Hearst Press,[28] in attempting to censure what it considered a "pinko"[29] film, failed to seal its fate.

THINK PINK

Equality is a concept near the top of the abstraction ladder, not down here on earth with humanity. A political and economic system such as communism must, by necessity, be imposed from above. John Sims originally decided to invite ten men with usable farm trades to join his efforts, somewhat stacking the "each-to-his-abilities" deck. However, he quickly abandoned this plan in favor of accepting all comers—undertaker, barber, politician, pants presser, or cigar salesman—once he saw the workability of the "I'll build your fireplace if you'll build my foundation" philosophy. In one of the most poetically poignant moments in the film, the violinist bathes the surrounding hills in Tchaikovsky.

Did John's change of heart foreshadow the fact that he was just a man who can't say "no," or did his faith in people outweigh his faith in process? At some point John realized the necessity of getting the rest of the commune on board. With the Swede's help, he did exactly that. The only legitimate heir apparent who might have successfully challenged John's leadership was Chris (John Qualen), the only "real farmer" on the farm. Yet he demurred, demanding instead that John serve as "a big boss" for a "big job."

Pure communism, by its nature, must thwart personal ambition, initiative and incentive. Communist leadership finds it necessary to eradicate individualistic thinking by taking control of the media, churches and academe in the name of the state. Even though life at the Sims commune was fairly simple, 100 souls focused on providing for the bread-and-butter needs of the group, "groupthink," the mechanism necessary to maintain communal identity, was not consistently enforced.

For example, one of the members skulked off to sell community goods just because "his wife wanted a radio! Can you beat that! With that kind of stuff, we'd last about a week." Problems such as this remained unresolved precisely because Sims tolerated personal idiosyncrasies.

There was a limit to the individualistic thinking tolerated by the commune, though. The community didn't take kindly to the slinky and solitary Sally (Barbara Pepper): "This ain't no place for your kind." She had horrified her neighbors by the "citified" behavior of playing jazz on her phonograph (symbol of technology) just a few hours after her father's death. Also, although desperately in need of funds, the community wouldn't hear of the jailbird's (Roy Spiker) offer to give himself up for the $500 reward on his head.

To the visionary is awarded the power. The character of John Sims was born in 1900, the dawn of a new century. He declared to the world in *The Crowd*, "My Dad says I'm going to be somebody big." John's leadership is demanded through a majority vote, a means of governing he would have preferred over exercising exclusive executive authority. The group also refused the deed to the farm property, not so much as diffident communists but as reluctant recipients of what they considered "welfare." Like Communist Party members in practice, however, the community in *Our Daily Bread* ended up creating an elite of one in John, an anathema to the egalitarianism championed in theory by the *Communist Manifesto*.

John is forced to engage in two moral battles, the first with the corrupting nature of power and the second with the allure of materialist reward. He asks, "What do these guys expect me to do? I'm only human." The slattern Sally seems to tempt on both fronts. By turning in the ex-convict, she intends to keep the reward to lure John into running off to some big city with her. John allows himself to become infatuated with the glamorous, eyebrow-penciled vamp, who serves as a metaphor for the lure of urban materialism, and turns his back on his self-sacrificing, apron-bedecked, "OK by me" helpmate. When he comes to his senses and renounces Sally, it is not the image of his loyal wife but the selfless felon that rivets his attention, stimulating his resolve to attend to his duty and ideals. The commune needs John with Mary; John does not need Mary. The ex-convict, anticipating the outcome of a combination of money plus Sally on the weak and inconsistent John, requests that the reward check be made out to "Mrs. John Sims."

With internal and external difficulties besieging the cooperative from the outset, force proved more effective than persuasion. A bully undertaking to corner a premium plot of land is cowed by the tough escaped prisoner. Do you make a convicted felon the community's cop? The sheriff selling a farm at public auction is outfoxed by neighbors who physically intimidate outside bidders, buying back deeds for a few cents on the dollar. It is unreasonable to expect a bank to be sympathetic to folks going through foreclosure? Moral arguments dealing with ends-means justification have always been tricky but never more so than in the case of communism. An abundance of evidence worldwide confirms that communist leaders consider force, blackmail, murder and deception acceptable methods of operation.

The audience of *Our Daily Bread* is left wondering whether the Sims commune is a short-term effort, an internal counterweight within the system itself, or a veritable breakout from Big Business domination altogether. What happens to these naive folk when their abundant corn crop increases the supply and drives down prices? Vidor ignored Alexander Legge's warning in a *Reader's Digest* article, "Back to the Land," "For these are city people. . . . [T]hese newcomers will inevitably sink to the bottom."[30] Vidor's nostalgic wish for an agrarian populist solution to the Depression seems to demonstrate the power of wishful thinking more than anything else.

The reason the Sims co-operative worked so hard to bring in the money crop was to "get cash so you can be a consumer again." Durgnat and Simmon provide the reality check: "Everything depends on the co-operative producing an abundant corn crop during the Depression, but that was a period of catastrophically *low* demand. Farmers were notoriously burning the very crop Vidor's cooperative labored so mightily to produce."[31] Unless Sims's intention was to create a self-sufficient culture (and evidence in the film counters this), John should have been as aware of market forces as the Russian communists. Under the Soviet Union's first five-year plan, meeting export quotas took priority over feeding the starving peasants. All citizens were required to submit to an austerity program requiring self-sacrifice, including food rationing on a daily basis until 1935. Morale was sustained by propaganda and force when necessary. One-third of the national income was reinvested to keep the country competitive in a world economy. Unfortunately, the Sims' co-op, as Vidor envisioned it, was bound to fail. While hunting and a truck garden could support the present population during the summer months, there would have been a food shortage during the rest of the year, and because market demand for corn had sunk, the cash crop would have yielded little or no profit.

Communists discourage and in some cases, ban religion, "the opium of the people,"[32] in order to eliminate every allegiance that might compete with the state. Many of Vidor's early silents articulated a religious idealism uplifting the moral strength of the mind or faith in rural society. An idealistic twenty-year-old King Vidor wrote in his diary, "I see the hand of fate call me to reform the world. It will start with the movies."[33] Vidor held a lifelong fascination for his mother's religion, an enchantment that to his immense frustration, stopped short of true belief. Christian Science provided the loose conceptual structure on which he would hang his attraction to the incompatible notions represented by puritanism, transcendentalism and pragmatism. His image of mankind as an extension of but separate from and subordinate to God/Nature provided a tenuous thread through all three for Vidor.

Emerson's transcendentalism provided the link connecting Vidor to the individualism of Ayn Rand. *Our Daily Bread* provides glimpses nostalgic of both Thoreau's rural idealism and Emerson's celebration of intuition as a portal to the spiritual. The "white flight" of the 1990s, currently two million Americans strong, harks back to those same philosophical roots. Unlike the 1950s middle-class relocation from the cities to the suburbs, the 1990s migration is a spiritual escape to small towns and rural counties, 75 percent of which are growing after decades of deterioration. *Time*'s Eric Pooley attributes this reinvention of lifestyle not only to the "powerful technological forces that are decentralizing the American economy," but also to the attraction of place "where the landscape is emptier, the housing costs lower, the culture more gentle— places where Martha Stewart manqué can slow down long enough to create the gilded topiaries they've dreamed about for years."[34] Yet it is important to note that while the Simses were looking for a spiritual Eden, economic frustration provided their primary impetus; in contrast, the contemporary urge to relocate stems from spiritual poverty in the midst of materialistic plenty.

Vidor was not afraid to dish out Mary Baker Eddy-type humanism (if victory were to come, it would require enormous self-sacrifice) with religious rituals such as Chris (John Qualen) blessing the land or the carpenter (Frank Hammond) leading the commune in prayer. Meeting the commonly held expectation of any puritan morality tale, Vidor's hero John Sims may have been initially tempted but eventually resisted the siren call of Sally. Reminiscent of Frank Capra's frequent biblical allusions, Vidor started out spinning the story of Job, offered up a Christ-like sacrificial lamb in the character of the ex-convict, who was himself a redeemed sinner, and ended with, if not a literal parting of the Red Sea, a miraculous diversion of the stream.

THE AUDIENCE RESPONDS

While *Our Daily Bread* remained a far cry from a blockbuster (*Variety* reported that "on the matter of the box office, . . . its chances seem thin") the critics were unfailingly kind to Vidor, seeming to operating on the same premise as the *New York Times* reviewer, namely, that cinema qualified "as a social instrument"[35] capable of changing viewers' convictions. Vidor makes a somewhat disingenuous assertion in his autobiography that he "tried to influence opinion neither one way nor the other," but his leftist agenda remains fairly transparent.[36]

Yet, in order to persuade, movies need an adequate audience. Other studios were craftily cashing in on Depression patrons who favored glitz on the screen. *Variety* groused, "It seems a petty objection to cite that such a worthy production lacks pretty, pretty glamour, that is too grim for people already somber from responsibility, that Americans will not patronize anything so serious."[37] The no-name cast didn't help the film's prospects, and it fared little better when rereleased as *Hell's Crossroads*.

Our Daily Bread, Vidor's shortest sound film at a mere seventy-four minutes long, zigs along with quick pans and zags by with angular wipes. Considering the seemingly tedious subject matter, Vidor's pacing proved inspired. The viewer is constantly stimulated by cinematic shifts during which characters amble out of frame or the camera backtracks.

In the final scene in which the diverted water surges into the cornfield, Vidor reminds the audience that economic anguish cannot help being alleviated in America. The unrestrained demonstrations of emotion, with adults turning somersaults and splashing each other with mud, found their genesis in Vidor's recollection of silent movie depictions of ecstasy. He hired former Mack Sennett stunt actors proficient in pratfalls for the expressed purpose of portraying exquisite joy in that manner.

Although threatened by the 1930 Production Code, which, at the time, pretty much determined content, the early 1930s could hardly qualify as a squeaky-clean period in film-making. Sex, violence and verbal hints of improprieties regularly went unpenalized. *Our Daily Bread*'s perceived purity was such a change of pace that the *Film Daily* reviewer singled out that quality as worthy of comment: "Taking up a very timely subject, King Vidor has turned out a really worthwhile screen document that not only makes satisfactory entertainment but has . . . the currently important merit of absolute cleanliness, which should get it support from various groups," but not, however, any organizations concerned with the communist threat.[38]

Early Vidor films, including *Our Daily Bread*, seem fairly straitlaced if not downright prudish when compared to subsequent efforts such as *The Fountainhead*. In fact, Vidor signed a lengthy pledge distributed in a Vidor Village investment brochure, vowing to direct only pictures without sex and violence, a pledge he later regretted as naive.[39] The wholesomeness of *Our Daily Bread* resulted in some interesting comments, especially once the picture was released in Europe. Vidor recalled in an interview: "The headline on the Paris papers said, 'King Vidor prefers food to sex.' Sex was supposed to be the biggest theme for pictures and I was talking about the idea that being able to eat came first for people, and sex was second."[40]

Speaking of food, perhaps David O. Selznick's theory of "the icebox element" anticipated the appeal this movie has for later generations. Selznick believed that after the family returns home from the theater, a good film ought to provoke a conversation so animated that the participants feel compelled to grab a midnight snack in order to continue the discussion. Vidor invites the audience to join him in nibbling from a variety of choice tidbits in *Our Daily Bread*. Some morsels, such as self-reliance, democratic humanism, and rural populism, are comfort foods, calling up fond memories of the down-home cooking that make us feel a part of something bigger than ourselves, while other foil-wrapped packages, initially appearing as remnants from a foreign food establishment, say, Chinese or Russian previously pushed to the back of the refrigerator, may turn out to be as American as apple pie. The communal teamwork exhibited in *Our Daily Bread* stops considerably short of communism, an ideology that will never get on the menu in America.

What did the average family chat about after viewing *Our Daily Bread*? Vidor offers up a single serving in his autobiography: "An explanation of this heroic struggle that we are living, a film story giving humanity reassurance that the good fight is not in vain and showing the individual that he is not alone in his quest for the good life would be received by receptive hearts everywhere."[41]

Our Daily Bread continues to shimmer as that kind of flick.

NOTES

1. Raymond Durgnat and Scott Simmon, *King Vidor, American* (Berkeley: University of California Press, 1988), 10.

2. In 1915 to Vitagraph silent star Florence Arto, whom he divorced in 1924; in 1928 to actress Eleanor Boardman of the William Randolph Hearst entourage, whom he divorced in 1932; and in 1932 to writer Elizabeth Hall, who died in 1973.

3. Turin produced *Turksib* or *The Earth Thirsts* (1929), the famous documentary depicting the building of a railway linking Turkistan with Siberia.

4. Colin Shindler, *Hollywood in Crisis: Cinema and American Society 1929–1939* (Routledge: London 1996), 69.

5. King Vidor, *A Tree Is a Tree* (New York: Harcourt Brace, 1952), 221.

6. Interview by Nancy Dowd and David Shepard in *King Vidor: A Directors Guild of America (DGA) Oral History* (Metuchen, NJ: Scarecrow Press, 1988), 144.

7. Alexander Legge, as told to Neil M. Clark, "Back to the Land?" *Reader's Digest* 22 (November 1932), 45–48; see also Malcolm McDermott, "An Agricultural Army," *Reader's Digest* 21 (June 1932), 95–97.

8. Dowd and Shepard, *King Vidor*, 148.

9. King Vidor, 224.

10. Ibid., 224.

11. Ibid., 226.

12. The word "communism" was introduced in the 1830s when it was used by clandestine worker societies in Paris.

13. Karl Marx, *Critique of the Gotha Program* (Moscow, Russia: Foreign Languages Publishing House, 1947).

14. In his contribution to *Contemporary Political Ideologies* (edited by Roger Eawell and Anthony Wright, Boulder, CO: Westview Press, 1993) titled "Marxism and Communism," Joseph V. Femia argues Marxism-Leninism as the *theory* and communism as the *practice* in light of Marx's ambiguous legacy, a permanent source of conflict among his ideological descendants.

15. Dowd and Shepard, *King Vidor*, 150.

16. R. R. Palmer and Joel Colton, *A History of the Modern World*, 5th ed. (New York: Alfred A. Knopf, 1978).

17. Durgnat and Simmon, *King Vidor*, 151.

18. Ibid., 759.

19. Ronald Brownstein, *The Power and the Glitter: The Hollywood-Washington Connection* (New York: Pantheon, 1990), 67.

20. Hollywood remained safe from further federal investigation until after the war, although in 1944 a California HUAC investigation chaired by Jack Tenny turned up nothing worth press coverage.

21. Shindler, *Hollywood in Crisis*, 55.

22. Richard Maltby and Ian Craven, *Hollywood Cinema* (Oxford, England: Blackwell, 1995), 10.

23. Brownstein, *The Power and the Glitter*, 49.

24. Gore Vidal, *Screening History* (London: Abacus, 1993), 49.

25. Durgnat and Simmon, *King Vidor*, 152.

26. Hoover's former chairman of the Federal Farm Board is the same Alexander Legge credited with the *Reader's Digest* article, "Back to the Land?"

27. "Our Daily Bread," *Variety*, October 9, 1934, 18.

28. William Randoph Hearst believed the picture was communist propaganda. Although Vidor had made successful films with Marion Davies, his theory was that Hearst's censure resulted from Hearst and Davies remaining loyal to Vidor's former wife, Eleanor Boardman.

29. Vidor, *A Tree Is a Tree*, 227.

30. Legge, "Back to the Land?" 45.

31. Durgnat and Simmon, *King Vidor*, 154. Emphasis added in original.

32. Karl Marx, *Critique of the Hegelian Philosophy of Right* in *Early Writings*,

edited and translated by T. B. Bottomore, foreword by Erich Fromm (New York: McGraw Hill, 1963, c. 1844).

33. Durgnat and Simmon, *King Vidor*, 27.

34. Eric Pooley, "The Great Escape," *Time* (December 8, 1997), 54.

35. Andres Sennwalk, *New York Times* (October 3, 1934), 2.

36. Vidor, *A Tree Is a Tree*, 227.

37. *Variety* (October 9, 1934), 18.

38. "Our Daily Bread," *Film Daily* (August 8, 1934), 7.

39. "A Creed and Pledge—I believe in the motion picture that carries a message to humanity. I believe in the picture that will help humanity to free itself from the shackles of fear and suffering that have so long bound it with iron chains. I will not knowingly produce a picture that contains anything that could injure anyone, nor anything unclean in thought or action. Nor will I deliberately portray anything to cause fright, suggest fear, glorify mischief, condone cruelty or extenuate malice. I will never picture evil or wrong, except to prove the fallacy of its lure. So long as I direct pictures, I will make only those founded upon the principle of right and I will endeavor to draw upon the inexhaustible source of Good for my stories, my guidance, and my inspiration. Signed, King Vidor."

40. Dowd and Shepard, *King Vidor*, 149.

41. Vidor, *A Tree Is a Tree*, 273.

Raymond Massey in the office of *The Banner* in *The Fountainhead*. Courtesy of the Academy of Motion Picture Arts and Sciences.

Chapter Nine

Anticommunism in *The Fountainhead*

Beverly Merrill Kelley

More than 30 million copies of Ayn Rand's works have made their way onto private bookshelves since *The Fountainhead* was published in 1943. First lady Hillary Rodham Clinton, Federal Reserve Chairman Alan Greenspan, Libertarian presidential candidate John Hospers, author Charles Murray, Ronald Reagan's chief adviser Martin Anderson, and Supreme Court Justice Clarence Thomas have publicly acknowledged the influence of Ayn Rand on their personal political evolution. Similarly, individuals polled by a joint Library of Congress-Book of the Month Club survey of "lifetime reading habits" published in 1991 ranked *Atlas Shrugged* second only to the Bible in its significant impact on their lives.[1]

Yet even more foes than fans have queued up to dismiss Rand's Objectivist philosophy. Rand is frequently criticized for avoiding vigorous scholarly analysis and her popularity as a best-selling novelist is often minimized as a "cult" following, the faithful cinching that claim by their mindless adherence to the self-absorbed lifestyle role-modeled by her fictional characters.[2] Intellectuals smirkingly point out that Rand's hold is limited to the philosophically naive and puerile. In Gary Kamiya's review of the recently released *Journals of Ayn Rand*, he asserts: "There may be some mature souls who find themselves stomping along to her brazen one-note samba, but her ideal readers are college sophomores who are trying to reinvent themselves as jutting-jawed Heroes of Reason."[3] Further, Rand made lasting enemies by flippantly dismissing the arguments of her opposition on impertinent moral or psychological grounds. Her anticommunist, pro-capitalist politics infuriated the Left at the same time the Right took umbrage with her atheism and civil libertarianism.

AYN RAND

It should come as no surprise to those who struggled in real life with her heavily accented monologues or to devoted readers who had to slog through her lengthy novels that Ayn Rand, born Alissa Zinovievna Rosenbaum in St. Petersburg on February 2, 1905, was thoroughly Russian. While little Alissa believed her character owed less to the accidental details of her private life than to the content of her brain (as reflected in the pages of books such as *The Fountainhead*), this writer believes it unwise to discount the influence of social relationships on the development of her thinking. As a young girl, little Alissa fell in love with the logic and precision of the sciences in spite of the rote learning drills forced on her by her early teachers. She effortlessly wrote short stories when she became bored with her lessons, a screenplay at the age of eight, adventure novels at the age of ten. Czarist tyrannies preceding the Russian Revolution provided her with ample material.

She found a spiritual ally in her lifelong battle to preserve human freedom in her father. When the family pharmacy was nationalized, the Rosenbaums, terrorized by the Bolsheviks, disgusted with street violence and despairing that food and fuel shortages would ever end, fled to the Crimea. There young Alissa was instructed by old-fashioned, Czar-loving matrons, and Alissa, hoping to become a professional mathematician, in turn, tutored classmates in geometry. She chose a series of American history classes as electives. During this period, because she found the concept of God rationally unprovable, she embraced atheism, rejecting both the Christian God and mystical collective God-state of the communists. Clasping a Russian passport dated 1925, Alissa took a roundabout tour via Latvia, Berlin, and Paris to New York, reporting a sojourn with Chicago relatives as the reason for her journey.

Alissa Zinovievna Rosenbaum abandoned her mother country and rechristened herself Ayn Rand within months of glimpsing the Statue of Liberty. Convinced that the airtight environment of brutality and repression in Russia could result only in physical and spiritual death, Alissa scurried to the land of opportunity, failing to return to her homeland as assured. Her parents, denied permission to leave the Soviet Union, did not survive the siege of Leningrad.

Typical of literary figures in the Soviet Union, Alissa set out to integrate her artistic, social critic and philosopher selves through her writing. Alissa Rosenbaum came of age during the rise of the Bolsheviks, graduating from the University of Leningrad with a social science degree and a heavily Kantian philosophy minor the year Lenin died. An interesting note: The few formal philosophy courses in which the Objectivist philosopher enrolled dealt entirely with intellectual history. The onslaught of communist propaganda encountered in her college classrooms, however, prompted her to develop critical listening skills and a methodology she dubbed "thinking in principles," which she committed to philosophical diaries. She burned her journals as well as her fiction outlines prior to her exodus from Russia.

Alissa Rosenbaum remained deeply scarred by the expulsion of fellow students to Siberia, which she reconstructed in the novel *We the Living*. She escaped imprisonment only because of her status as a graduating senior. Rand claims this autobiographical work, originally titled *Air Tight: A Novel of Red Russia*, was written in order to get the Soviet Union out of her system. *We the Living* chronicles Petrograd University engineering student Kira Agrgounova's struggle with the harsh conditions of Soviet dictatorship, further complicated by a romantic triangle involving Leo Kovalensky, a tuberculosis-stricken counter-revolutionary, and Andrei Taganov, an idealistic communist so sickened by communist corruption that he commits suicide. In Taganov, Alissa Rosenbaum foreshadows *The Fountainhead* figure Gail Wynand, whom she also condemns for seeking power by manipulating the masses.

At the university, she was forced to study economic determinism, which essentially argues that the material forces of production, ownership, exchange and distribution shape human history. Three decades later, while viewing Nikita Khrushchev's 1959 appearance on American television, Rand recalls being immediately struck by the eerie manner in which his credo of dialectical materialism echoed the precise language taught at her alma mater, an ironic observation in light of the fact that Rand's literary and philosophical ideas, formulated very early in life, also remained substantially unchanged.[4]

OBJECTIVISM

Rand jettisoned key Russian traditions while accenting others. She rejected Marxism, equating it with Russian mysticism. Yet in postulating revolution as organic to the establishment of her utopian society, Rand in essence mimicked the modus operandi of the Leninists she claimed to abhor.

She affirmed the dialectical revolt against formal dualism. Dialectic, the Aristotelian counterpart to rhetoric (often exemplified by the Socratic method) provided her with a means to avoid pitting opposing theses against each other. Nicholas Onufrievich Lossky, Rand's philosophy professor at the Petrograd University, introduced her to Aristotle, which ultimately shaped the form and content of her thought. The aspect of Rand's philosophy that proved most attractive to King Vidor, who would later direct the screen version of her best-seller, was her ability to fuse opposites by isolating the integral relationship between them.

She used a "both and" formulation to unite what had previously been held separate and distinct. For example, while her countrymen stressed community over the individual, Rand viewed ethics and politics as mutually supportive, that is, the Aristotelian synonymy of the good man and the good citizen.

OBJECTIVISM AS POLITICAL IDEOLOGY

Rand integrated dialectical methodology with libertarian politics in Objectivism. Her rebuff of statism and collectivism led her to defend individual rights and free-market capitalism.[5] She also took the Russian concept of *sobornost*, meaning "conciliarity" (N. O. Lossky illustrated *sobernost* as "the combination of freedom and unity of many persons on the basis of the common love for the same absolute values"[6]) and redefined it, with the individual becoming both a source and product of the whole.

In *The Fountainhead*, Rand endorsed a quasi-Lockean/Jeffersonian view of the natural rights of the individual. She further interpreted human ego as one's ability to choose, pursue and work to achieve personally articulated happiness, as long as the same right was respected in others, while rejecting Marx's atomistic conception of humanity, which condoned the use of force.

Rand's conceptualization of capitalism, a byproduct of an Aristotelian philosophical base, was neither an expression of the Protestant work ethic nor compatible with any religious system of thought. She held that capitalism and altruism are philosophical opposites, incapable of coexisting in the same man or society. She contended that although the United States, the most secular Western country in her estimation, had achieved the greatest economic progress, it would continue to pay the price for preserving significant elements of altruism and collectivism in its cultural base.

Discrediting the religious traditions of her mother country as well as the secular collectivism of the Marxists, she remained Russian in her thinking and just as much a social utopian as the communists she despised, despite her denial. The radical who transplanted herself to the United States championed individual rights and a laissez-faire economic policy to the degree that she seemed determined to out-democratize democracy and out-capitalize capitalism.

BEST-SELLING NOVEL

In *The Fountainhead*, Howard Roark (Gary Cooper) is a gifted architect who envisions projects outside of the conventional master builder box. His insistence on individualism, as expressed in personal sovereignty with respect to artistic expression, brought him mockery from the media ("BUILDING OUTRAGE EXPOSED While many are starving") led by

Banner publisher Gail Wynand (Raymond Massey) and resentment by the architectural establishment, chiefly *Banner* building critic Ellsworth Toohey (Robert Douglas). Even Roark's mentor is resentful of those who have the power to force the artist to color inside politically correct lines. Henry Cameron (Henry Hull) advises Roark to compromise in order to survive. Left without an ally save Dominique Francon (Patricia Neal), who is engaged to Roark's fair-weather friend Peter Keating (Kent Smith), Roark ignites Dominique's ardor. Her fear of losing the man she loves, Howard Roark, causes her to forsake her heart, flying into an unhappy marriage with Wynand. Keating, finding himself in over his architectural head in accepting a public housing project, begs Roark to bail him out, continuing a dependence established in college. Roark, who cares little for dollars or distinction, assents with the simple proviso that his blueprint be realized without alteration. The self-important and somewhat bitter critic Toohey sees to it that Roark's design is compromised, eventually resulting in the destruction of the edifice. Wynand unsuccessfully attempts to mobilize his newspaper behind Roark; however, the great unwashed, roused by Toohey, vote with their feet and Wynand's newspaper files for bankruptcy. In the storybook ending, Roark's rousing courtroom defense, railing against the "collectivist . . . parasites," convinces the jury that egoistic principles, when weighed on the scales of justice, outweigh the law. Wynand takes his life, leaving Dominque free to love Roark.

The Fountainhead was originally intended as a philosophical magnum opus defending individualism. Rand's working title for the book, *Second-hand Lives*, was discarded as her vision of ego evolved into "the fountainhead" of human progress. Twelve publishers rejected the self-serving tome, dismissing it as not only excessively intellectual but as too controversial to merit a substantial readership. Rand purportedly wrote the novel to chisel her profile of the ideal man: "The portrayal of a moral ideal, as my ultimate literary goal, as an end in itself—to which any didactic, intellectual or philosophical values contained in a novel are only the means."[7] Despite her self-avowed enmity of collectivism, *The Fountainhead* bears more than a faint resemblance to its ideological opposite, the propagandistic literature produced by Stalinist Socialist Realists.

Heavily influenced by novelist Fyodor Mikhailovich Dostoyevsky, Rand attempted to imitate the way he integrated themes and plots with his belief system. Rather than state her philosophic notions in the abstract, Rand used stories, screenplays, dramas and novels to flesh out her portraiture of Mr. Perfect as he related to the conditions that made him possible.

Setting such high aims for herself resulted in a writer's block so paralyzing that at one point, the eventual best-seller seemed hopelessly blocked. Rand professed vehement opposition to the practice of dedicating books, insisting instead, like her protagonist Howard Roark, on addressing her work to any reader proving worthy of the material. However, Rand was so grateful to her husband, Frank, for his persistent encouragement when she was blocked that she inscribed *The Fountainhead* to him as its savior.

Critic Gary Kamiya isn't sure that this "comic book with Wagnerian dialogue" should have been saved, yet he admits that the

> lack of development, psychological depth and flexibility is so absolute that it is fascinating. You keep waiting for something light, something human, something different to appear and it never does. Rand's formula is a rigor mortis-like adherence to her icy first philosophical principles, combined with grandiose wish-fulfilling plots. The results are simultaneously banal and hysterical: like Aristotle (the only philosopher she respected, despite his many "errors") crossed with Mickey Spillane (her favorite contemporary novelist).[8]

Rand outlined the plot and characters of her first genuine commercial success in 1935. Offered up as an oblation to Rand's quest for an integrated (non-dualistic) understanding of humanity, the book hit the *New York Times* list in 1943. Warner Brothers snatched up the screen rights[9] and tapped King Vidor to direct. Vidor insisted that Rand draft the screenplay, which she offered to do free, providing, again emulating Roark, that no dialogue was changed without her consent.

An incident testing her resolve ensued during the filming of the courtroom summation. Rand discovered Vidor shooting a somewhat abbreviated version of the six-page speech so that the memory-impaired lead actor could deliver the difficult monologue. Indifferent to the fact that Gary Cooper couldn't handle more than a few lines at a time, Rand marched over to Jack Warner's office and demanded that he enforce her contract terms with Vidor.

KING VIDOR

With Gary Cooper miscast in the lead by the producer Henry Blanke, Vidor needed a new cinematic language to translate the tensions inherent in *The Fountainhead*.[10] In training his lens on the torment of the individual, Vidor emphasized the stark composition, oblique camera angles, and deeply shadowed lighting used in *film noir* yet atypically included virtual vistas of vertical skyscrapers extending across the frame. Studio hairdressers grumbled about the extra work created by frequent shots of each character from the rear and set decorators might have followed suit had they been required to keep genuine glass walls fingerprint-free.

Vidor also helped himself to various elements of expressionism. He used an elephantine dining table for the scene in which Wynand callously buys off Dominque's suitor, Peter Keating. A colossal candelabra, ablaze with flickering tapers, provided the physical depiction of the psychological barrier between the betrothed couple.

He suggested the megapower of the media by a wall-size world map. The forced perspective so reminiscent of the cinematic populism in Vidor's silents was also visually depicted in the *Banner* editor's office scene as the camera pans across an ocean of reporters. Vidor also employed the image of elitists walled off from the workers by a slender sheet of glass to establish the structural reality of the American class system.

Vidor's interest in architecture began with the Cedric Gibbons-designed building in *The Crowd*. Vidor wanted to hire Frank Lloyd Wright but Wright requested 10 percent of the film's entire budget to draft the fictional Roark's renderings.[11] Vidor disappointed film critics by employing Edward Carrere to design the futuristic exteriors, which more closely resembled Los Angeles International Airport than the mystical geography of Manhattan.

Vidor utilized *The Fountainhead* as a vehicle for his own beliefs, seemingly unconcerned with where Rand's *weltanschauung* ended and his began. Despite having declared himself an ardent Democratic Party supporter, Vidor pledged, "That picture is so much of what I believe, I could die happily, knowing that I had made it."[12]

Vidor didn't seek out *The Fountainhead* as a pet project, although the timing of the cinematic undertaking, on the heels of an all-consuming psychological exploration of his life, appeared more than coincidental to him. He had just undergone Jungian analysis in the midst of his third marriage and a marked-up copy of *Psychology of the Self* attested to his oneness with the principles of Objectivism: "I was then very conscious of this recognition of the self, the dignity of the self, and the power and divinity one has."[13] He particularly delighted in training the camera on the friction between Roark's true individualism and obvious counterfeits such as Wynand, whose journalistic incursions, first for and then against Roark, evidenced his disingenuousness to Vidor.

Vidor sharply diverged from Rand, however, when it came to exploring the religious dimensions of the belief system that seems to have found a second home with the Me Generation. His brand of spirituality was grounded in the moral strength of the mind as well as an agrarian faith in the healing power of open spaces. Vidor held that "self" offered definitive proof of the existence of God and sought to mellow Rand's hyperpure individualism (made all the more off-putting by her ardent atheism) with his conception of healthy autonomy. He explained,

We've been thrown off by repentance, long suffering and the ideas of the church—eternal sin and all that has been putting man down. Where do you find God—in a church, a priest, a Pope? Truly it is a man's consciousness and his own self that represents God, that speaks for God in its own way. None of the other outside authorities can ever do that. It is really a fine basic theme.[14]

While even minor changes to Rand's dialogue were verboten, Vidor was able to insinuate spirituality through the eye of the camera. A thick red cross of compassion etched on the ambulance window becomes superimposed over one of the skyscrapers designed by Henry Cameron (Henry Hull) as the vehicle speeds by. As the car cruises down Cameron's *via doloroso*, Roark symbolically accepts the cross too heavy for his mentor to carry.

Rand couldn't stop Vidor from visually highlighting moments during which characters transcend self. For instance, Dominque's near death as she dynamites Roark's compromised building is unveiled as a self-sacrifice and Roark's release of Dominique to give her time to learn her life lesson, "not to be afraid of the world" appears selfless for an Objectivist.

Vidor didn't completely adopt the naked egotism inherent in Objectivism. When Cameron rips apart copies of the *Banner*, a symbolic attempt at besting Toohey-style collectivism, he pays for the privilege. Contrast that diminutive ethical gesture with the scene in which Dominique, acting as agent for Roark, commits a felony by detonating property belonging to someone else.

Vidor could never resign himself to Rand's dynamite climax; he felt it bombed morally. While he didn't argue that Rand's "ideal man" should compromise himself, Vidor impertinently inquired whether Roark's persuading Dominique to substitute as saboteur, asking her to act in his stead, didn't actually amount to the same thing. It didn't seem to Vidor that a self-actualized egoist would have broken the law or acted out like a child in the throes of the terrible twos. Vidor held that such extremism is just as negating as it is morally repugnant.

Vidor believed Roark could have remained victorious had he simply held the line against the small minds who seem to infect big business. After the *Banner* smear campaign, Roark survived by designing structures somewhat smaller than an Enright-type architectural monument, such as shops and filling stations for men of modest means. At that time he declared, "No building is unimportant. I'll build for any man who wants me, anywhere, so long as I build my way." When faced with the studio's insistence that he stick to Rand's bombastic turning point, Vidor contended that if Roark could legitimately destroy his own creation, *The Fountainhead*'s director should be free to burn the negative of a film he felt compromised as well. Warner Brothers was said to have responded, "Right, and we'll see if a jury exonerates you."[15]

By the early 1940s, a sufficient number of Americans still cherished the myth of the self-made man to make a best-seller out of Rand's novel.

Rand's novel and the movie end with Dominique (Patricia Neal) being transported to the deified Roark (Gary Cooper) astride the summit of his greatest architectural achievement. While Rand might argue that Objectivist tenets should properly eclipse the character development of any of the characters of her book, it is ironic that it was her somewhat stilted, two dimensional figures that tended to muddy her thesis. Durgnat and Simmon summarize, "It's surprising that the combined professionalism of Gary Cooper, Vidor, and Jack Warner could do so little to modify Ayn Rand's comic-strip dialogue."[16]

ANTICOMMUNISM AS IDEOLOGY

The termination of World War I brought out a slew of conflicting attitudes toward the Soviet Union. Americans unfamiliar with or scarcely bothered by the moral implications of communist principles chose to believe that the Russians had simply sold out to the Germans. President Woodrow Wilson fantasized about a world in which communism could coexist with capitalism without violating the principle of national self-determination. Internationalists refused to endorse relations with any regime instigating insurrection, relying instead on withholding free-market democratic resources to check communism. Rumors of human rights violations in the 1930s, offensive to even the most leftist of Russia's supporters, were dwarfed by concerns for its country-wide famine. In fact, the full and indisputable truth about Lenin's reign of terror, like that of Stalin decades later, failed to come to light for decades.

In the 1940s, Stalin found Lenin's bloody footprints a perfect fit for his size-ten jackboots. The Truman Doctrine appended an anticommunist proviso to the liberal internationalism that, in tension with isolationism, remained an underlying precept of American foreign policy from the Wilson years on: America would intervene only if the ideology of a foreign power agitated the world order.

The Truman Doctrine stated:

Nearly every nation must choose between alternative ways of life. One was based upon the will of the majority, and is distinguished by free institutions, representative government, free elections, guarantees of individual liberty, freedom of speech and religion, and freedom from political oppression. The second way of life is based upon the will of a minority forcibly imposed upon the majority. It relies upon terror and oppression, a controlled press and radio, fixed elections, and the suppression of personal freedoms.[17]

In a speech to the National Association of Evangelicals on March 18, 1983, President Ronald Reagan reddened the visage of the Soviet Union with the sobriquet, "evil empire," prophesying: "The real crisis we face today is a spiritual one at root; it is a test of moral will and faith. I believe that communism is another sad, bizarre chapter in human history whose last pages even now are being written." He left the Oval Office maintaining his opposition to communism.

How did America get from liberal internationalism to an extended Cold War? George F. Kennan, former U.S. ambassador to the Soviet Union, encapsulates the view of Americans for whom the threat of Soviet world domination was deadly serious, the slogan, "Better red than dead" was abhorrent and the contest between the two world powers apocalyptic:

> It [anticommunism] then tends to attach to its own cause an absolute value which distorts its own vision of everything else. *Its* enemy becomes the embodiment of all evil. *Its* own side, on the other hand, is the center of all virtue. . . . If *we* lose, all is lost; life will no longer be worth living; there will be nothing to be salvaged. If we win, then everything will be possible; all problems will become soluble; the one great source of evil—*our* enemy—will have been crushed; the forces of good will then sweep forward unimpeded; all worthy aspirations will be satisfied.[18]

Americans who vigorously opposed communism were viewed as fascists populating the nightmares of civil libertarians across the nation or conspiracy-obsessed neurotics who painted towns from Los Angeles to Washington a vivid shade of red. Even today's history texts still routinely equate anticommunism with McCarthyism.

American adversaries conducted their crusade for seventy years before tasting victory. Anticommunist ideology *in toto* was complex and pluralistic, differing from previous nativist movements in that the primary enemy was both international and foreign-directed. Despite the damage done by McCarthy and other conspiracy theorists who still tend to monopolize remembrances of the "Red Scare," anticommunists prevailed largely because they offered a more accurate picture of the world than did their ideological antagonists. The United States in the 1940s was moving into the era dominated, as President Dwight D. Eisenhower termed it, by "the military industrial complex." Radicalism required reliance on self, yet the American spirit conceived of itself as pious, pragmatic and populist.

Anticommunism should scarcely require a scholarly defense, yet the disservice done by the excesses of the radical Right as well as the power of the academic Left to denigrate the moral and intellectual legitimacy of anticommunism left a bad taste in the mouth of the nation. To this day, Hollywood reviles the Elia Kazan-types who turned over communist colleagues to avoid the blacklist. Despite absolving nearly every other sin, Tinseltown refuses to forgive fellow artists who acted as stool pigeons during the House Un-American Activities hearings of the late 1940s and early 1950s.

While the House Un-American Activities Committee of the 1930s was initially interested in fascists, during 1947, HUAC zeroed in on communists, targeting the movie industry with its high public profile to provide maximum publicity for the committee and its work. In October 1947, HUAC called for an investigation of communism in motion pictures but appeared less interested in the subversive content of films than in the political affiliations of the filmmakers.[19] Determined to rid Hollywood of communist infiltration, HUAC subpoenaed dozens of prominent writers, actors and directors, and pressured them to publicly disavow communism as well as people they had allegedly known in the party.

Committee Chairman Parnell Thomas engaged in the sort of media posturing later honed to a fine art by Senator McCarthy. Friendly witnesses such as Jack Warner, Walt Disney, Ronald Reagan, Gary Cooper and Ayn Rand were allowed to read prepared statements, use notes and offer testimony without supporting evidence, while the protests of unfriendly witnesses had to be shouted over the rulings of Chairman Thomas, making it appear that they were challenging HUAC's authority as well as refusing to answer the committee's questions. In the first round of hearings, the Hollywood Ten, jailed for refusing to testify, served as examples to those who were to follow. Studio moguls initially requested the cooperation of actors with the "are-you-now-or-have-you-ever-been" crowd, later negatively reinforcing the reluctant by blacklisting those who declined to name names. By the time the hearings were over, the Bill of Rights was in tatters. In all, over 200 movie industry employees were named by HUAC and innumerable others found themselves labeled guilty by association.

Richard Gid Powers, on the other hand, presents American resistance to communism as an essentially honorable, if not noble cause. The title of his 1996 book, *Not without Honor*, comes from the Gospel according to Matthew: "A prophet is not without honor, save in his own country, and in his own house." Powers, indoctrinated by academe with the notion that anticommunism represented America at its worst, unearthed evidence to the contrary while researching his tome; he concluded that the anticommunist movement evidenced America at its best.

During the seven decades anticommunists sought to alert their fellow countrymen to the communist threat, they were vilified with every epithet from "crackpot" to "red baiter" in an attempt to minimize and marginalize their voices. Powers differentiates sharply between "responsible" anticommunists, who served as reasonable proponents of the mainstream political movement, and those he labels "radical countersubversives." Powers singled out the opportunistic senator from Wisconsin, Joseph R. McCarthy, whose reckless and irresponsible behavior contributed irreparable damage to the cause, for the greatest censure.

Despite the tendency to characterize opposition to communist dogma as monolithic McCarthyism, this protest movement incorporated Americans of diverse worldviews, methods, goals and motives, who, in fact, brawled among themselves with nearly as much fire as they battled communism. What they shared was an total knowledge of the enemy coupled with the all-consuming belief that communism wasn't just a life-or-death issue, it was far more important. Opposition to communism resonated with the American resolve to foster the growth of democracy all over the planet, a cause the United States has backed with its blood and bounty against threats from Germany, Japan, the Third Reich as well as European and Asian totalitarian states. As Rand fleshed out the bickering and badgering mouthpieces for her philosophic polemic, she also inadvertently personified the major anticommunists strains (liberals, radical rightists and former communists) as well.

LIBERAL ANTICOMMUNISTS

By 1949, Arthur M. Schlesinger Jr.'s *The Vital Center* was immediately co-opted as the manifesto of liberal intellectuals opposing communism. With so many of the devoted suspected of being fellow travelers, the Left needed to slap a new face on liberalism. Schlesinger redefined anticommunism as a means of securing democracy against the new enemy, totalitarianism, thereby providing common ground with the Right and pre-empting any antifascist name-calling by the communists. The Left held that to abridge civil liberties, as HUAC had done in order to resist the "Red Menace" (not to mention coming up virtually empty-handed), was to betray the cause of freedom. The liberal point of view by the end of the 1940s returned to the peaceful coexistence perspective of the Wilson era and fastened the conservative position, with Velcro in this instance, to the Left.

Ayn Rand modeled Howard Roark after the unorthodox architect Frank Lloyd Wright, who felt quite at home with American anticommunists leaning to the left. Although Wright had never been expelled for an unwillingness to conform to traditional architectural styles as Roark had been, Wright, too, would have thumbed his nose at the dean who arrogantly informed Roark, "There's no place for originality in architecture." Wright and Roark upheld the preservation of individual rights and the maximization of choice, especially with respect to the freedom to pursue happiness as deemed personally appropriate.

Roark superseded Aristotle's "magnanimous man" and even Nietzsche's *Ubermensch* with respect to the degree of self-actualization achieved ("Frankly, my dear, I don't give a damn—except about me"). Roark would have had a difficult time fitting in with mere mortals. So frequently did Rand have the other characters refer to him as "a genius" that Gary Cooper found bonding with the audience nearly impossible.

American communists spent decades patiently infiltrating centers of democratic power; some supported Henry Wallace's 1948 presidential bid while others became entrenched within the ranks of the Democratic Party and/or organized labor. Like them, the opportunistic Ellsworth M. Toohey (Robert Douglas) conducted a long-term campaign to capitalize on the unrest already present among the readers of the *Banner*. Employing a time-honored capitalistic goal, the need to build circulation, as a ruse, Toohey used tried-and-true propaganda devices to malign Roark in the same way that American communists marshaled public support for Sacco and Vanzetti: snob appeal, scare tactics and sob stories.

Toohey's true mission, ominously foreshadowed in the line, "Nobody knows what I'm after but they will when the time comes" was not lost on Roark, who realized that the diminutive dilettante, swaggering and sucking on an extra-long cigarette holder, sought to thwart any ambition, initiative and incentive among the constituents of the architectural community. When the greedy and unprincipled Peter Keating (Kent Smith) confesses that Roark actually designed Courtland, Toohey gloats in his success at finally fashioning Keating into the "totally selfless man" (party loyalist). Toohey, particularly troubled by the unconventional Roark, rants, "Artistic value is achieved collectively, by each member subordinating himself to the will of the majority." After the Enright enterprise, Toohey intervenes to prevent Roark from winning lucrative contracts. Recognizing Roark's ability to creatively solve the economic problems plaguing the Courtland project, Toohey ensures that Roark's plans are seriously compromised, thus violating Roark's only condition for permitting Peter Keating to get credit for the design.

Rand created unforgettable archvillains, often giving them ignoble features and an ambiguous masculinity. Toohey's character was allegedly based on the acerbic Alexander Woollcott, who, according to King Vidor, "exercised a certain control [power] with his column and he had a certain dominant attitude about everything."[20] When a beaten-down Roark, viciously smeared by Toohey's "One Small Voice," which endlessly attacked individualism, was asked, "Why don't you tell me what you think of me?" Rand has Roark parrot the Objectivist Party line (actually quoting Rand's husband), "But I never think of you." This is one of those "so there!" lines that never quite achieve the desired effect in real life. Rand *always* thinks of those she despises, probably because Rand despises so many.

As unfettered by ends-means justification as most communists, Toohey admits, "Maybe I want to dishonor and discredit all greatness." He realizes a notable nemesis like Roark cannot be ruled by an interloper who weaseled his way into power. The leading architectural critic at the *Banner* proved himself the sort of parasite to which Roark refers in his courtroom summation, a man who creates nothing, capitalizing (no pun intended) instead on the work of other architects. Toohey sought to create a spiritual communism in which the individual is subordinated to the collective in every way conceivable, a form of social domination achieved through the tremendous power of numbers. "There are thousands against one," observes Toohey as he prepares to turn public opinion against Roark.

Like George Kennan, the architect of America's "containment policy," who hypothesized in a 1947 *Foreign Affairs* article that if the United States could merely contain Soviet expansion, the Soviet Union would self-destruct via economic over-extension in ten to fifteen years, Roark didn't feel compelled to actively fight Toohey. While the wall didn't fall until 1989, Kennan was ultimately vindicated; and Roark, like his skyscraper, rose over Toohey's defeat.

Rand's Objectivism would not permit Roark to operate out of altruism or fear. Unyielding as quarry marble, he chooses honest sweat, wielding a pneumatic drill, to the anxiety-induced compromise suggested by the weak-willed Peter Keating. Dominque, paranoid that the Enright House will prove Roark's undoing, is sent away, not for her own good but with the admonition, "You must learn not to be afraid of the world. You will come back to me when you've learned it."

Roark remained faithful to his ethical code in the same way that liberal intellectuals adhered to democratic principles while patiently resisting aggressive communist behavior. With $14.57 in his pocket and without a watch to mark the rapidly approaching eleventh hour, Roark noted the strings attached to the Security Bank of Manhattan Building commission, its final approval of design and building plans. Abruptly rejecting the deal, Roark explained that a building, like a man, must have integrity—there must be no compromises in artistic expression.

Roark's love-hate relationship with Dominique allows an exploration of the dynamic between liberals and former communists. Leftists remained curiously silent during the HUAC hearings of 1947, believing, like Roark, in giving individuals the freedom to make their own mistakes. These folks are bewildered to learn that former communists and fellow travelers, returning from self-imposed exiles abroad or forced to use "fronts" to work in this country, continue to rail against them for failing to speak up on their behalf.

THE RADICAL RIGHT ANTICOMMUNISTS

Contemporary right-wing intellectuals, like those holding forth during the 1940s, deny that conservatism is a neatly packaged ideology. It wasn't until Dewey's 1948 loss that the far Right embraced anticommunism as the vehicle to electoral and conceptual victory. William F. Buckley Jr.'s *National Review* would not give the Right a virile voice until 1956. Early conservatives, precariously perched to the left of far Right extremists such as Senator "Tail Gunner Joe" McCarthy, scapegoated liberalism, relentlessly resisting the political revolution ushered in by the New Deal.

Opposed to liberal internationalism in general, radical rightists overreacted against a specific enemy in each decade: (1) communist front organizations and Bolshevists supporting labor unrest in the 1920s; (2) advocates of the New Deal in the 1930s; (3) backers of a wartime alliance with the Soviet Union in the 1940s; and (4) those rumored to be subverting the U.S. government in the 1950s.

As our tolerance of communism ebbed and flowed, the radical rightists attempted to convince anyone who might listen that the American Communist Party was a danger in itself, not just as an agent of a foreign power contaminating the country with collectivist values, but because its goal was to impose Soviet-style government on the United States, which would destroy our traditional religious and patriotic values. This brand of anticommunist didn't think there was enough room in the United States for both communism and democracy.

Radical rightists maintained that the government was free to employ any means necessary to ferret out and lock up communists and their sympathizers who identified themselves as criminal conspirators by the clandestine nature of their activities. Their demand for domination would have never amounted to much had the invasion of South Korea on June 25, 1950, by North Korea not thrown the world in a state of emergency. McCarthy's addlepated accusations hit the Senate agenda at the same time Julius and Ethel Rosenberg were arrested for treason, and the United States seemed headed for a direct confrontation with the Soviet Union. Like Parnell Thomas, chairman of the 1947 HUAC, McCarthy gave the public an identifiable foe on which to focus during uncertain times.

Joseph R. McCarthy's name eventually became stigmatized and appended to the ignominious "ism" typifying all that was extreme and evil among the radical rightists. Richard Powers maintains that McCarthy's speech at the 1950 Lincoln Day dinner in Wheeling, West Virginia, "was, in retrospect, the greatest disaster in the disastrous history of American anticommunism."[21] During that address, McCarthy supposedly held "in his hand" a list of 205 communists (not even fellow travelers) securely entrenched in the State Department. Before tumbling off his pedestal, the most feared man in America had placed his indelible mark on radical rightism.

The American religious Right, celebrating God's existence and human spiritual redemption, still stands as a formidable natural enemy to communism. Ironically, the faith practiced in Rand's mother country, which she rejected along with communism, offered the only enduring organized Russian opposition to the Bolsheviks. From the time of Lenin through the Gorbachev era, Americans on the Right have vigorously defended religious freedom and church sovereignty. Nonetheless, influential Americans of faith and spiritual leaders opposed providing Soviet communists with military assistance, even in order to withstand Nazi invaders. Distrust of the Soviet Union was most vociferous among American Catholics. The Vatican had faithfully taken an anticommunist stance from the Bolshevik Revolution of 1917. In March 1937, Pope Pius XI issued an encyclical censuring Soviet atheism and forbidding Catholics to cooperate with communists, no matter how worthy the endeavor. Pope Pius XII proved at least as anticommunist as his predecessor, condemning both Nazism and communism, regarding the latter as an incomparable menace to religious liberty.

Vidor's resolute inclusion of religious imagery in *The Fountainhead* aside, Rand was particularly troubled by movie-goers who chose to view Roark as a profoundly religious man, presenting his courtroom summation as the basis for that conviction. In the introduction to the twenty-fifth anniversary printing of the novel, the ardent atheist, in listing possible *The Fountainhead* rewrites, mentions a

> possibly misleading sentence in Roark's speech, "From this simplest necessity to the highest religious abstraction, from the wheel to the skyscraper, everything we are and everything we have comes from a single attribute of man—the function of his reasoning mind." This could be misinterpreted to mean an endorsement of religion or religious ideas. I remember hesitating over that sentence, when I wrote it, and deciding that Roark's and my atheism, as well as the overall spirit of the book were so clearly established that no one would misunderstand it, particularly since I said the religious abstractions are the product of man's mind, not of supernatural revelation.[22]

Despite Rand's rejection of religion, Gail Wynand (Raymond Massey) is clearly a character on a spiritual quest. Like Senator McCarthy, Wynand sprouted from modest means, secured by austere adherence to the Puritan work ethic. Wynand floated out of a gutter in Hell's Kitchen on the newsprint pages of the *Banner*. Wynand initially seeks salvation by worshipping at the shrine of Dominique. In fact, in commissioning Roark to build her a rural residence, Wynand employs the term "temple" to describe the project. He then risks his beloved *Banner* in a crusade to extricate Roark from legal difficulties, trusting the sacrifice will lead to his redemption. After closing down the newspaper, Wynand resolves that instead of building the Wynand Building as a monument to himself, he will commission Roark to construct a memorial to spirit. Then he takes his life. So much for spirit.

The origins of McCarthy's anticommunism do little to explain his zealotry in the extreme. Working-class Irish commingled their Catholic faith and gung-ho patriotism into an idealistic yet self-assured Americanism. While Father Coughlin's diatribes broadcast against the empire most evil were wildly popular with these folk, few held significant qualms that communism, socialism or even liberalism would not ultimately prove doomed. During his 1946 campaign for the Senate, the opportunistic McCarthy echoed the GOP's attack on Truman (whose administration supposedly harbored communists) and began his practice of smearing opponents as "pinko." As a Senate freshman in 1947, he appeared in the media warning against the communist threat to world peace and dug in with such ardent anticommunists as J. Edgar Hoover, the Kennedys, and a Georgetown Jesuit, Father Edmund Walsh, in Washington.

McCarthy's red-baiting rhetoric for the Wheeling audience was contrived by *Washington Times-Herald* reporters Ed Nellow and George Waters, with *Chicago Tribune* writer Willard Edwards from HUAC communications, a Nixon speech on Alger Hiss and FBI reports to the Senate Judiciary Committee. There was, of course, no list of 205 names—indeed, the political fortune-hunter McCarthy, as Joseph N. Welch of the Army-McCarthy hearings surmised, had no shame. The Wheeling speech launched McCarthy's furious yet futile hamster wheel course, forcing him, then his defenders, to escalate their audacious and irresponsible claims and counter-claims. Truman summed up McCarthy's true impact on communism when he quipped to the press that McCarthy was the "Kremlin's greatest asset in America."[23]

It seemed, at least initially, that McCarthy succeeded in manipulating public opinion through intimidation and mendacity. Gail Wynand, the power-mad publisher of the *Banner* (a "fountainhead" of yellow journalism), also operated under the misapprehension that he could force the masses to submit to his dictates. The newspaper magnate's might, won by pandering to the public with columns such as Toohey's, was just as transient as McCarthy's. Wynand's failure to salvage the same man he once shattered was ascribed to the Objectivist dictum that one becomes the slave rather than the master of the masses. Toohey lectures Wynand that one "rules the mob only as long as he says what the collective wants him to say." On the other hand, Toohey triumphs over Wynand by hang-gliding on the winds of public opinion and patiently conducting a long-term campaign, like the American communists, to lay a foundation for his anti-individualism vision.

The brand of anticommunism that now carries McCarthy's name was evident long before "Tail Gunner Joe" became a household name. Conspiracy theorists started spinning their webs not long after the Bolshevik Revolution. In fact, Blair Coan, a former operative in the Justice Department during the Teapot Dome Scandal, pulled together evidence of Communist infiltration, supposedly disclosed by a Comintern source, as early as 1925. Using rather McCarthyesque rhetoric, he warned:

> The people of the United States, their government and their Presidents, since the war "to make the world safe for democracy" was fought, have been deliberately and unconscionably tricked by the mob-minded apostles of that very "democracy," aided, abetted, goaded and, in some instances, financed by the red oligarchy of Moscow and its American addicts and dupes.[24]

Congressman Hamilton Fish, a Democrat from New York, traveled to a dozen American cities chairing hearings on communist investigations from 1930 to 1931. He invited real and countersubversive-type experts on Russian and American communism to testify. Although Ayn Rand wouldn't make an appearance before HUAC hearings until October 20, 1947, her interest in Fish's activities would have been piqued by her lifelong abhorrence of communism. Rand first outlined a McCarthy-like character, Andrei Taganov, in her 1936 novel, We the Living, who would later be fleshed out as Gail Wynand, the miscreant manipulating the masses in The Fountainhead.

Film turns on visual shorthand. Vidor covers an entire wall of the Banner CEO's office with a map of the world, symbolizing Wynand's rather extravagant estimation of his import and potency. The dirty-dealing senator from Wisconsin also utilized the same sort of hyperbole while witch-hunting American communists. Gail Wynand, wheeling and dealing behind the guise of Fourth Estate, symbolizes the radical Right's opposition to communism. McCarthy, expanding 1947 HUAC Chairman Thomas's modus operandi, turned individuals, whether or not card-carrying members of the party, into faceless symbols he could berate, humiliate and eventually eliminate. Like McCarthy, Wynand, who informed Dominique that "there are no men of integrity," also projected his lack of integrity onto others.

Although Wynand believed every individual to be false, he discovered the exception that proves the rule in Roark. Just as McCarthy attempted to destroy General George C. Marshall, Wynand, bulldozed by Toohey, tried to break Roark. McCarthy aspired to demonize the man who served as commander of the American military in World War II, the former secretary of state and then-secretary of defense. On June 14, 1951, McCarthy took the floor of the Senate to proclaim Marshall a lifelong minion of the Soviet Union. Richard Powers described the speech, as "the red web thesis raised to the grandiose levels of cosmic madness."[25]

Wynand stands as the most tragic Randian figure, just stopping short, as he commits suicide, of deliverance. McCarthy also leaves little to pity, having exited the Senate in disgrace and lived out his few remaining years as an alcoholic. McCarthy led the anticommunist cause astray not just by assaulting communists, but by assailing the anticommunist Left. Like ultra-patriotic radical rightists, McCarthy felt free to release his full fury at the radical Left's seeming disloyalty. McCarthy's loathing of liberals, particularly Roosevelt, hinged more on a tradition of class envy than anything else. In addition, McCarthy had no love for the liberal elite, who he believed were bent on destroying the independence of the Catholic Church. Gail Wynand, who loathed Roark at first sight, was challenged by Roark's steadfast integrity, even in the face of great personal loss.

The "on again-off again" relationship between liberal intellectuals represented by Roark and radical rightists by Wynand proved tenuous at best, the only ties binding them being their belief in democratic principles and their joint revulsion for totalitarianism. Knowing Dominique had dynamited Roark's mutilated masterpiece, Wynand arrives at her hospital bedside to celebrate their three-way victory. Later in the 1950s, all strains of grass-roots American anticommunism would band together to ready global opposition to a militant and expansive communist movement.

FORMER COMMUNISTS AS ANTICOMMUNISTS

As a Russian refugee, Ayn Rand joined Sidney Hook (founder of the American Congress for Cultural Freedom), Eugene Lyons (author of a Stalin exposé), Isaac Don Levine (ghostwriter for defectors, spies and KGB agents), and Elizabeth Bentley (Hoover's prize informant) as former communists who were able to provide damning data attesting to communist subversion. Communist propaganda might have succeeded in concealing Lenin's and Stalin's heinous deeds from the Left but the disquieting truth was revealed to Americans on the rise in the American Communist Party hierarchy. Powers contends that the U.S. contingent as well as the various fronts became virtual schools for anticommunism, whose graduates, like recent religious converts, provided the most zealous challenge to the communists. Powers comments:

> If there is any truth in the old merchandising maxim that the best way to kill a bad product is with good advertising, the Communists' formidable public relations skills were killing communism. The more the Communists succeeded in attracting Americans to join their political and cultural campaigns, the more these erstwhile

communists and fellow travelers violently recoiled from them, bringing their experience to the anticommunist movement.[26]

Former American communists added their harrowing personal experiences to the intelligence already gathered by other adversaries of communism.

Ayn Rand was the product of a society lacking any sort of evolved notion of the individual, in fact, her Russian dictionary at that time contained no word for "privacy." The religious and political culture of the Soviet Union failed to recognize any semblance of the individual. She testified that communism defeated "the living" by embezzling the very qualities that made Russians human beings.

Her undiluted enmity for communism stayed with her for the rest of her life. In 1947, she served as a friendly witness to HUAC, instructing the committee members in methods of countering communist brainwashing. While a civil libertarian such as Rand would not normally aid a government agency engaging in HUAC-type prying, she simply couldn't resist the public forum.

Dominique Francon, Rand's alter ego, dispensed Objectivist dogma throughout *The Fountainhead*. Just as former communists were forced to confront the failures of their leaders once the excesses of Lenin and Stalin became common knowledge, Dominique turns her back on the prosperous world of her father once she understands the price tag is integrity. In choosing to write a small column, "Your House," for the *Banner*, Dominique attempts to isolate herself from the repressive culture of famous architects like her father. As a journalist, she could serve as a vocal conscience to the collectivists, pointing out when they missed the mark in their endeavor to squelch the new and the different.

Guy Francon owed his considerable financial success to churning out structures as similarly overhung with faux classic gingerbread as every other designer in demand. Dominique's betrothed procured a partnership in her father's firm by limiting himself, in her estimation, to being a "third rate architect." When Gail Wynand asks her to recommend a master builder for one of his projects, she informs him, "I have no desire to help Peter's career." In fact, she lost no sleep when her fiancé unceremoniously dumps her in a deal with Wynand to gain an architectural commission.

For Ayn Rand to choose the name Dominique (from the French for "of the Lord") for her female protagonist and *The Fountainhead* character most like herself is ironic, to say the least. However, as believers contend, it takes far more faith to assert that no God exists than to adopt the atheistic position, especially as noisily as Rand does. Furthermore, wasn't it Dominique who threw a three-dimensional likeness of a god down the airshaft because "it's the things we admire and want that bring us into submission"? Perhaps the lady doth protest too much.

Bear in mind, "dominus" also provides the Latin root for "dominate." Vidor cast the statuesque Patricia Neal, visualizing her playing the scene in which Dominique gazes down into the quarry at her quarry. Ayn Rand initially requested Greta Garbo for the part, who apparently rejected the idea. Neal was the better choice, memorably depicting the character who most mirrored Rand's need to physically bend another to her will.

The power struggle between Howard Roark and Dominique Francon also sheds some light on the love-hate relationship between liberal intellectuals and former communists. The sexual pheromones released by Roark's sweaty physique may have called out to Dominique at an elevated level of animal magnetism yet her glimpse into his highly developed intellect (revealed during an impromptu lecture on marble) is what allowed Roark to hold her in an amoristic half-nelson for the rest of the movie.

Similarly, intellectually honest American communists could no longer square rumored atrocities with idealistic principles; the bloom that had bathed communism-cum-egalitarianism in a romantic glow for American liberals was definitely off the Russian rose. Stalin was ultimately found responsible for exterminating tens of millions of peasants in the Ukraine and murdering or banishing millions more who, however remotely, threatened his power to Siberia. The Left, initially repulsed by the smugly self-satisfied financially secure, found out the hard way it was always a mistake to cooperate with communists, especially when they admitted Sacco and Vanzetti could do more for the cause dead than alive.

The audience in *The Fountainhead* was left to judge whether individualism rapes or enraptures. A late-night session in Dominique's bedroom allows for both smacks and smooches between Roark and Dominique before the demure fade-to-black. Rand's notes to director Vidor indicate that Roark "raped her because he knew she wanted it."[27] Little wonder the amorous feelings displayed by Patricia Neal and Gary Cooper appeared so genuine onscreen; they fell in love during the filming. King Vidor recollects witnessing their off-camera romance developing before his eyes, claiming the love affair positively influenced their performances: "When they looked at each other in the picture, it really meant something. It was very convincing."[28]

The Objectivist outlook concerning love and sex, as interpreted by Rand's former lover, psychologist Nathaniel Branden, makes connections between the conscious and subconscious, the mind and the body, as well as the material and spiritual. In *The Psychology of Romantic Love*, Branden outlines a middle ground between promiscuity and platonic love, defining sex as a distinctly human activity, neither exploitative nor submissive. Objectivist sex and love, on one hand, treat the self as an object worthy of desire and apprehension, while on the other, they require self-assertion, self-responsibility, self-respect and self-esteem, none of which are generated through sexual conquest. "To say I love you, one must first know how to say the I," Roark later instructs Dominique.

Why does Dominique leave Roark to wed Gail Wynand? She foreshadows her decision when she tells Wynand, "If I ever decide to punish myself for some terrible guilt, I'll marry you." Tying the knot with Roark's worst enemy enrolled Dominique at a university from which she graduated *summa cum laude*, after passing a final exam in Objectivism. Had Wynand realized, as Roark did, that only an offer of freedom could win Dominique, he might not have been forced to settle for such an empty conquest.

THE AUDIENCE RESPONDS

Although Vidor selectively remembers *The Fountainhead* as a popular movie, critics were not impressed with the cinematic treatment of Rand's philosophical novel. The stellar cast, headed by Gary Cooper, newcomer Patricia Neal and the ever-pernicious Raymond Massey, failed to suck the excess hot air out of Rand's long-winded script. Singling out the dialogue as unnecessarily complicated and preachy, Bosley Crowther of the *New York Times* wisecracked, "Wordy, involved and pretentious . . . and a more curious lot of high-priced twaddle we haven't seen for a long time. . . . *The Fountainhead* is a picture you didn't have to see to disbelieve."[29]

The reviewer from *Variety* was equally unenthusiastic: "It is a film with an idea and it clings to it with such complete tenacity that the end result is a cold, unemotional, loquacious feature."[30] Vidor's clever cutting, backed by a Max Steiner score, couldn't rehabilitate Rand's turgid scenes, which were grimly overacted. The result, according to Nora Sayre of the *New York Times*, "is a thrillingly bad movie."[31]

Viewers were jarred by the doctrine of selfishness preached by Ayn Rand, especially put off by the immorality of destroying another's property without moral justification or putting one's name on someone else's work. Whether Vidor did, in fact, violate the production code by allowing a crime to go unpunished in this film prompted serious inquiry by Warner Bros. Vidor didn't land in jail; however, Roark's winning an acquittal by elevating personal integrity above the law didn't wash with moviegoers, and Vidor was forced to defend Rand's ending despite his strenuous objections in later years.

The motivations of Rand's characters are not believable. While her philosophical premises may be provocative, her fictional arguments remain tautological. Since Objectivism permeates all her writing, Rand's characters can't be permitted to behave in a self-sacrificial manner. Peter Keating presents a perplexing plot problem when he begs Roark for his assistance with the Courtland project. Rand's solution is less than elegant; while Roark knows Keating is his only chance to bypass Toohey and the board of directors, his incentive, which derives from wanting to see a worthy public works project accomplished, has to be forced by Rand as induced by "loving the doing." Rand is more driven to make the point that art is an individual expression of genius untainted by mortal self-interest or earthly reward than to provide the audience with grounds for identification.

When Henry Cameron beseeches Roark to incinerate his papers after his demise, Cameron, in essence, selfishly destroys Roark's inheritance. The scene doesn't make sense. The spiritual battle, which has raged between collectivists and individualists for aeons, depends on both the torch and its passing. Honoring Cameron's request forces Roark, in essence, to extinguish the flame and like the Heaven's Gate cultists who enforced celibacy by castration, hampers the philosophy from attracting a great many adherents.

With communism looming large on the national agenda and the world at war for the second time, Hollywood storytellers followed *The Fountainhead* with even darker and more troubling fantasies of a praetorian world populated by cynical heroes and seductive heroines. Fifteen years after making *Our Daily Bread*, Vidor undertook the filming of *The Fountainhead*, which seemed so utterly and ideologically contrary to collectivism. How the same individual could direct two films pointing in such opposite political directions is enigmatic, yet the answer is simple. Americans perceive individualism as receptive to communal endeavors as long as "collective" is defined in terms of teamwork, specific individual effort rather than abstract societal movement.

Whether you argue that art reflects life or the reverse, these two movies, *The Fountainhead* and *Daily Bread*, with their polar points of view illustrate the ambiguity America employs in pondering political matters. Rand's Objectivist philosophy veers too far to the libertarian Right (espousing an extreme individualism) to recommend it. Vidor, who eschews dichotomy, broaches the extremes in an attempt to affirm the center. He counterbalances collectivist images with Rand's egoist words in much the same way that American political thought is better conceived in terms of a spectrum rather than a duality. Just as contemporary congressional legislation has only to tout itself as bipartisan to win the approval of the public, we are learning that most weighty matters rarely reduce to either/or issues. If genius is supposedly the ability to hold two contrary thoughts in one's mind simultaneously, then America must be a nation of superior intellects. Of course it is.

NOTES

1. Quoted in Chris Matthew Sciabara, *Ayn Rand: The Russian Radical* (University Park: Pennsylvania State University Press, 1995), 1.

2. Including the penchant of Rand's heroines for rough and explosive sex, unsupported as an integral component of her philosophy.

3. Gary Kamiya, executive editor of *Salon Internet* (http://www.salonmagazine.com), "Book Review," *Los Angeles Times* (January 4, 1998), 10.

4. See Barbara Branden's *The Passion of Ayn Rand* (Garden City, NY: Doubleday, 1986); and Rand's introduction to the twenty-fifth anniversary edition of *The Fountainhead* (New York: Penguin, 1968).

5. For Rand's defense of capitalism, see her collection of essays, *Capitalism: The Unknown Ideal* (New York: New American Library, 1967).

6. N. O. Lossky, *History of Russian Philosophy* (New York: International Universities, 1951), 41.

7. Ayn Rand, *The Fountainhead* (New York: Penguin, 1968), vii. Twenty-fifth anniversary edition.

8. Kamiya, "Book Review," 10.

9. Throughout the 1940s, Rand wrote several screenplays, including the film version of *The Fountainhead, You Came Along* starring Robert Cummings and Lizabeth Scott, and *Love Letters* with Jennifer Jones and Joseph Cotten.

10. Clark Gable or Humphrey Bogart would have been much more believable as the arrogantly self-actualized Howard Roark.

11. Wright's 1930 vision of Broadacre City mirrors the thinking principles espoused by nineteenth-century Transcendentalists much admired by King Vidor.

12. Dowd and Shepard, interview by Nancy Dowd and David Shepherd in *King Vidor, Directors Guild of America (DGA) Oral History* (Metuchen, NJ: Scarecrow Press, 1988), 235.

13. Ibid., 227.

14. Ibid., 232.

15. Durgnat and Simmon, 268.

16. Ibid., 263.

17. Quoted in Richard Gid Powers, *Not without Honor: The History of American Anticommunism* (New York: Free Press, 1995), 198.

18. George F. Kennan, *Russia and the West* (New York: New American Library, 1960), 11. Emphasis added in original.

19. *Mission to Moscow* remained the single film conforming to official communist ideology. Made during wartime to glorify America's Russian ally, *Mission to Moscow*, a film with poor production values, was based on Ambassador Joseph Davies's book of his experiences in Russia during the late 1930s. Roosevelt sent Davies to assess the Soviet willingness to fight and he learned that there is little difference between Soviets and Americans on a personal level. Ayn Rand felt

MGM's *Song of Russia*, portraying Soviet children laughing and playing, qualified as propaganda.

20. Dowd and Shepard, *King Vidor*, 237.

21. Powers, *Not without Honor*, 235.

22. Rand, *The Fountainhead*, viii.

23. Powers, *Not without Honor*, 242.

24. Blair Coan, *The Red Web* (Belmont, MA: Americanist Classics, 1925), viii, ix.

25. Powers, *Not without Honor*, 244.

26. Ibid., 115.

27. Quoted in Durgnat and Simmon, *King Vidor, Directors Guild of America (DGA) Oral History*, 265.

28. Dowd and Shepard, *King Vidor*, 236.

29. Nathaniel Braden, *The Psychology of Romantic Love* (New York: Bantam, 1980). Bosley Crowther, *New York Times* (July 9, 1949), 3.

30. "The Fountainhead," *Variety* (June 29, 1949), 14.

31. Nora Sayre, "Silents and Talkies by King Vidor for the Centennial of his Birth," *New York Times* (February 11, 1994), C7.

Jimmy Stewart observing the young boy reading the Gettysburg Address aloud to his grandfather from the wall of the Lincoln Memorial. Courtesy of the Academy of Motion Picture Arts and Sciences.

Chapter Ten

Conclusion

Beverly Merrill Kelley

What relevance do movies documenting a bygone era in American history have today? Contemporary film protagonists caught in the backwash at the end of the Cold War seem to be slipping behind the megaforce of special effects or are relegated to playing anti-heroes as quirky and loathsome as Jack Nicholson's misanthrope in *As Good as It Gets*. Today's movie protagonists, mirroring the prevailing Generation X individualistic orientation, are mostly pessimistic loners. What a contrast to the "let's-stay-up-all-night-and-write-a-bill" teamwork of Jefferson Smith and Clarissa Saunders or the ebullient collaborative appeal John Sims uses to inflame his fellow farmers.

Yet Lesley Poles Hartley tells us in the prologue to *The Go-Between* that "the past is a foreign country and they do things differently there." As we look back on the films of the 1930s and 1940s, we may find their corny sentimentality a bit off-putting but cannot disregard the attraction we feel, despite affecting the sophisticated veneer of the 1990s, to healthy portions of unadulterated American spirit, which are cinematically embodied in the little guy who stands heroically tall as he strives for the ultimate good of the community.

As Jacques Barzun reminds us in *God's Country and Mine*, anyone wanting to know the heart and mind of America had better learn baseball, especially as played by high school students or small-town teams. Our nation's pastime provides the consummate metaphor for a country in which each player must succeed as an individual for the team to prevail. Baseball rewards personal achievement with a champion's laurel, while sometimes entreating a sacrificial offering, allowing someone else to be commended for the winning score. The objective remains, in the long run, to return home. Small towns across the nation, populated by real-life Smiths and Ambersons, Kanes and Sims, continue to authenticate the way in which our citizens handle one of the defining characteristics of democracy, the tension between individual and community.

The dicey dichotomy between singular and collective persists in our technology-driven, globalized, post-industrial society for good reason. Oppositional points of view, which enhance the pluralistic goal of democracy, will continue to compete in the public square just as they did between 1929 and 1950. At the present time, the *e pluribus unum* folk at one end of the political spectrum mourn the tragedy of educators no longer inculcating American values, while at the other, multiculturalists, arguing for empowerment, celebrate salad bowl individualism.

In the 1930s and 1940s, however, when a dispirited nation needed cheering, the movie industry abandoned its offensive against traditional values and began pouring rugged individualism into new bottles labeled "one for all and all for one." The studios engaged America's ardor for the simpler lifestyle extolled at the beginning of *The Magnificent Ambersons*, when life had not yet been scrambled by the baffling complexities of war, industrialization and economic blight. Like the mood of national politics, 1930s and 1940s films reflected the abrupt transition from the midnight of Hoover's gloom to the daybreak of FDR's Pollyannaism.

Like the Swede in *Our Daily Bread* who admits, "I don't even know what those words [*isms*] mean," many Americans refuse to encumber themselves with political labels, content to remain simultaneously fragmented yet somehow united by a fundamental essence they can't quite define but, like obscenity, readily recognize.

In his revisionist biography, *Frank Capra: The Catastrophe of Success*, Joseph McBride asserts that Capra espoused communism, fascism, Marxism, populism, conservatism, McCarthyism, New Dealism, jingoism, socialism and capitalism at various points in his film career.[1] Attributing this tangle of ideologies to a clash between rigid Capra conservatism and his liberal screenwriters (as McBride contends) isn't as credible as maintaining that Capra, like the majority of Americans, momentarily entertained all sorts of notions before returning to the spirit Jefferson Smith attempts to articulate in telling Clarissa Saunders:

Boys forget what their country means—just reading "land of the free" in history books. And they get to be men and they forget even more. Liberty is too precious to be buried in books, Miss Saunders. Men ought to hold it up in front of them every day of their lives and say, "I am free—to think—to speak. My ancestors couldn't. I can. My children will."

Furthermore, Capra's nostalgic montage of monuments served as a better vehicle for driving this abstraction home then any thousand words of dialogue.

James Madison's dirty little secret was that the Constitution and pure democratic principles are inherently inconsistent. Despite supposedly seating power in the people, the Founding Fathers feared that the populace might be persuaded by some silver-tongued demagogue's rhetoric just because he expressed the popular will or mimicked the national sentiment. The framers neglected to mention that America was actually a republic and the documents they wrote provided a necessary if not perpetual brake on true popular participation.

However, one wonders when film-goers will finally revolt against seeing themselves endlessly portrayed—nowhere better illustrated than the recent *Wag the Dog*—as the mindless masses or ignorant plebiscite. Back in 1939, the political machine in *Mr. Smith* dupes citizens by clogging the print communication channel between the senator and his uneasy constituents. Whether the voters heed Smith's wakeup call is uncertain; Capra ends his movie without resolving the plot.

Although we will continue to dispute *who* we are, the advent of film permitted us to visualize *what* we are. This medium was the first to translate, however loosely, a transcendent and homogeneous collective unconscious, which has been sporadically characterized as the American "can-do" attitude: No obstacle is considered too immense, no challenge too vast, no goal too distant or sacrifice too weighty, and never more aptly realized than in one of Vidor's or Capra's films.

The ten million jobless during the Depression could laugh through their tears even if that meant squandering twenty-five cents to escape their cares. Movies dominated popular culture at the time a quarter bought a ticket to a double feature, a couple of cartoons and a newsreel. The Supreme Court had yet to dismantle the studio system, which held sway from shooting to showing, and television would not end Hollywood's grip on pop culture until the mid-1950s. At their 1940s peak, a mere eight dream factories released more than 400 pictures a year and the nation's moviegoers purchased nearly 90 million tickets per week.[2] While the ideological impact of a single film may be negligible, nevertheless, each frame remains a tangible reflection of who we are and what we believe.

Movies provide a circular cultural flow; viewers are influenced by the story at the same time screenwriters respond not only to mass trends but also to the realization that they cannot overturn the prevailing social consensus if they wish to become richly remunerated. Rivaling politicians as barometers of public attitudes, filmmakers understand only a narrow window for significant cultural initiative exists. When the final credits roll, the crowd exercises the lion's share of control over the content by purchasing the commodity of entertainment.

Hollywood is in the business of producing fantasy. Its task is to ascertain the longings and ambitions of the audience, reducing them to a formula and then repeating the formula in picture after picture, a prosperous practice providing a role model for its more prodigious stepchild, television.

Studio heads rarely harbor furtive cravings to serve as social revolutionaries. They are, instead, opportunistic entrepreneurs who, in the 1930s, discovered that a postwar generation, bored with causes and convention, was ripe for a glimpse into the glittering world gossiped about in newspaper columns.

Postmaster General Will Hays, a prominent Republican and Presbyterian elder, drafted by movie moguls to police the sex and violence excesses that sold tickets, bragged in 1934,

> No medium has contributed more greatly than the film to the maintenance of the national morale during a period featured by revolution, riot, and political turmoil in other countries. It has been the mission of the screen, without ignoring the serious social problems of the day, to reflect aspiration, optimism, and kindly humor in its entertainment.[3]

He was more right than he realized. Depression audiences demanded glitz and glamour; the grim reality of films like *Our Daily Bread* simply didn't "pack 'em in" during that decade.

The 1920s through 1940s were bookended by two world wars, with the Great Depression taking up the bulk of the middle. Prior to the fall of 1929, life was propelled by a stream of new technology, government became increasingly irrelevant (if not highly suspect), and the national culture cleaved between prohibitionists and pleasure-seekers. The 1921 collapse of agricultural prices and structural unemployment due to mechanization were assumed aberrations rather than harbingers of impending doom. Postwar factories, with more efficient management, intensive research and ingenious sales methods, nearly doubled industrial production. National income soared from $480 in 1900 to $681 per capita in 1929.[4] Calvin Coolidge and Herbert Hoover donned rose-colored spectacles to preach about the end to poverty. Except for the occasional psychic, nobody envisioned the economic avalanche that would bury shortsighted risk-takers and old money alike, not to mention the full-fledged global depression, a political upheaval and a second world war even more monstrous than the first.

In the 150 years following the signing of the Declaration of Independence, despite a number of financial reverses and economic recessions, an insistence by the American dreamers that any impediment to the pursuit of happiness could be overcome remained cheerfully and confidently intact until October 29, 1929. The stock market crash and ensuing Depression proved a defining experience for every survivor, whether rich or poor, urban or rural, black or white. They also began a critical period during which the country poised between coalescing as a community or being permanently ripped apart.

For the first time, the national psyche was sent careening toward alien political ideologies. By 1931, it became transparent to everyone but President Hoover that the economy was not just experiencing a routine downturn; Marxist prophesy (that capitalism, driven by the corporate profit motive, was by nature unsound) seemed to be coming true. In 1933, the Hays Office, whose predominant purpose was to stave off state and federal control of the film industry, became involved with the production of the politically provocative *Gabriel over the White House. The Nation*'s William Troy feared that the motion picture, bearing the hamhanded William Randolph Hearst touch, might "convert innocent American movie audiences to a policy of fascist dictatorship in this country."[5]

This era was also marked by a renewed fervency for community values. Strengthened family order transformed private life. Americans rediscovered the merits of unity, sacrifice, teamwork and social discipline as they simultaneously lost patience with self-oriented behavior, impotent traditions and a splintering culture. Government was deputized to enforce the swing of the pendulum away from individualism, a word coined and used by de Tocqueville in *Democracy in America*, with new publicly financed institutions, novel economic proposals, atypical political alliances and unique global treaties. The local theaters responded by projecting exactly what the public wanted—images of the ritzy well-to-do, fatuous shysters and inept politicians—as well as halving admission prices and offering attendance incentives from china to bicycles to silk stockings. When the banks closed down for four days in March 1933, neighborhood theaters honored personal promissory notes and accepted payments (chickens, fruit, and other edibles) in kind.

By the mid-1930s, America was awash in the political revolution known as the New Deal. To the strains of "Happy Days Are Here Again," Franklin D. Roosevelt, whose watch extended from 1933 to 1945, linked pragmatism with reviving the American spirit. Instead of tolerating diversity, he cultivated consensus. Deliberately invoking individual/community dualism, he reaffirmed the existence of "we, the people" in order to reconstitute trust in government. In fact, his March 1933 Inaugural censured a "generation of self-seekers" while plugging unity and confidence to fight a common foe: "The only thing we have to fear is fear itself."

FDR didn't wheedle voters with promises of minimal sacrifice; he summoned them with "no pain, no gain"-like admonitions and commanded every available resource for community survival. Similarly, Frank Capra elevated characters like Jefferson Smith, gifted only with common sense and homespun virtues; the disarmingly honest senator's victory over his political enemies echoed the country's mastery of the Depression.

The newly inaugurated Judd Hammond in *Gabriel over the White House* makes this promise with fingers crossed: "America will weather this [unemployment and racketeering] through the spirit of Valley Forge and Gettysburg." Prior to the 1930s, the American ethos existed in stock oratorical phrases such as Hammond's; the cinema gave it flesh and blood representation. Via metaphorical reduction, cinematic characters physicalized the "we, the people" esprit.

An alliance between Washington and Hollywood, initially established during FDR's first term, harnessed the propagandistic potential of cinema by enlisting Hollywood in America's war effort. The thirty-second president seemed to possess an unprecedented instinct for exploiting its promise for persuasion. It was no accident that New Deal make-work endeavors such as the Federal Theater Project subsidized filmmakers.

By 1939, a new sense of urgency swept the country: Hitler was on the march in Europe while across the Pacific, Japan was invading China. Roosevelt set out to muster support for the Allies. At the end of the New Deal, capitalism remained undiminished yet enough largess had been distributed to make Roosevelt a hero to millions. By 1941, Germany had invaded Soviet Russia and the American Communist Party changed its tune, at least the words, by rechristening the Allied-Axis imperialist conflict "a people's war against fascism."

Pearl Harbor redirected the new national unity overseas, enjoining our youth to exchange their Civilian Conservation Corps (CCC) uniforms for GI garb. The government met little resistance in imposing heavy burdens on both battlefield and homefront participants as the American work force, on the payroll once again, began to build weapons of mass destruction, motivated by the desire to secure a lasting victory.

By 1941, the domestic scene was bathed in rosy tones: Unemployment hit single digits, crime was down and FDR's policies restored faith in government. Instead of flirting with alternative philosophies, we focused on enemies of democracy in strictly moral terms, refusing to compromise with the twin evils incarnate, Hitler and Mussolini. The communist-riddled Hollywood Anti-Nazi League went to town in Tinseltown and movies with antifascist themes such as *Citizen Kane* became increasingly prevalent. The Roosevelt administration established a Bureau of Motion Pictures, which requested that every producer respond to the prime directive, "Will this picture help win the war?"

American foreign policy fluctuated from an isolationist stance adopted after fighting the "war to end all wars" to an interventionist response brought on by intensifying pressures to vanquish the international bullies wearing various visages of totalitarianism. Isolationism impelled by economic frustrations was initially illustrated by the social anomie and alienation depicted in Vidor's *The Crowd*, followed by the desperation and despondency in his sequel, *Our Daily Bread*.

Even though the veterans of World War I had been home for a dozen years, the powerful "futility of war" message in *All Quiet on the Western Front*, emblematic of dominant isolationist and pacifist impulses, kept America out of foreign conflicts until December 7, 1941. Anti-interventionists, mainly from the Right, found themselves linking arms with the anticommunist folk during this period. Currently, America seems to be sliding into a neo-isolationism, probably because generations born since Pearl Harbor lack the memory or experience of isolationism's liabilities and have allowed the acrid aftertaste of military defeat to linger.

Casablanca had its premiere on Thanksgiving Day, 1942, only nineteen days after U.S. forces landed at the Moroccan city in the first direct American strike against the Nazis. The original play, *Everyone Comes to Rick's*, written by Murray Burnett, was antifascist yet hardly pro-war. Warner Bros. employed the leftist screenwriter Howard Koch to give Rick a political conscience and help him perceive the folly of America's prewar isolationism in a manner parallel to the response of a jilted and jaded lover who crosses paths once again with his inamorata.

With Roosevelt's death and the advent of the Cold War, anticommunism began to enjoy fresh credibility in light of Stalin's empire-building, the rise of communist China and domestic spy scandals. While the seductiveness of communism originated in the economic and spiritual wreckage wrought by the Depression, the 1930s were largely a period of political incoherence for Hollywood radicals. The powers-that-be in the motion picture industry, a trade that amalgamates art and commerce, remained unconvinced that spotlighting politics either to the Right or to the Left paid off at the ticket counter.

HUAC communist-hunters in the late 1940s and Senator Joseph McCarthy in the early 1950s submitted the federal government, academia, the Army and mass media to scrutiny, with Hollywood providing the most visible bull's-eye. While the initial hearings in 1947 called for an investigation of communism in the movies, the committee actually targeted the movie-makers.

The Hollywood blacklist is now almost as legendary as the cinematic output during that period. Later features such as *The Front* and *Guilty by Suspicion* documented a sorry narrative of loyalty oaths, political repression, unjust treatment, crushed careers and copies of the First Amendment sailing out of HUAC windows.

It's not surprising that the 1947 committee and its successors failed to establish that communist propaganda had ever been injected into a Hollywood film, including previous propaganda, *Mission to Moscow* or *Song of Russia*, meant to extol the antifascism of America's Russian allies. American cinema never successfully marketed either the fascist ideology or the political and economic principles of communism, both of which translate into lousy box office. Furthermore, the people of the United States, as a matter of course, distrust grand ideas and idealistic schemes.

The irony is that Hollywood itself was built on a failed Christian utopia founded by Horace Henderson Wilcox and his wife, Daeida. They purchased a 120-acre parcel fragrant with orange blossoms, jasmine and eucalyptus eight miles northwest of Los Angeles, now dominated by larger-than-life letters that make up the Hollywood sign.

Americans contend there is more than one way to make the world a better place. An inflexible insistence on the rightness of one's "big idea" may, in the case of a Lenin or a Hitler, shift the course of history in a negative direction. Communist regimes have sounded the death knell for more than 90 million people in this century, including 65 million in China and 20 million in the former Soviet Union, while Hitler's Germany ranks second or third in total genocide.[6]

Those who aspire to straighten the crooked timber of humanity find themselves stopped cold by the demand to exclude rival theories. The fact that totalitarianism united the Right and Left in this country against the powerful allure of its claims gives new meaning to "strange bedfellows." The Depression may have shaken American confidence in elitism as well as our economic and political foundations but few were sold on fascism even when dressed up as benevolently as the Angel Gabriel. Likewise, communism failed to sell even while operating under the guise of a farming commune or labor activism.

In King Vidor, we find individualism stretching to include a singular as well as a collective response to solving economic enigmas. Free-market capitalism failed in 1934. While the New Deal fell considerably short of socialism or communism, Vidor's *Our Daily Bread* demonstrated the charm of collectivist schemes during a period of chaos and confusion. Fifteen years after producing *Our Daily Bread*, Vidor embraced Ayn Rand's ode to libertarianism, *The Fountainhead*, an antithesis of the agrarian communal society featured in *Our Daily Bread*. Like Capra, Vidor could simultaneously hold contradictory notions in tension via the elastic language of the cinema. Just as Rand made anti-dualism work in objectivism, the permeable medium of film indulges symbols with multiple meanings, including the visualization of dichotomies. Continental "isms" disappoint when attempting to accurately define and contain the American understanding of politics. That doesn't blot out their relevance; it points to the necessity for these ideologies to be reconfigured into a generic American view if they are to merit consideration.

America's best hope rests in the continued evolution of a terminology that not only regards labels as pointless but proves capable of pragmatic shape-shifting. What is required is a medium that backs away from black-and-white formulation while promoting the mixing and matching of pigments from an ever-expansive political palette. What methodology might allow the mirroring of political realities such as the recently published UCLA study finding college freshmen less willing to identify themselves as Republican or Democrats, with some 55 percent of university students calling themselves "middle of the road," the highest such mark in a decade?[7] How about checking what's playing at the neighborhood multiplex?

Film not only provides a looking glass that reflects political reality but also functions as an X-ray, permitting us to see beneath the artificial categories we impose but disallowing a clarity we had hoped for. It is imparative to note that ideological window panes are sticky with the fingerprints of those who would hardsell a one-size-fits-all view of the world.

The major value of the film study is the provision of an unconventional venue for analysis. Summarily dismissed by highbrow culture as well as the academy until the 1960s, cinematic studies have now earned a modicum of respect, but the potential for academic analysis in general and political investigation in particular has remained undeveloped. Instead of lamenting the paucity of ideological features, scholars armed with the ability to decode could be met with a superabundance of material, available at any local theater or video store. Analysis, however, must proceed through a glass darkly, so to speak. To assail filmmakers for neglecting political persuasion is nonproductive. Demanding more message films clearly violates Hollywood's bottom line philosophy. Stated simply, didacticism doesn't sell. Americans expect, first and foremost, movies to entertain.

Furthermore, political analysts must redefine their theories, the boundaries of which, at least in this country, seem so confused that any filmmaker who heeded the call of academe and attempted to teach a cinematic civics lesson would be engaged in an exercise in futility. American audiences would not only stay away in droves but those who did plunk down the price of admission would leave feeling cheated as well as not the least bit entertained.

Yet it is precisely because movies reflect indirectly that their use as a primary source for studying American politics becomes so valuable. *Casablanca* succeeded as good entertainment, not to mention effective propaganda, because of its unique combination of identification, ideology and dialectic. Fantasy themes such as "land of opportunity" (*The Fountainhead*), "good will toward men" (*Gabriel over the White House* and its polar opposite, *Citizen Kane*), "simple life" (*The Magnificent Ambersons, Our*

Daily Bread and *All Quiet on the Western Front*) and "log cabin to White House" (*Mr. Smith Goes to Washington*) were symbols that already held meaning in the American subconscious, a reality hardly lost on Presidents Franklin D. Roosevelt and Harry S. Truman. These two presidents advanced their rhetorical visions (New Deal and Fair Deal) by employing the silver screen and its seductive images. Political persuasion, which requires creative coalition-building, flourishes with the ambiguous appeals found in film.

Movies give us access to the unintentional, rather like moving the focal point from the well-lighted center to the foggy, yet consequential periphery. While *The Fountainhead* is ostensibly a vehicle for Objectivism, Ayn Rand's characters inadvertently embodied the various voices of anticommunism struggling to be heard throughout the 1940s and 1950s. *Kane*, the unflattering portrait of a fascist who poses as an ordinary citizen, also casts back the character of Orson Welles.

Would an off-kilter locus permit us a glance behind to spy ahead? Despite a robust national economy and a stratospherically soaring stock market, most Americans remain troubled about the direction of the country and deeply apprehensive about the federal government's ability to solve the problems of deepest concern.[8] Disquieted by the insufficiency of morality these days, we cherish our freedoms but recognize that liberty must be tempered by personal responsibility.[9] We are enchanted by assertions that family, even in a mobile society, should be paramount, spirituality essential, and despite the fact that Tocqueville never said it, this country is great because this country is good. We realize the political process is currently hog-tied by a dependence on special-interest capital and our preoccupation with the personal weaknesses of politicians distracts us from addressing endemic corruption. Conventional wisdom tells us that real reform originating from elected officials is a pipe dream rivaling Hollywood's best efforts.

If you buy William Strauss and Neil Howe's thesis that around the year 2005, American will embark on a "fourth turning" parallel to events that unfolded during the 1930s and 1940s, you may want to re-examine the cinematic documentation provided by Capra, Welles, La Cava, Curtiz, Milestone and Vidor for a handy post-millennial forecast.

Although twenty-first-century America might seem more affluent, diverse and technologically evolved than the society devastated by the stock market crash of 1929, Strauss and Howe, who gave us best-sellers *Generations* and *13th-GEN*, foresee a national crisis playing out in any number of surreal scenarios. As they look into their crystal ball they envision America's former civic order,

> ruined beyond repair. People will feel like a magnet has passed
> over society's disk drive, blanking out the social contract, wiping

out old deals, clearing the books of vast unpayable promises to which people had once felt entitled. The economy could reach a trough that may look to be the start of a depression. With American weaknesses newly exposed, foreign dangers could erupt.[10]

Sound familiar?

You've already taken a Strauss and Howe-type excursion "back to the future," through the eight old-fashioned flicks presented in this book. Those who choose to prophesy are presently protected by time. Strauss and Howe might eventually turn out to be prognostically-challenged, however, as George Santayana reminds us, "those who cannot remember the past are condemned to repeat it." The lessons laid out in these eight classic films will prove more relevant than first realized.

The problem with the future is that we can't elude it, the problem with the present is that we can't preserve it and the problem with the past is that we can't concur about it. With cinematic images, we share common ground. At least film provides a new language that we can use to discover, discuss and dream about politics, American-style.

Finally, who says academic inquiry has to be arduous and agonizing? Please pass the popcorn.

NOTES

1. Joseph McBride, *Frank Capra: The Catastrophe of Success* (New York: Simon and Schuster, 1993).

2. In 1997 figures, 270 releases with the sale of 25 million tickets per week, the current population is twice what it was in the 1940s. Colin Shindler, *Hollywood in Crisis: Cinema and American Society, 1929–1939* (London: Routledge, 1996), 213.

3. Steven Mintz and Randy Roberts, editors, *Hollywood's America: United States History Through Its Films* (St. James, NY: Brandywine Press, 1993), 92.

4. Shindler, *Hollywood in Crisis*, 7.

5. William Troy, *The Nation* (April 26, 1933).

6. Quoted by James P. Pinkerton, "Macro or Micro, Socialism Is a Bad Idea," *Los Angeles Times* (January 15, 1998), B15.

7. Tom Kisken, "Apathy Rising Fast," *Ventura County Star* (January 13, 1998), 1.

8. According to an August 1997 *Washington Post*-ABC News poll. Richard Morin, "Poll Finds Wide Pessimism About Direction of Nation," *Washington Post* (August 29, 1997), 28.

9. According to a *Los Angeles Times* poll, 77 percent of the populace doesn't think this is a moral nation. Daryl Kelley, "Venture County Leans Toward Political Center," *Los Angeles Times* (October 12, 1997), 1.

10. William Strauss and Neil Howe, *The Fourth Turning: An American Prophesy* (New York: Broadway Books, 1997).

Selected Bibliography

Abbott, George, Maxwell Anderson, and Dell Andrews. "All Quiet on the Western Front." In *Best American Screenplays*, edited by Thomas Sam. New York: Crown, 1986.

Allen, Robert C., and Douglas Gomery. *Film History: Theory and Practice*. New York: McGraw-Hill, 1985.

Alpers, Benjamin Leontief. "Understanding Dictatorship and Defining Democracy in American Public Culture, 1930–1945." Ph.D. dissertation, Princeton University, 1994.

American Film Institute. "Frank Capra: One Man—One Film." In *Frank Capra*, edited by Richard Glatzer and John Raeburn. East Lansing: University of Michigan Press, 1974.

Baker, C. R., and R. W. Last. *Erich Maria Remarque*. Lanham, MD: Barnes & Noble Books-Imports, 1979.

Bakewell, W. *Hollywood Be Thy Name*. New York: Methuen Publishers, 1991.

Balio, Tino, ed. *History of the American Cinema*. Vol. 5. *Grand Design: Hollywood as a Modern Business Enterprise*. New York: Charles Scribner's Sons, 1993.

Bance, A. F. "*Im Westen nichts Neues*: A Bestseller in Cultural Context." *Modern Language Review* 72 (April 1977), 359–73.

Basinger, Jeanine. *The World War II Combat Film: Anatomy of a Genre*. New York: Columbia University Press, 1986.

Bell, Jeffrey. *Populism and Elitism: Politics in the Age of Equality*. Washington, DC: Regnery Gateway, 1992.

Bergman, Andrew. *We're in the Money: Depression America and Its Films*. New York: New York University Press, 1971.

Bernstein, Matthew. *Walter Wanger, Hollywood Independent*. Berkeley: University of California Press, 1994.

Berson, Arnold. "Erich Maria Remarque." *Films in Review* 45 (September/October 1994), 28–35.

Bogdanovich, Peter. "The Kane Mutiny." *Esquire* (October 1972), 99–105, 180–90.

Bogdauer, Vernon, ed. *Blackwell Encyclopedia of Political Science*. Oxford, England: Blackwell Publications, 1991.

Boller, Paul F., Jr., and Ronald L. Davis. *Hollywood Anecdotes*. New York: Ballantine, 1987.

Braden, Nathaniel. *The Psychology of Romantic Love*. New York: Bantam, 1980.

Brownstein, Ronald. *The Power and the Glitter: The Hollywood-Washington Connection*. New York: Vintage, 1992; Pantheon, 1990.

Butler, Ivan. *The War Film*. New York: A. S. Barnes, 1974.

Capra, Frank. *The Name above the Title*. New York: Bantam Books, 1972.

Carnes, Mark C., ed. *Past Imperfect: History According to the Movies*. New York: Henry Holt, 1995.

Carringer, Robert L. *The Making of Citizen Kane*, rev. ed. Berkeley: University of California Press, 1996 (1985).

Chalmers, John Whiteclay, II. "All Quiet on the Western Front (1930): The Antiwar Film and the Image of the First World War." *Historical Journal of Film, Radio and Television* 14 (1994), 4.

Christensen, Terry. *Reel Politics: American Political Movies from Birth of a Nation to Platoon*. New York: Basil Blackwell, 1987.

Clanton, Gene. *Populism: The Human Preference in America 1890–1900*. Boston: Twayne, 1991.

Coan, Blair. *The Red Web*. Belmont, MA: Americanist Classics, 1925.

Cragan, John, and Don Shields. *Applied Communication Research*. Prospect Heights, IL: Waveland Press, 1981.

Creel, George. *How We Advertised America: The First Telling of the Amazing Story of the Committee on Public Information That Carried the Gospel of Americanism to Every Corner of the Globe*. New York: Harper and Brothers, 1920.

Crowther, Bosley. *Hollywood Rajah*. New York: Henry Holt, 1960.

Crowther, Bruce. *Hollywood Faction: Reality and Myth in the Movies*. London: Columbus Books, 1984.

Cutts, John. "All Quiet on the Western Front." *Films and Filming* 9 (April 1963), 565–58.

Diggins, John P. *Mussolini and Fascism: The View from America*. Princeton, NJ: Princeton Press, 1972.

Dowd, Nancy, and David Shepard. *King Vidor: A Directors Guild of America Oral History*. Metuchen, NJ: Scarecrow Press, 1988.

Drinkwater, John. *The Life and Adventures of Carl Laemmle*. New York: William Heinemann, 1931.

Durgnat, Raymond, and Scott Simmon. *King Vidor, American*. Berkeley: University of California Press, 1988.

Edmonds, I. G. *Big U: Universal in the Silent Days*. New York: A. S. Barnes, 1977.

Eksteins, Modris. "War, Memory and Politics: The Fate of the Film *All Quiet on the Western Front*." *Central European History* 13 (March 1980), 60–82.

———. "*All Quiet on the Western Front* and the Fate of a War." *Journal of Contemporary History* 15:2 (April 1980), 345–66.

———. *Rites of Spring: The Great War and the Birth of the Modern Age*. New York: Doubleday, 1990.

———. "All Quiet on the Western Front." *History Today* 45 (November 1995), 29–35.

Etzioni, Amitai. *The Spirit of Community: The Reinvention of American Society*. New York: Simon and Schuster, 1993.

Femia, Joseph V. "Marxism and Communism." In *Contemporary Political Ideologies*, edited by Roger Eawell and Anthony Wright. Boulder, CO: Westview Press, 1993.

Firda, Richard Arthur. *All Quiet on the Western Front: Literary Analysis and Cultural Context*. New York: Twayne, 1993.

Fitzgerald, F. Scott. *The Last Tycoon: An Unfinished Novel*. New York: Charles Scribner's Sons, 1941.

France, Richard. *The Theatre of Orson Welles*. Lewisberg, PA: Bucknell University Press, 1977.

Fussell, Paul. *The Great War and Modern Memory*. New York: Oxford University Press, 1975.

Galbraith, John Kenneth. *American Capitalism: The Concept of Countervailing Power*. Boston: Houghton Mifflin, 1956.

Giannetti, Louis, and Scott Eyman. *Flashback: A Brief History of Film*, 3rd ed. Englewood Cliffs, NJ: Prentice Hall, 1996.

Gitlin, Todd. "After the Failed Faiths." *World Policy Journal* 12:1 (Spring 1995), 61–68.

Glatzer, Richard. "A Conversation with Frank Capra." In *Frank Capra*, edited by Richard Glatzer and John Raeburn. East Lansing: University of Michigan Press, 1974.

Gomery, Douglas. *Movie History: A Survey*. Belmont, CA: Wadsworth, 1991.

Goodwyn, Lawrence. *Democratic Promise: The Populist Movement in America*. New York: Oxford University Press, 1976.

Gray, J. Glenn. *The Warriors: Reflections on Men in Battle*. New York: Harper & Row, 1970.

Grieder, William. *Who Will Tell the People: The Betrayal of American Democracy*. New York: Simon and Schuster, 1992.

Guttmacher, Peter. *Legendary War Movies*. New York: Metrobooks, 1996.

Hellman, Geoffrey T. "Thinker in Hollywood." *The New Yorker* 16 (February 24, 1940), 23–28.

Hicks, John D. *The Populist Revolt*. Lincoln: University of Nebraska Press, 1961.

Higham, Charles. "Orson Welles as Poet and Historian." In *Hollywood's America: United States History Through its Films*, edited by Steven Mintz and Randy Roberts. St. James, NY: Brandywine Press, 1993.

Hirschorn, Clive. *The Universal Story*. New York: Crown Publishers, 1983.

Hoffman, Preston. "All Quiet on the Western Front" (Sound recording reviews). *Wilson Library Bulletin* 69:8 (April 1995), 104.

Hollihan, Thomas A. "Propagandizing in the Interest of War: A Rhetorical Study of the Committee on Public Information." *Southern Speech Communication Journal* 49 (Spring 1984), 240–46.

Houseman, John. *Run-Through: A Memoir*. New York: Simon and Schuster, 1972.

Hughes, Robert. *Film*. Films of War and Peace, Book 2. New York: Grove Press, 1962.

Isenberg, Michael T. "An Ambiguous Pacifism: A Retrospective on World War Films, 1930–1938." *Journal of Popular Films and Television* 4:2 (1975), 98–115.

————. "The Great War Viewed from the Twenties: *The Big Parade* (1925)." In *American History/American Film: Interpreting the Hollywood Image*, edited by John E. O'Connor and Martin A. Jackson. New York: Frederick Ungar, 1979, 17–38.

————. *War on Films: The American Cinema and World War I, 1914–1941*. Rutherford, NJ: Fairleigh Dickinson University Press, 1981.

————. *Interpreting Film: Studies in the Historical Reception of American Cinema* 99:2 (April 1993), 296.

Jefferson, Thomas. *Writings*. Edited by Merrill D. Peterson. New York: Library of America, 1984.

Jones, Dorothy B. "War without Glory." *The Quarterly of Film, Radio and Television* 8 (Spring 1954), 273–89.

Kael, Pauline, ed. *The Citizen Kane Book*. Boston: Little, Brown, 1971.

Kazin, Michael. *The Populist Persuasion*. New York: Harper Collins, 1995.

Kelly, Andrew. "*All Quiet on the Western Front*: Brutal Cutting, Stupid Censors and Bigoted Politicos, 1930–1984." *Historical Journal of Film, Radio, and Television* 9:2 (1989), 135–50.

Kennan, George F. *Russia and the West*. New York: New American Library, 1960.

Klein, Maury. "Laughing Through the Tears: Hollywood Answers to the Depression." In *Hollywood's America: United States History Through Its Films*, edited by Steven Mintz and Randy Roberts. St. James, NY: Brandywine Press, 1993, 87–92.

Koch, Howard. *The 50th Anniversary Edition of Casablanca: Script and Legend*. Woodstock, NY: Overlook, 1992.

Lamb, Robert Paul. "*Citizen Kane* and the Quest for Kingship." *Journal of American Studies* 19 (August 1985), 267–70.

Larson, Cedric, and James R. Mock. "The Lost Files of the Creel Committee of 1917–19." *Public Opinion Quarterly* 3 (1939), 5–29.

Lash, Joseph P. *Eleanor and Franklin*. New York: New American Library, 1971.

Legge, Alexander, as told to Neil M. Clark. "Back to the Land?" *Reader's Digest* 22 (November 1932).

Lossky, N. O. *History of Russian Philosophy*. New York: International Universities, 1951.

Lundberg, Ferdinand. *Imperial Hearst: A Social Biography*. New York: Equinox Cooperative Press, 1936.

Macnab, Geoffrey. "Video: *All Quiet on the Western Front*." *Sight and Sound* 5:7 (July 1995), 60–61.

Maltby, Richard, and Ian Craven. *Hollywood Cinema*. Oxford, England: Blackwell, 1995.

Marx, Karl. *Critique of the Gotha Program*. Moscow, Russia: Foreign Languages Publishing House, 1947.

————. *Critique of the Hegelian Philosophy of Rights*. In *Early Writings*, edited and translated by T. B. Bottomore. Foreword by Erich Framm. New York: McGraw Hill, 1963, c. 1844.

Mast, Gerald, and Marshall Cohen, eds. *Film Theory and Criticism: Introductory Readings*, 3rd edn. New York: Oxford University Press, 1985.

Mast, Marshall, and Kawin F. Bruce. *A Short History of the Movies*, 6th edn. Boston, MA: Allyn and Bacon, 1996.

McBride, Joseph. *Frank Capra: The Catastrophe of Success*. New York: Simon and Schuster, 1993.

———. *Orson Welles*. New York: Da Capo Press, 1996.

McConnell, Robert. "The Genesis and Ideology of *Gabriel over the White House*." In *Cinema Examined*, edited by Richard Dyer MacCann and Jack C. Ellis. New York: E. P. Dutton, 1982.

McDermott, Malcolm. "An Agricultural Army." *Reader's Digest* 21 (June 1932).

McKenna, George. *American Populism*. New York: G. P. Putnam & Sons, 1974.

McLean, Iain, ed. *The Concise Oxford Dictionary of Politics*. Oxford, England: Oxford University Press, 1996.

Millichap, Joseph R. *Lewis Milestone*. Boston: Twayne Publishers, 1981.

Mills, C. Wright. *The Power Elite*. New York: Oxford University Press, 1956.

Mintz, Steven, and Randy Roberts, eds. *Hollywood's America: United States History Through Its Films*. St. James, NY: Brandywine Press, 1993.

Mitchell, G. T. "Making *All Quiet on the Western Front*." *American Cinematographer* 66 (September 1985), 34–43.

Mulvey, Laura. *Citizen Kane*. London: British Film Institute, 1994.

Naremore, James. *The Magic World of Orson Welles*, rev. ed. Dallas, TX: Southern Methodist University Press, 1989.

Nichols, Bill, ed. *Movies and Methods*. Berkeley: University of California Press, 1976.

Nimmo, Dan, and James Combs. *Mediated Political Realities*. New York: Longman, 1983.

Nordlinger, Eric A. *Isolationism Reconfigured: American Foreign Policy for a New Century*. Princeton, NJ: Princeton University Press, 1995.

Palmer, R. R., and Joel Colton. *A History of the Modern World*, 5th ed. New York: Alfred A. Knopf, 1978.

Pinkerton, James P. *What Comes Next: The End of Big Government and the New Paradigm Ahead*. New York: Hyperion, 1995.

Powers, Richard Gid. *Not without Honor: The History of American Anticommunism*. New York: Free Press, 1995.

Quirk, Lawrence J. *The Great American War Films: From the Birth of a Nation to Today*. New York: Citadel Press, 1994.

Remarque, Erich Maria. *All Quiet on the Western Front*. Translated by A. W. Wheen. Boston, MA: Little, Brown, 1929.

Richards, Jeffrey. "Frank Capra and the Cinema of Populism." In *Movies and Methods: An Anthology*, edited by Bill Nichols. Berkeley: University of California Press, 1976.

Rousseau, Jean Jacques. *The Social Contract and Discourse* (1792), Book III, Chapter 4. London: Dent, 1973.

Rowley, B. A. "Journalism into Fiction: *Im Westen nichts Neues*." In *The First World War in Fiction*, edited by Holger Michael Klein. London: Macmillan, 1976.

Schatz, Thomas. *The Genius of the System*. New York: Metro/Henry Holt Books, 1986.

Schumacher, R. "Remarque's Abyss of Time: *Im Westen nichts Neues*." In *Focus on Robert Graves and His Contemporaries*, edited by J. W. Presley, 1 (Winter 1990–1991), 24–36.

Sciabara, Chris Matthew. *Ayn Rand: The Russian Radical*. University Park: Pennsylvania State University Press, 1995.

Shafritz, Jay M. *Harper Collins Dictionary of American Government and Politics*. New York: Harper Perennial, 1993.

Shindler, Colin. *Hollywood in Crisis: Cinema and American Society 1929–1939*. Routledge: London, 1996.

Simmons, Jerrold. "Film and International Politics: Banning of *All Quiet on the Western Front* in Germany and Austria, 1930–1931." *The Historian: A Journal of History* 52:1 (November 1989), 40–46.

Simon, Callow. *Orson Welles, The Road to Xanadu*. New York: Viking, 1993.

Sklar, Robert. *Movie-Made America: A Social History of American Movies*. New York: Vintage Press, 1975.

Slide, Anthony. "Hollywood's Fascist Follies." *Film Comment* (July/August 1991), 62–67.

Smith, Adam. *The Theory of Moral Sentiments*. Indianapolis: Liberty Fund, 1982.

Soderbergh, P. A. "Aux Armes! The Rise of the Hollywood War Film, 1916–1930." *South Atlantic Quarterly* 65, 4 (1964), 509–22.

Spears, Jack. "World War I on the Screen." *Films in Review*, Part 1, 17:5 (May 1966), 275–92, and Part 2, 17:6 (June–July 1966), 347–65.

Stott, William. *Documentary Expression in America*. London: Oxford University Press, 1973.

Straiger, Janet. *Interpreting Film: Studies in the Reception of American Cinema*. Princeton, NJ: Princeton University Press, 1992.

Strauss, William, and Neil Howe. *The Fourth Turning: An American Prophesy*. New York: Broadway Books, 1997.

Street, Sarah. "Citizen Kane." *History Today* (March 1996), 48–52.

Swing, Raymond Gram. *Forerunners of American Fascism*. Freeport, NY: Books for Libraries Press, 1969 (1935).

Taylor, Harley U., Jr. *Erich Maria Remarque: A Literary and Film Biography*. New York: Peter Lang, 1989.

Thompson, David. "*All Quiet on the Western Front*." In *Movies of the Thirties*, edited by Ann Lloyd. London: Orbis Press, 1983.

Thorpe, Margaret Farrand. *America at the Movies*. New Haven, CT: Yale University Press, 1939.

Tocqueville, Alexis de. Democracy in America, edited by J. P. Mayer. Translated by George Lawrence. Garden City, NY: Doubleday Anchor, 1969.

Tonnies, Ferdinand. *Community and Society*. East Lansing: Michigan State Press, 1957, 33–34.

Travers, M. P. A. *German Novels on the First World War*. Stuttgart, 1982.

Unger, Irwin "Points of View: Were the Populists Backward Leaning." In *Firsthand America: A History of the United States*, Vol. 2, 3rd ed., edited by Virginia Bernhard, David Burner, Elizabeth Fox-Genovese and John McClymer. St. James, NY: Brandywine Press, 1993.

Vidal, Gore. *Screening History*. London: Abacus, 1993.

Vidor, King. *A Tree Is a Tree*. New York: Harcourt Brace, 1952.

Vines, Joe Edwin. *Wings vs. All Quiet on the Western Front: Two Views of War on Film*. Unpublished master's thesis, University of Georgia, 1981.

Warshaw, Robert. "The Western." In *Film: An Anthology*, compiled and edited by Daniel Talbot. Berkeley: University of California Press, 1970.

Welles, Orson and Peter Bogdanovich. *This Is Orson Welles*. New York: HarperCollins/HarperPerennial, 1993 (1992).

Wenden, D. J. "Images of War 1930 and 1988: *All Quiet on the Western Front* and *Journey's End*: Preliminary Notes for a Comparative Study." *Film Historia* 3:1–2 (1993), 33–37.

Winter, J. M. *The Experience of World War I*. New York: Oxford University Press, 1991.

Wolin, Sheldon S. "Violence and the Western Political Tradition." *America Journal of Orthopsychiatry* 33:1 (January 1963), 15–28.

Wood, Michael. *American in the Movies: Or, "Santa Maria," It had Slipped My Mind*. New York: Basic Books, 1975.

Index

Acton, Lord, 35
Adams, John, 33
Adoree, Renee, 98
"Agricultural Army, An," 118
Alexander, Ben, 28
Alger, Horatio, 17
Algiers, 82
Alland, William, 61
Allison, Joan, 81
All Quiet on the Western Front, xvi, 95, 97–103, 107–11, 169, 172; awards, 109, 111
America-Firsters, 78–79
American, 64
American Capitalism, 34
American Congress for Cultural Freedom, 155
American Federation of Labor, 124
American Movie Classics, 2–3, 5 n.1
American President, The, 4
American Revolution, 33
anarchism, 67, 122
Anderson, Martin, 137
Anderson, Sherwood, 98, 105, 108, 110
anti-big government, 14–15
anticommunism, 3–4, 124, 137, 169; former communists, 155–58; as ideology, 145–48; liberal, 148–50; radical right, 150–55
antifascism, 3–4, 50, 62, 65–72, 82, 122, 168–69
anti-individualism. *See* collectivism
anti-intellectual, 15
anti-materialist, 14
anti-media, 15–16
anti-technology, 16
antiwar. *See* pacifism
aristocracy, 34
Aristotle, 13, 17, 31–32, 139–40, 142, 148
Armistice Day, 97
Army-McCarthy hearings, 153
Arnold, Edward, 16, 69
Arthur, Jean, 6, 16, 21
As Good as It Gets, 163
"As Time Goes By," 82, 88, 91, 93 n.10
Atlas Shrugged, 137
auteur, 30
Ayres, Lew, 101, 110, 112 n.6

"Back to the Land," 130
Barber of Seville, The, 69
Barkley, Alben W., 21
Barnes, Howard, 80

About the Author and Contributors

BEVERLY MERRILL KELLEY is a full professor and chair of the communication arts department at California Lutheran University in Thousand Oaks, California. She holds bachelor's and master's degrees from San Diego State University and a Ph.D. in communications studies from UCLA. In addition to numerous academic articles and papers, she writes a newspaper column, hosts a weekly radio show on a National Public Radio affiliate, and a weekly television show on the local educational television channel. She is a regular contributor to the Ventura County opinion page of the *Los Angeles Times*.

JOHN J. PITNEY, JR. is an associate professor of government at Claremont McKenna College in Claremont, California. He holds a bachelor's degree from Union College and a Ph.D. in political science from Yale. He has written a number of academic studies, as well as articles for *The New Republic, Los Angeles Times, The Weekly Standard*, and *The Wall Street Journal*. Also, he is a contributing editor for *Reason* magazine.

CRAIG R. SMITH is a full professor in speech communication and chair of the journalism department at California State University, Long Beach. He holds a bachelor's degree from the University of California, Santa Barbara and a Ph.D. in speech communication from Pennsylvania State University. He presides over the Freedom of Expression Foundation based in Long Beach, California. He has written speeches for President Gerald Ford, President George Bush, and Lee Iacocca as well as managing the 1980 campaign of Senator Robert Packwood. The author of 15 books and a multitude of journal articles, he has garnered a number of prestigious awards for both his teaching and scholarship.

HERBERT E. GOOCH III is an associate professor of political science at California Lutheran University in Thousand Oaks, California. He holds a bachelor's degree from the University of California, Berkeley, master's degrees in both political science and business administration as well as a Ph.D. in political science from the University of California, Los Angeles. He directs the masters degree program in public administration at California Lutheran University. He has managed political campaigns in California and Nevada, as well as authored a number of scholarly articles in addition to a documentary on the space shuttle program for NASA.

ISBN 0-275-96018-8

EAN

9 780275 960186

90000>

HARDCOVER BAR CODE